THE LIFE OF FRED ARCHER

THE
LIFE OF FRED ARCHER

by

E. M. HUMPHRIS

Edited by
THE LATE LORD ARTHUR GROSVENOR

With a Preface by
ARTHUR F. B. PORTMAN

9th THOUSAND

London:
HUTCHINSON & CO. (PUBLISHERS), LTD.

PRINTED IN
GREAT BRITAIN,
AT THE ANCHOR
PRESS, TIPTREE,
:: ESSEX ::

The shoppy slang of Turf is hushed to-day,
  No cry of "Tinman won, sir, by a head !"
The dull November seems to all more grey,
    For Archer's dead !

The glories of the Downs are shadowed o'er,
  'Twill seem a link has snapped in Memory's chain,
When Epsom comes without the deafening roar,
    "Archer again !"

The punter mourns the man who brought him luck
  Who, heedless of the Ring's resounding din,
Would bursting come from out the hopeless ruck,
    And land a win !

                                        .

Farewell, best jockey ever seen on course ;
  Thy backers weep to think by Fate's decree
The rider pale upon his great white horse
    Hath beaten thee !
                              —EDGAR LEE

PREFACE

THE author has flatteringly asked me to write a Preface to this book on the famous Fred Archer, and as I knew him well and saw him ride a vast number of his races it gives me great pleasure to do so ; and I will commence by speaking of the five Derbys he won, all of which I witnessed.

Archer had his first Derby success on Silvio, who started at 100 to 9, in 1877, and, after a pretty finish, won by half a length from Glen Arthur, both the pair outstaying the favourite, Rob Roy, who was beaten three-quarters of a length for second place, with Rhidorroch fourth, a head behind Mr. Mackenzie's colt. His next win at Epsom was in 1880, when he rode a most remarkable race on Bend Or, as he was greatly handicapped by having had his arm badly injured through Muley Edris savaging him after he had ridden that ill-tempered brute in a gallop on Newmarket Heath a short time before, and also by Bend Or coming badly down the hill to Tattenham Corner owing to having sore shins. Archer, for all that, rode with such judgment that, bringing his mount with one long run, he caught Robert the Devil, on whom Rossiter certainly should have won as the race was run, in the last two strides, to beat him by a head.

The following season Archer had little difficulty in steering Mr. Lorillard's American colt Iroquois to victory, as owing to the Two Thousand Guineas winner, Peregrine, with his heavy-loaded shoulders, coming badly down the hill, the half-length by which Iroquois reversed their Newmarket running was easily gained.

Not until 1885 did Archer again ride a Derby winner, and he then, on Melton, rode what was probably the greatest race of his life. Paradox having got Royal Hampton and

Xaintrailles dead-settled at the Bell, and being then well clear of Melton, seemed to have the verdict safe, but, besides showing greenness, being left alone, he commenced to slow down, as lazy horses such as he was are apt to, and Archer, riding Melton for all he was worth, brought him up like a flash of lightning, so that, although Paradox responded most gallantly when challenged, the other had just got the first run, and won one of the greatest races I have ever seen by a head.

Archer's other Derby winner, the mighty Ormonde, in 1886, did not give him much trouble to score on, as although The Bard made a gallant effort the big horse outstrode the little one from the distance and his length and a half victory was easily gained.

My father thought Archer the greatest jockey he ever saw, from 1850 up to the time of his death, in 1890, and I believe personally that he would have more than held his own against such acknowledged great exponents of the art of riding in this century as Maher, O'Neill, Sloan, Carslake, Donoghue, Frank Wootton, Joe Childs, Stern, and Frank Bullock. Although their style is different, they would have found poor Fred hard indeed to defeat, and he was marvellously quick at grasping the best way possible to win a race, and seldom if ever lost what he should have won.

Probably the worst-judged race Archer ever rode was when he was beaten for the Cambridgeshire of 1886 on St. Mirin, as he nearly "starved himself silly" to get down to 8 stone 7 lb., this being one pound more than "Mr. Manton's" colt was weighted at. Archer had never succeeded in winning this event and was rather nervous and, after having apparently got the best of the struggle, St. Mirin was caught again in the last ten strides by The Sailor Prince and beaten a head.

Fred told me his fear of Melton cost him the race, but more likely it was because he had only eaten three bits of dry toast and had two half-pint bottles of champagne to drink for twenty-four hours before this race, and was extremely anxious owing to having backed his mount to win a very large sum of money, as during the season he had been losing a great deal at betting, some £30,000 or more ; and if St. Mirin had got home he would have been a winner on the year.

Archer's riding of Galliard in the Derby of 1883 caused much discussion, and some people, especially the more suspicious, were inclined to favour the idea that he had not done his best to win on the colt.   There was no doubt that his brother, Charles Archer, who trained Highland Chief for Lord Ellesmere, and only died in 1922, had backed that son of Hampton to win a huge sum, which gave colour to the stories that Fred Archer pulled Galliard; but although apparently unlucky, he was an animal of uncertain temperament, and I do not really think there was much wrong, whilst Epsom is such a peculiar and fluky course that any horse may show different form over it from what it does elsewhere.   I believe Lord Falmouth, who was furious at the time and most suspicious of Archer's honesty, was afterwards quite satisfied with the explanation given.

Fred was almost crazy about this time to ride the winner of virtually every big race (and, by the way, only the Cambridgeshire and Gold Cup at Ascot, for which latter race he was second on four occasions, ever escaped him), so in 1881, thinking Peter was sure to win if he rode him, he wanted to ride the horse for the Manchester Cup; but his owner, Sir John Astley, would not take Charlie Wood off the horse. Consequently Archer rode Captain Machell's Valour, and by his marvellous riding on him upset by a neck Sir John's great plunge on Peter.

Upon this last-named uncertain horse Archer accomplished a great feat only a few days later at Ascot when winning the Royal Hunt Cup by three-quarters of a length from Sword Dance after Peter had stopped to kick at the foot of the hill, and thereby lost lengths which it seemed impossible he could make up.

Archer was a man with faults—who of us has not got them?—but take him all round he was a splendid fellow. One of the secrets of his great success as a jockey—and he certainly never had a superior—was the strictest attention to business in every detail, added to keen observation, as a guide to future events, of what other horses besides his own mounts were doing in races.

I know no more notable instance of this than Mr. Everitt's Offenheit, a half-brother to that brilliant mare, Geheimniss.

The colt, who, when backward, was brought out first for the Windsor Castle Stakes at Ascot in 1885, was entrusted to John Watts, a very excellent jockey, and finished third for the race, won by Fullerton, odds of 75 to 20 being laid on Archer's mount, Storm Light, in a field of eight.

Watts informed the owner afterwards that his mount only failed because he was not quite fit, and Mr. Everitt, who asked Archer what he really thought of Offenheit, was told by him, "Not a bad sort, but a sure non-stayer," and this he proved himself to be.

Added to these powers of observation Archer had a keen, intelligent brain and iron nerve which enabled him to hug the rails round such dangerous descents as Tattenham Corner or the hill at Brighton without fear, and thereby win many a race which a less intrepid rider would have failed to do. He showed the most wonderful courage when riding, although otherwise he was a very highly strung man. This was probably brought about by excessive wasting, which naturally affected his nerves, and also by the terrible amount of strong medicine which he was constantly taking to get off a pound or half a pound in weight when there was really nothing to take off, for he was a mere bag of skin and bones, and Dr. Coulson, who usually looked after him, told me that the liberties which Fred would take with his constitution were appalling.

Archer was not an elegant rider : he crouched too much for that ; but he gained an advantage by it, for Tom Cannon and his school sat upright, and even began to lean back and meet the resistance of the wind. Archer rode long, whereas modern jockeys ride short, as Sloan did, and are right forward on their mounts' withers, and crouching as well.

I am sure, however, that Archer would have held his own among modern jockeys. He was the best jockey I have ever seen, and I should say he was probably the best all-round jockey on every type of racecourse who has ever lived.

Conditions have changed since Archer's time, just as they were different when he was so superlative from those of Frank Buckle years before him, and this makes comparisons between one period and another difficult ; but the feats Archer accomplished, and the number of races which he won that less skilful riders would have lost, were enough to convince me that he was an absolute genius in the saddle.

One rather amusing story told of Archer was that when quite a boy he was found crying because he could not ride both winners in a dead-heat ; and it was this temperament which made him work so hard and waste so much in later life.

Of course, Archer having a great influence, and being permitted to do things by people above him socially which no other jockey had ever dreamed of doing previously, was very much inclined to bully other jockeys, and especially the smaller boys. He almost invariably weighed out first or, if not doing that, got to the post first so as to take the most advantageous position on the course, there being no draw for places at the start as is now the case. In fact, Archer, at the zenith of his fame, might with truth be described as a Dictator of the Turf, quite to the same extent as either Lord George Bentinck or Admiral Rous before him.

Very clever and a very close observer of all that was going on around him, Archer certainly had a sufficiently brilliant brain, had his education been profound enough, to have made him a better Prime Minister of England than some of the people who have held that exalted post since his days.

He was a very intimate friend of the late Captain Machell, with whom he went out a good deal, and a pet story of Machell's was that Fred said to him respecting an exalted lady having proposed marriage to him : "I don't think I had better do it, do you, Captain ? And, anyhow, it would not make me a duke !"

I will conclude now my all-too-inadequate comments upon a very remarkable personality, but I must add ere closing how much the author, and everyone who knew him, regretted the death on November 22, 1922, of that delightful man, Sir Willoughby Maycock, who, at the age of nearly seventy-four, succumbed after a few days' illness to a violent chill caught by going out on the night of the General Election. Sir Willoughby kindly gave the author all the assistance he could in this work, and this, it goes without saying, was much, as he possessed a wonderful memory and also had a great number of records of every kind.

Thanks are also due to Mr. W. H. Clarke, the Editor

of the *Sporting Chronicle*, who was kind enough to edit part
of the MS, and to go through the proofs.

ARTHUR F. B. PORTMAN.

P.S.—I wrote the above when the book was first published,
years ago, but the following may be of interest for the latest
edition.   The comparisons made last year by most of the
Press between Archer and Richards were rather foolish,
as the former, from 1878 up to the close of his career in 1886,
could never ride less than 8 st. 7 lb., and Gordon Richards,
without wasting, can do nearly a stone less, with the scale of
weights now far higher than in Archer's day—Fred rode
long, and Richards—who beat Archer's record of 246 wins
in 1885, when scoring on Mr. Frank Hartigan's Golden King
in the Wavertree Plate at Liverpool on November 8, 1933,
curiously enough the very day in the month that Archer shot
himself—rides very short.   Both being great and brainy
jockeys, I will leave it at this, without any further criticism.

A.F.B.P.

THE LIFE OF FRED ARCHER

CHAPTER I

BACK in the Georgian era, the rosy dawn of Cheltenham's prosperity, in the days when ladies rode about on pillions, William Archer had a livery stable in St. George's Place, Cheltenham. His house was, and is, something like a white-washed Noah's Ark, and still has an old-world appearance of perfect tranquillity. William Archer I. did a thriving business, principally in letting out "double horses", and his brother Frederick was a well-to-do man who kept the Foley Arms at Malvern. St. George's place is a small thoroughfare leading from the High Street opposite the Fleece Hotel into Bayshill Road.

The quaint little home of at least three generations of the Archers is very difficult to photograph, as the street is narrow and the cottage very much built in. Thus a picture of it makes the house look like a funny little box, and proves that the camera can sometimes lie. Fred Archer's sister Alice looked at the hardly won presentment of her grandfather's old home, and said scornfully : "Father was a well-to-do steeple-chase rider at the time, and you'd think to look at this that Fred had been born in the gutter." This unpretentious yet highly respectable cottage stands much as it stood in the times of the earlier Georges. The front of the house may have been a little altered, but the yard at the back retains some of the aspects of an old posting-place.

Cheltenham has small respect for real celebrities and their dwellings, but the love of sport has got into the town's very bones, and could not even be eradicated by Dean Close, "The

Pope of Cheltenham", who fought with Colonel Berkeley for supremacy, and prevailed for a time, so that he broke up the grandstand on the racecourse and sold it for firewood. He is likewise said to have engineered the prosecution of George Jacob Holyoake.

In Cheltenham there are many people who officially disapprove of racing yet take a great pride in the Prince of Horsemen, who rode into his fellow-townsmen's respectable hearts so that the love of his memory crops up in most unlikely soil. Men and women who have hardly ever seen a racehorse and, if they had, wouldn't know its head from its tail, are interested in Archer, and perhaps they will read this book.

When William Archer II., Fred's father, and his brothers and sisters were boys and girls at St. George's Cottage, the Cheltenham Gas Works were of modest dimensions, and some of the shops and offices were lighted by rows of oil lamps. On the night when George IV. died there was a fearful thunderstorm and, appropriately as some thought, a strong smell of sulphur. The infant Gas Works suffered grievous injury, and considerable damage was done in Compton Abdale, one of the smallest and most beautiful of the Cotswold villages. Just where the Gas Company now makes bricks, and also on the site of St. Peter's Church, was a large piece of waste ground where pony and galloway races were held. In these William Archer II. is said to have competed "in his pinafore", and it is recorded of the infant jockey that he often won.

The future steeplechase rider had come as a New Year's present to his parents in 1826. Both St. George's Place and the Lower High Street were at that time more fashionable localities than they are nowadays. Dr. Jenner lived in St. George's Place, and at his house there Charles James Fox once said to him : "And what is this cowpox like that everybody is talking about ?" "Like a dewdrop in a section of a roseleaf," replied the enthusiast. Tom Oliver, the steeplechase jockey, is said to have once lived in the Gloucester Road, and not far away lived the La Terrières, who were friends of Adam Lindsay Gordon in their boyhood, and in later years watched over young Fred Archer's career with the greatest interest.

William Archer I. had thirteen children, one of whom,

18

Albert, died in 1920 at Prestbury. Another son was Richard, who followed the family calling, riding for Alderman Coupland. Reuben, a very charming young man and a good horseman, died very early of consumption.

The Georgian pillion-riding establishment of William Archer I. boasted one great attraction in "the double-backed mare", whose back had been admirably adapted by Nature to the double burden she had to carry. She was a beast with her likes and dislikes and with a will of her own. With the elder Fred Archer (the great jockey's uncle) she would always turn back into the yard, but with William Archer II. she never came back until William chose.

At the time when William Archer II. was born, the Cheltenham Races (first established upon the Cleeve Hill Downs in 1819 as an annual fixture, and previously held occasionally on Nottingham Hill) were amongst the most popular meetings in the country. The last Duke of Gordon was in the town for the first annual meeting and gave a card-party in celebration of the event, to which he invited most of the fashionables then at the Spa. The stewards on this occasion were Lord Rosslyn and Colonel Berkeley:

Two followers of th' Ephesian Dame;
One pays his bows as haughty Nimrod drest,
The other worships in a jockey's vest.

His Royal Highness the Duke of Gloucester was also at Cheltenham in 1819. He had come in 1807, and enjoyed himself so vastly that he came every year for the races until he died twenty-seven years later. A simple-minded and very kind man, not very clever perhaps, but clever enough always to do the right thing in the right way, he was greatly beloved in Cheltenham, and was one of the founders of the prosperity of the Spa. On his way back to town after the races the Duke sometimes visited his friend Warren Hastings at Daylesford. Like George IV. and others of his family, the Duke of Gloucester was a good friend in adversity.

In 1825, 40,000 people were on Cleeve Downs for the races, and Mr. S. H. Brooks says in his charming little book, "The Three Archers," that Claude Loraine and Mr. Lake's

19

Cain won the principal stakes. Sir Willoughby Maycock, however, said : "Claude Loraine won the Gloucestershire Stakes at Cheltenham on July 20, 1825, and he was ridden by T. Howard. No record of Cain having won there in 1825. A horse of that name running in 1825 belonged to Mr. Yates. Cain did win the same race at Cheltenham on July 19, 1826, ridden by Spring."

At this time William Trant and Howard Arnull, Chifney, Robinson and Buckle were celebrated jockeys. Trant died at Prestbury in 1825 from over-training.

Neither William Archer I. nor his wife, a Winchcombe girl, had ever intended that William Archer II. should be a jockey. Under these circumstances it was surely tempting Providence when the elder William taught his little boy of six to ride. The child never had any doubt as to his future calling. He meant to be a jockey. In after days his daughter Alice said of him : "My father used to say that he never had more than two days' schooling in his life." But of course he did have more than that, though he and another little boy used to start off and walk to every race-meeting that was within any sort of a distance of Cheltenham, and someone would nearly always give them a lift one way or another.

He had his first mount in a hurdle race at Elmstone Hardwicke, near Cheltenham, at the age of nine, and rode in a way that the critics approved of. As he could not persuade his parents to let him be a jockey, he ran away from home when he was fourteen and engaged himself with a Mr. Eccles, who lived at Birmingham. He weighed only four stone at this time, and soon made a hit as a featherweight rider.

William was employed in the Midlands for about three years, and after he left his first employer he engaged himself to various owners, and had several winning mounts at minor meetings in Warwickshire and Staffordshire. Amongst others, he rode for Alderman Coupland (who owned King Cole, winner of the Chester Cup in 1839), who employed him for a year, giving him one suit of livery and £6.

Though offered an increased salary, Archer refused to stay another year, as he had had a quarrel with Mr. Walters, who trained for Alderman Coupland.

Archer, when grown up, was a very short man with

exceedingly small hands and feet, but though he was a pigmy jockey as a boy, he in later years put on a considerable amount of flesh.

After leaving Birmingham, Archer, now a first-rate horseman, was taken up by George Taylor (Alec Taylor's grandfather), who at that time trained for Lord Chesterfield, one of the great supporters of the Cheltenham Races.

Though William Archer had ridden successfuly for Alderman Coupland, he had hitherto been very poor, for the best of jockeys in those days only earned what would nowadays be considered a mere pittance. After a skilful win at Hednesford, he was congratulated by Lord Chesterfield and by Mr. Thomas Taylor, who was then buying horses for the Russian Government.

His next employer was Mr. Bradley, at Hednesford, to whom he engaged himself for a term of years, riding for the stable and acting as head lad. His luck was in, and his services were in great demand, but he was putting on weight rapidly, and he began to turn his thoughts towards steeplechasing, as did Fred Archer years afterwards. Billy, however, went farther than *thinking*; he *became* a steeplechase jockey, and often also rode in hurdle races. At this time he rode with great success at Prestbury Park as well as at Hednesford.

He is said by a leading sporting paper to have been one of the most respectful and best-mannered jockeys on the Turf, and though his temper was short and his language forcible, he was popular with all classes.

One morning Mr. Thomas Taylor said to him: "Archer, would you like to go to Russia ?" Bill said he would. He was given splendid testimonials by Lord Chesterfield and also by the Marquis of Anglesey, who had left a leg behind him at Waterloo and who often acted as starter at Hednesford Races. Soon he started off to Russia under engagement to ride for Nicholas I., Tsar of Russia, at a salary of £100 a year, with board, lodging, and all expenses paid.

On a bright May morning he sailed from Hull, taking with him a string of English thoroughbreds, among them being Lady Adelia, a filly by Touchstone, and Fishfag, by Billingsgate, and his stud safely landed at Cronstadt, and proceeded to Tsarskoe-Selo Palace, some twenty-five versts from St.

21

Petersburg, where the extensive plains afforded ample training-grounds. The Emperor Nicholas I. was greatly interested in horse-racing, and an interesting article in *The Times* for July 27, 1914, on "The Turf and the Army" gives an account of the Tsar's efforts to encourage in his officers that love of sport which he considered a necessary part of military training.

William Archer is said to have been for some time at Thirsk, near Moscow, where the frost and snow were awful. The severity of the climate tried his health, and he returned home in 1844. Nine years later the Tsar Nicholas issued a decree ordering horse-racing for officers of the Guard at Tsarskoe-Selo, and granting stakes valued at Rs.1,000 (£100).

In the autumn of 1844, William Archer landed at St. Catherine's Docks, London, and at once went to his old master, Mr. Bradley, at Hednesford, as he had promised that if he did not like Russia he would return to him.

For the next few years he rode in many steeplechases and hurdle races, and at length settled down in Cheltenham as a professional horseman.

He rode for Lord Strathmore and for several well-known owners, among them Prince Baratzky, who offered him a splendid engagement in Hungary if he would go abroad again. But Archer preferred his native town to any other part of England, and he had resolved in any case never to leave his own country.

Owing to the vigorous denunciations of Mr. Close, the incumbent of Cheltenham, the races had languished and had been discontinued. Indeed, the "Gloomy Dean" of those days also banned the theatre and almost all amusements.

In 1838, however, the local race-meeting was reorganized as the Cheltenham and Cotswold Races on an improved course, with Lord Chesterfield as one of the stewards. In this year old Sam Darling won the Gloucestershire Stakes, and the year following Mr. E. Griffiths's Lugwardine, ridden by Chapple, beat The Skater in a big field of horses.

About this time the Cheltenham Races were held in Prestbury Park, where we find both Archer and old Tom Oliver in the pigskin. Here, on one occasion, Archer had two mounts, one of Captain Alleyne's, The Nigger, getting fourth, and another on Thurgarton, winning the race, Oliver on Vanguard being second.

In the spring of 1847, Archer took part in the wonderful race for the Cheltenham Grand Annual, on which Lindsay Gordon is said to have founded "How We Beat the Favourite". William Archer evidently regarded it as one of the most exciting events in which he ever took part. The late Mr. Holland, of Prestbury, Archer's connection and lifelong friend, once described the Noverton Steeplechase on the actual course which he said was flagged out by Lord Fitzhardinge, and it was the most difficult one over which the Cheltenham Steeplechases were ever run. The winning-post was situated in a field at the back of Mr. Robinson's mill, and the course was over the lane leading from Prestbury to Noverton House, over a stone wall, through Gyngell's Meadows to Hewletts Hill ; on again to Prestbury Wood, and back *via* Hewletts. There were stiff brier fences, twenty-four in number, and the course was reckoned a little over four miles. There were thirteen starters for the principal handicap ; Tramp, a Liverpool Steeplechase winner, was made favourite, but Stanmore, ridden by William Holman, won the race, Archer being only defeated a length on Mr. Evans's Daddy Longlegs. Tramp, running through an orchard, cannoned against a tree and dashed his brains out, and Turner, his rider, was much injured. The Hewletts, or Agg's Hill, is thought by some people to be the hill mentioned by Byron in *The Dream*. On the top of it is the house where, in 1809, William Hickey, of the Memoirs, visited his friend Major Agg.

Soon after this Archer rode Mr. Gambier's brown pony The Weasel (9 stone) against Mr. Trelawny's grey gelding, Cheese, ridden by Mr. William Fitzhardinge Berkeley, at that time a cornet in the Horse Guards, afterwards Member for Cheltenham and subsequently Lord Fitzhardinge. The match was for 100 sovereigns, three miles over the steeplechase course ; the betting was 3 to 1 on The Weasel, which won easily, Mr. Berkeley's mount, Cheese, repeatedly refusing to negotiate the obstacles. "Lord Fitzhardinge never forgot this race," says Mr. Brooks, "and when he met William Archer always shook hands with him and invited him to share his hospitality."

About this time Archer won a race at Stratford-on-Avon on Eagle, belonging to Mr. William Hurlstone, and among the competitors was Mr. Nelson Powell, a well-known lawyer of Chipping Sudbury, a bold and fearless rider who steered many horses to victory. Mr. Powell afterwards emigrated to Australia, and died there from the effects of an accident.

Archer also remembered a big match at Prestbury Park between Captain Dickson's McOrville and Sir John Malcolm's Dunlavon, when the former was ridden by Oliver and the latter by F. Jacobs. Dunlavon won, and Oliver had a nasty fall, but recovered in time to get third on Prince George in the Liverpool Steeplechase the next year. In 1849, Archer won the Newport Pagnell Steeplechase on Charity. Mr. Brooks says that in 1849 Archer was living at Cintra House, though he still kept up his old quarters in St. George's Place.

There was another attraction for the jockey in Prestbury ; he had fallen in love with Miss Emma Hayward, the handsome elder daughter of William Hayward, then the highly respected landlord of the King's Arms. On the day before St. Valentine's Day, 1849, Archer was married to Emma Hayward by the Rev. John Edwards (later De la Bere), whose son's letters to Fred Archer are published in this book. The wedding party was a very merry one—and no wonder, for Black Tom Oliver was best man, possibly attended by his satellite Lindsay Gordon, but this last is pure conjecture. Mr. William Holman, the celebrated trainer, and Mr. Hawkins, the owner of Theresa, were also present. The bride's father gave a gorgeous wedding feast at the King's Arms, at which the vicar and all who had been at the wedding were present, and afterwards the bride and bridegroom went off to London, where they stopped with Host Wright of the Anglesey Hotel in the Haymarket. Mrs. William Archer was a tall, dark girl, whose beauty was rather of the Oriental type. She was eminently aristocratic-looking, and "Archer's parents were indeed thought to have some good blood in their veins from somewhere," remarked a famous trainer. "Must have, to get that," he said, as he gazed at his "best" portrait of Archer. For the "best" pictures of Archer are like the sands of the sea or the hoofs of Eclipse in number.

Emma Hayward came of a family long and highly esteemed

in Prestbury, and whether she had aristocratic forebears or not, she certainly looked the part. Her father was church-warden at Prestbury for over forty years, and was much liked by the two vicars, whom he served as vicar's warden. Mr. Edwards took a great interest in George Stevens, and is said to have given a picture of him to the landlord of the King's Arms after one of Stevens's five Grand National victories, though after mature deliberation it was decided that the church bells should not be rung to celebrate the event.

His son, Mr. De la Bere, was very fond of Fred Archer, both for his own sake and because of his mother and grand-father.

When Mr. Hayward's daughters were little girls, some Miss Hugheses came and set up a school in the village. Mr. Hayward was a great man in Prestbury, and he helped the sisters, who got together quite a flourishing little school. As a rule they only took the daughters of professional men and some of the better-class tradesmen, but they took also the children of the landlord of the King's Arms, who had been so kind to them, and they gave the Hayward girls a very good education.

Mrs. William Archer used in after years to tell her children stories of her schooldays and of Prestbury in the days of her youth. She was fond of telling them of a wonderful old house called Broxteth House, which still exists in Prestbury under another name. It was a very, very old-fashioned, rambling place, and when Emma Hayward used to go there an artist was decorating the dining-room. On every one of the panels round the room he was painting scenes in "The History of the Racehorse". With this animal Emma Hayward had in those days little acquaintance, though she was in after years to be so much mixed up with its destinies.

"The pictures may be there now, for all I know," said Archer's sister (in about 1914), "but you see it's a long time ago. Mother has been dead five years, and she was nearly eighty-six when she died.* It's a pity she didn't write down her reminiscences; she could have told you about every-thing. She was a fine-looking girl, with very good features,

* Note by Sir Willoughby Maycock: "Fred Archer's mother died at Withington, near Cheltenham, in Septemberr, 1908."

25

and this artist at Broxteth House who was doing the race-horses made a sketch of mother. My sister had it, and she left it to my Emmie. She had always promised she should have it because Emmie has such a look of her grandmother. It's just as the artist gave it to mother, this narrow gold frame and all. These two oil-paintings are of father and mother. He was a very small-made man ; look at his tiny hands and feet. His mutton-chop whiskers look so odd nowadays. Mother was dark, you see, but Fred, though he had grey eyes, was very like her."

William Archer took his bride to live in the old family house in St. George's Place.

CHAPTER II

FREDERICK JAMES ARCHER was born in St. George's Place, Cheltenham, on January 11, 1857, and in the year of Blink Bonny's Derby. Blink Bonny, by the way, was bred and owned by Mr. I'Anson, Mathew Dawson's connection and one-time neighbour. In Fred's birth certificate his father is described as a steeplechase rider. This document had a peculiar interest for sportsmen, who were always discussing Fred's age. "For," said Fred's charming sister Alice (the late Mrs. Pratt), "Fred was apprenticed so young that he was out of his time when he was a mere boy, and famous too. People often made bets about his age, and sometimes they would write to mother, enclosing a five-pound or ten-pound note, and ask her to decide the matter. At last she kept by her a number of copies of Fred's birth certificate, and would post one off whenever anyone wrote to her about his age."

Police-Superintendent MacRae remembered seeing the Archers' furniture being taken away in vans from St. George's Place when they moved to Cintra House, Prestbury. This happened when Fred was a baby in long clothes, so that only by three or four weeks did he escape being a Prestbury man by birth. All William Archer's children but the youngest, Charles, were born at St. George's Place, though they left it so young that they always seem to be more connected with Prestbury than with the old family home. There were three sons, William, Fred, and Charlie, and two daughters, Emily and Alice.

Cintra House is now the Vine Tree Inn, a pretty old-fashioned place standing in the Burgage at Prestbury. A great vine grows up it, hence its present name, though "Cintra House" is still painted on the side of it.

27

In 1858, William Archer won the Grand National on Little Charley, and as he was born on December 2 in that same year Charles Edward Archer was appropriately named after Mr. Capel's horse. Mr. Capel also owned Anatis, the mare on which the late Mr. Tom Pickernell won one of his three victories at Aintree. The Capels have lived at Prestbury House for many years, and the family is mentioned in some of the earliest accounts of Cheltenham Spa. Tom Pickernell, not long before his death, read an article by the late Finch Mason in *Baily's*. "It brought back," he said, "many happy old times to my mind. For old Capel and Fog Rowlands and the rest of the old 'uns were all great friends of mine." An old friend of Fred Archer's said that during Mr. Capel's last illness he saw him, and he talked much of his and Lindsay Gordon's friend, the much loved Thomas Pickernell, and he had Mr. Pickernell's photograph of him.

They are all dead now—Mr. Capel and Tom Pickernell and Fog Rowlands, and another admirer of Mr. Pickernell's, Bob James, Tom Oliver's old jockey, who spent his last days in the beautiful old almshouses at Prestbury. "The Gift of Anne Goodrych for the Religious Poor." Bob James also treasured up a photograph of "Mr. Thomas", and would talk of nothing but him and the horses he rode.

Fog, or Fothergill, Rowlands was the sporting doctor from Wales who settled down in Prestbury and trained steeplechase horses for his friends, among them being King Edward. His son was Cecil Raleigh, of Drury Lane fame, who died in the early days of the Great War. Mr. Raleigh had a boundless admiration for Fred Archer, and was fond of talking of the old Prestbury days. He said that in Prestbury Fothergill Rowlands was one day taking some horses, heavily clothed, to trot round a ploughed field, which was the old-fashioned way of sweating them, when a very small boy opened the gate for him and seemed to take a keen interest in the horses. Asked if he liked horses, he replied in the affirmative with a broad smile.

Good (and especially small) stable-boys were always rather difficult to get, so Dr. Rowlands looked up the boy's employer, who let him come to the stable, where it was soon discovered he was a born horseman. When breaking in yearlings he

28

seemed to enjoy being kicked off, and he actually rode in a four-mile steeplechase at Kidderminster when he only weighed 4 stone 7 lb. John Jones was his name, and a most excellent and trustworthy fellow he became. Eventually he married, and his son, Herbert Jones, became the King's jockey.

In talking of Tom Pickernell and "the old 'uns", one wanders a little way from Little Charley's Grand National. In this race Tom Oliver's mount, Escape, was knocked over at the next fence after Becher's Brook, and William Archer, riding a patient race, bided his time till close home and won fairly easily.

Years afterwards, Mr. William Villar, of Cheltenham, won his first race across country and came home through Andoversford, where William Archer then lived. To the boy's great delight, the old steeplechase jockey presented him with the whip he had used when he rode Little Charley at Aintree.

Soon after his Grand National victory the Archers seem to have left Prestbury for a time and lived in Cheltenham, in St. George's Place, and also, it is said, in the London Road. On the death of the old churchwarden, about 1860, William Archer returned to Prestbury and succeeded to the King's Arms as landlord.

Superintendent MacRae was then a young policeman who had not long come from Scotland. Though by no means brought up in an atmosphere of sport, he took kindly to it, and was, like many others, interested in the steeplechase rider and his family. He often used to call at the King's Arms on business or pleasure, and he remembered Fred Archer's brothers and his sisters all in pinafores, and how they used to go about Prestbury with a donkey.

The Superintendent must have found Cheltenham, and especially Prestbury, a change after the Spartan home from which he had come. There in the mornings the long family of lads and lasses waited round the porridge-bowl, spoon in hand, each ready to dip his or her implement into the national and common dish as soon as their father's long grace should be ended.

They walked long miles to church on Sundays, where they attended two services with scarcely a break between them, and which lasted hours and hours. The blinds of the house

29

were drawn down on Sundays, and if you had a girl, and met her out of doors, you had to walk on one side of the road while she walked on the other, and speak to her when nobody was in sight. Mrs. MacRae started her son off on the road southwards with a carpet bag and two bibles, one in English and the other in Gaelic. The latter volume was stolen *en route* by an English thief, who probably thought, said the Superintendent, that this book, written in a strange language and carried with little else in a carpet bag, was of great value from a worldly point of view.

This innocent youth managed to hold his own, and later on had to keep order on the Cheltenham Racecourse and among skylarking Yeomanry officers, and his name stood for law and order in Cheltenham for many years.

CHAPTER III

THE little Gloucestershire village of Prestbury nestles at the foot of Cleeve Hill, the highest of the Cotswolds.

In the first days of the war it is said that, when the Gloucestershire men joined up, recruits who were members of the Church of England were told to stand forward ; several did so, and so did the Roman Catholics and others. But when Presbyterians were asked for, some of the Church of England men again stepped out of the line. "But you are Church of England," it was objected. "So we be, sir, so we be ; but we be Presbyterians, too," said these inhabitants of no mean village.

Though steeplechasing was born elsewhere—Sir Willoughby Maycock said it took place in England as far back as 1792— St. Albans and Prestbury were its cradles. In Prestbury, Tom Oliver, pupil of Tommy Coleman, settled down after the Wanderjähre of his adventurous youth. His house and stables and lovely garden were just where the tramline swerves round beyond Prestbury village on the way to Southam. Here he trained men, as well as horses, and Mr. Raleigh said he prepared Tom Sayers there for his earlier fights, particularly for his terrific encounter with Harry Paulsen.

Black Tom Oliver gave Lindsay Gordon his first mount in the Trials on the racecourse, remarking afterwards : "There now, you young devil, you've rode a race." He gave Tom Pickernell his first ride in a steeplechase at Andoversford, and to him he said : "It's as well you were beaten, young squire, or you'd have thought you could ride."

In Tom's spare time he baited badgers in Queen's Wood where the primroses grow. He was fond of literature, and even encouraged Lindsay Gordon to recite in his voice of dolorous pitch his own and other people's poetry. In

31

Cheltenham Gordon wrote his "Hunting Song", which was possiblysent out to his publishers by Frederick Marshall, the sporting lawyer, who signed Fred Archer's indentures. Two verses of it are :

Here's a health to every sportsman, be he stableman or lord ;
If his heart be true I care not what his pockets may afford.
And may he ever pleasantly each gallant sport pursue,
If he takes his liquor fairly, and his fences fairly too.

He cares not for the bubbles of Fortune's fickle tide,
Who, like Bendigo, can battle, and, like Oliver, can ride.
He laughs at those who caution, at those who chide he'll frown,
As he clears a five-foot paling or he knocks a peeler down.

The village still rings with the glorious deeds and quaint remarks of Tom Oliver. "He was," said Cecil Raleigh, "a small, wiry man, with a fringe of iron-grey hair round the face which made him look rather like a marmoset monkey, the effect being further heightened by a sallow complexion (he was said to be half a gipsy) and by his extremely bright, black, twinkling eyes.

"He would say and write quaint things, as, for example, when an owner wrote to him and said :

" 'My horse has been under your care for three months. Do you think he can stay ?' "

"Oliver replied :

" 'Sir, your horse can stay, but he takes a damned long time about it.'

"On another occasion he was extolling the qualities of a horse he was selling, but the dubious buyer inquired :

" 'Doesn't he pull ?'

" 'Pull !' exclaimed Oliver. 'He wouldn't pull a sprat off a gridiron !'"

His last years were spent at Wroughton, in Wiltshire, where he trained the royally named descendants of The Bloomer, the mare that he had sold to Mr. Cartwright in Prestbury.

To Cheltenham Spa after Waterloo came the Duke of Wellington and many of his officers, and one of these, Colonel (afterwards General) Thomas Charretie, was married in Cheltenham parish church a year after the battle   From that time onwards this famous sportsman made Cheltenham his headquarters, and was continually at Prestbury and at the King's Arms. He had been an old patron of Oliver's at St. Albans, and Black Tom often rode for him at Prestbury and elsewhere. On the racecourse the Colonel had his affair of honour with Mr. Sanguinetti, and there, too, his famous horse Napoleon lost him his celebrated bet.

Hither, too, came Jack Mytton with his Longwaist and other horses to win the Cheltenham Grand Annual and many other races. Mr. Osbaldeston came also, and Major Ormsby Gore with Hesperus. At Prestbury, Lottery made such a name that subsequent winners of the Cheltenham Grand Annual were penalized in the Grand National.

In later times, on Cleeve Hill, above the village, bonfires were lighted to celebrate each of George Stevens's five victories in the Grand National, and on the hill between Prestbury and Southam a stone marks the place of his tragic death. Close to his grave in the cemetery is the place where once a grandstand stood instead of a chapel, and where young William Archer, Fred's brother, "a kind and generous-hearted lad", was killed at Cheltenham Races. Lindsay Gordon puts into the mouth of George Stevens the first verses of the steeplechase riders' classic, "How We Beat the Favourite."

In Prestbury village, almost under the shadow of the old church, stands the King's Arms, the beautiful old hostelry where William Archer's wife was born and where her children were brought up. Its rough old white walls, black oak beams and polished floors are defiant of time, and for more than four centuries it has stood, almost foursquare, in the very heart of Prestbury. The old smoke-room upstairs has queer little alcoves and a black corner cupboard, and, of course, oak beams in the ceilings. The staircases are very winding, with unexpected turns and twists and little recesses, and the whole place has a sort of lavendery, old-world peace. The black oak of the smoke-room is well-seasoned by the long churchwarden pipes of those Jacobites who escaped the Georgian vicar's searching eye, of many Hanoverians, and of all the Victorians who were anybody in the palmy days of Cheltenham Spa, when "Old Q." drove about Prestbury in such a yellow coach-and-four that the simple villagers thought he was the Prince of Wales.

In Fred Archer's boyhood the smoke-room was a sort of club, where nightly the squire, the parson, the doctor, the lawyer, the better-class tradesmen and the aspiring jockey, Cheswas, smoked their churchwardens, drank good ale and told tall tales. When William Archer was the landlord, Tom Oliver, Isaac Day and William Holman used to meet there and discuss sporting matters with their host, the famous steeple-chase rider. Jemmy Edwards, the middleweight champion, was often there. He used to train at Prestbury, where he and Tom Sayers used to spar with Lindsay Gordon, and once in Edwards's boxing saloon in the Lower High Street, Gordon, by a fluke, got the better of the unbeaten "Earywig". Mr. Tom Pickernell was there, and he told the tale and fought the battle over again in his little house at King's Heath with the syringas in the front garden.

Nowadays the aristocracy have more or less deserted the old inn where Jack Mytton, Charretie, the Berkeleys, the fascinating and luckless Berkeley Craven, Fulwar Craven and a host of other celebrities were formerly to be found. Nowadays the villagers congregate in the tap-room and spin yarns about the local heroes, and especially "Freddy". "And," said one of them, "that's where you should go o' nights if you want to hear tales of Archer from the men who knew him as a boy."

I was particularly fortunate some years ago to meet Fred Archer's sister Alice, the late Mrs. Pratt. I obtained from her the following recollections of her brother. They are put down just as she related them to me.

"It was a pretty, old-world place," said she, "and in the smoke-room every man had his own particular corner. I think there was a picture of this room in the *Sporting and Dramatic* at the time of Fred's marriage. The smoke-room was for the gentry, and most of the other people went into the tap-room downstairs, except John Cheswas, a steeple-chase jockey, a very superior man and all that. He could always be found in the smoke-room, smoking his long church-warden pipe with the best of his betters. I remember this used rather to annoy my father; he often said things about it; but John sat there all the same, and, in fact, he seemed to mix altogether with a ᴧss of people far above him. Sarah

Cheswas, John's wife, had been an old servant of ours, and she used to come in by the day and work for mother.

"In places like Prestbury there is always the village idiot, isn't there? And Sam Cheswas, Sarah's and John's son, was ours. He had fits, and we were rather afraid of him. We children used often to go down to Sarah's, but before we went in we'd always ask Sarah, 'Is Sam at home, and do you think he'll have a fit?' And Sarah would sometimes say, 'I don't think so. He had five in the night.'

"The King's Arms in this photograph of it looks just what it was—an old-fashioned country inn. I think the trams have rather spoilt Prestbury, and, of course, old Mr. Holland is gone, which makes a difference. He was such a nice old man, and so was his father, who lived to be ninety-five. Everybody respected them both; and as for the old father, children and dogs simply worshipped him; indeed, all animals fairly loved him. So did Sam Cheswas—he followed old Mr. Holland about like any dog. Wherever Mr. Holland went, there was Sam after him, and Mr. Holland would often give him a bit of meat or something to take home to his mother. Sarah had a relative who had been a servant, and she and the man she married were sent to Botany Bay for stealing something. I remember my mother telling me what an excitement it caused in Prestbury when their children—two of them—came to visit their mother's native village. She, though she had become quite prosperous, was not allowed to come back to England. Her son and daughter who came to Prestbury were very flourishing, too, and though I am not old enough to remember it myself, mother would often tell us the tales these people told of the life in Australia.

"There was only one wheel-chair in the village and no flys until father started his posting business, for he was very enterprising, and he thought that one wheel-chair was not enough for Prestbury to go about in. We bought two or three flys, and as they were very nice and he kept good horses he soon made a good thing out of it. But the fly-proprietors by Pittville Gates were very angry about it; they did not like it at all.

"We went to School in Cheltenham, for one Miss Hughes (from the school where mother used to go) had married a Mr.

35

Williams, and she and her sister had left Prestbury and started another school in Pittville. As my grandfather had helped Mrs. Williams and Miss Hughes to start their school in Prestbury they were always grateful to him, and after his death they were glad to take my sister and me, as they had been to take my mother. But when the people from the other inn at Prestbury wanted to send their daughters there Mrs. Williams said she did not care to take them. They said, 'Well, but the Archers go to your school !' Mrs. Williams replied that she knew the Archers well, and that made a difference. Mother would send the old wheel-chair man to fetch us home if it rained. We used to beg him to let us have the front down, but he always refused, saying, 'Now, what would your mother say if you got wet ?' and we were shut in, in a kind of glass case, with a window over the front. Still, we thought it a perfectly lovely thing, though he didn't, for he had to drag the great heavy chair, with my sister and me in it, right back to Prestbury.

"Tom Oliver did not live in Prestbury any longer in my young days, but I remember seeing him once, and when he looked at me he noticed how remarkably like my father I was, and then said : 'If William Archer were dead I could swear to his ashes.' I didn't quite know what he meant, but it was a funny expression, and it stuck in my memory always.

"Mr. Edwards and his son, who afterwards took the name of De la Bere, had known mother all her life, and they used to like to come in and yarn to my father. Sometimes old Mr. Edwards would say to my mother : 'If Archer had had a good education he would have made a name for himself in other things than steeplechasing and done great things in the world. My father, as I told you, had run away as a boy to get into some training-stables, and he used to tell us that he had only had two days' schooling in his life, though really he had more than that ; my mother, of course, had been very well educated besides being a very refined sort of woman.

"In my grandfather's time Mr. De la Bere was not so very High Church ; indeed, such an old-fashioned churchwarden as my grandfather wouldn't at all have approved of such changes, I expect. Mr. De la Bere was very fond of Fred ; you know he insisted upon coming to Newmarket to bury him. Mother kept all my father's accounts and generally wrote his letters. They were not a demonstrative couple, but my father thought all the world of my mother, and when anybody came to see him he would always say, 'Where's your mother?' and always seemed unhappy if she was not about. Father had a temper, but I never saw mother put out about anything.

"They were as different as possible; she had a very gracious sort of manner. They had a very good time when they were first married; they used to go about together to most of the race-meetings. Father was a very successful rider, and people took a good deal of notice of mother, both on his account and because everyone liked her. Though mother did all the correspondence, I remember that in later years, when Fred had letters from all sorts of 'swells'—and you know what a hand these people write—it was father that could generally read every word. For one thing, it was nearly all about horses, and father knew everything that had to do with them by a sort of instinct. Anyhow, he'd always drop on the word, and then he would say to my mother: 'There now, with all your fine education, I can read that and you can't.' And mother would smile.

"Father was very fond of boxing, and when Fred and Charlie were quite little boys he would set them to spar with one another in the club-room. They got on very well until they lost their tempers, which they often did. I once went to see Tom Sayers's grave in Highgate Cemetery. It has just one word 'Time!' on it. I thought it was very nice.

"Once a week a great event happened in Prestbury. *Bell's Life* came. It was sixpence then, and a weekly. Now it is joined up with the *Sporting Life* and is a daily paper. Well, when it came, father would shut himself up in the private room, or at any rate in a room where all the rest of us weren't, and he would read the paper in peace. After it had been lent all round the village, to Mr. Holland and all the rest, father would cut out all his own and Horatio Nelson Powell's and the Joneses' races and paste them on great sheets of brown paper. It was all very interesting, and we had them till about six years ago, when we lived in a house that had a damp kitchen, and these papers were all put away in a box there, and they all got into a sort of pulp and become quite illegible.

37

"The original of this picture of father on Thurgarton is at Newmarket. My brother had it. But I have one of him on his old cob as well. He had a good seat on a horse then, you can see, though he was getting an old man when that was taken.

"Father made a good deal of money for some years, but as he began to get too heavy for riding, and he had never managed to save any money, he began at one time to get rather 'under the weather.' He and mother both had comfortable homes when they were young, and hadn't had to save and screw, and they didn't take comfortably to it now. People used to say that such a well-known jockey as father should have let *Bell's Life*, or one of the other sporting papers, raise a subscription for him, but he always stoutly refused. Plenty of more important people than himself had done it, but he never would, though *we* didn't like being poor, and often thought he might just as well. My sister was older than I when the bad times came, and so managed to get more education. But I had to be taken away from school when I was only eleven, and there was very little money for anything just as we were all growing up and needed it.

"I remember Mr. and Mrs. Fothergill Rowlands very well. He was a very handsome man and she a most charming and fascinating woman. She had been married before, and had grown-up daughters but only the one little boy, and I shouldn't have thought he could remember so very much. He seemed so much younger than I, and was always about with a nurse, and yet I don't think there can be so much difference in our ages."

Another old Prestbury resident who remembered Mr. Raleigh as a child described him as "a sweet little boy"— to his great delight.

William Archer gave up riding about 1862, his last mount being at Beckford on Black Dwarf, the property of Mr. J. Taylor.

Fred Archer was for a time at a Mr. Cox's school in Cheltenham, and afterwards at Hygeia House, a well-known school opposite to the King's Arms. It was kept by a Mr. Vliemann, though Mr. Sam Brooks speaks of a Mr. Lewis who was at Hygeia House School, also in Archer's time, and says that he had a wooden leg with which he used to inflict corporal punishment on his pupils. Mr. Alfred Holman, the well-known trainer, was at Hygeia House, but not with Fred. He was a day boy, and used to stray over to the King's Arms to hear some of the wonderful yarns in which William Archer excelled. Mr. William Villar, the late Mr. Fred Taylor, and the late Mr. Herbert Mills were all at Hygeia House with Fred and Charlie Archer. Charlie is said by at least one competent judge to have ridden better than Fred as a boy. Fred apparently could neither read nor write much when he left for Newmarket. There he attended a night school.

Mrs. Pratt said :

"Mother was vexed because Fred would be away from school all but about two days a week. And father encouraged Fred in his riding. In spite of anything mother would say about wasted opportunities, father would retort : 'Let the lad alone ; he'll make more out of his riding than he ever will out of his book-learning.' But as a result of this Fred grew up very badly educated. He could sign cheques and write a good hand when he liked, but he generally employed somebody else to write all his letters, and I don't think we have kept any of those that he wrote himself. I remember that I tore one up not long ago that he sent me just after he won the Derby on Melton, when he sent me a present."

It is not surprising that young Fred Archer's thoughts were chiefly about horses. At three he was always riding on the back of his long-suffering uncle Hayward, while whenever he got a chance he would steal into the stables and climb on to the horses' backs. He used to look up at the groom in a wistful sort of way and say : "I shall ride when I am bigger, shan't I ?"

The accounts of eye-witnesses who saw and heard Fred Archer's education by his father show that the cross-country rider's teaching was distinctly of the rough and ready order, though none the less effective. Mr. Parker wrote :

"I was engaged at the King's Arms at this time as house-boy. When Fred was about ten years old he had a great liking for riding, so by this time his father bought him a dun-coloured pony with a black stripe down its back. It stood about 11 hands in height, and was a very smart pony. Every opportunity Freddy was riding it. There was a garden at the King's Arms, where his father taught him to ride, and on one occasion his father and brother William had the pony on a rope, with Fred riding, lunging it over a hurdle, when his father in a very angry voice, shouted : 'Sit back, you —— !' After this he soon learnt to handle the pony himself, and could ride her in good style on every possible occasion."

Another man who remembers later instructions on Prestbury racecourse says : "Old Billy Archer threw bits of grass and turf at young Fred, and his language was something awful. I don't think Fred was ever afraid of the *pony* !"

On Sunday afternoons the three Archer boys used to go out bird's-nesting with the house-boy, Henry Parker, who said Fred used to talk a good deal in those days, and was perhaps his favourite of the three. Parker said he once ran young William Archer down Prestbury Street for half a crown. William Archer's coachman was named Wilcox, and his sister said that when Fred was ten years old, or even younger, he used to come up on Sunday mornings with Wilcox to his house on Bushcombe Hill, where the coachman would put up the hurdles and Fred would jump his pony over them.

It was at Prestbury, when he was eight years old, that Fred Archer rode his first race, the occasion being some small local sports. His father, Mr. Raleigh said, rigged the boy out correctly in breeches and colours, with a little top-coat over them, and in these he walked about the village all day. In the late afternoon he rode a pony which had been matched against a donkey, the match being made one of the events of the sports.

The course was twice round an orchard at the back of a small inn called the Plough, and twice over a small brook. The donkey had a high reputation, and was ridden by a yokel with a thick stick. For a small and nervous boy, Archer rode remarkably well, but the donkey won by a neck !

Fred Archer's first win was in a donkey-race. There were three runners ; Fred was riding Southam Lass, a donkey which had belonged to the Earl of Ellenborough, and the others were Penarth and Peter Simple. This race was for a new bridle, and was run in the small paddock of the Plough Inn, Prestbury.

40

From his childhood Fred Archer was accustomed to ride across country on one of his father's ponies or on one borrowed from Cecil Rowlands, the doctor's little boy. About the time of his ninth birthday William Archer gave £5 for a pony for him, to Charles Pullen, who kept the Unicorn at Winchcombe, and this afforded the child great pleasure.

Freddy's pony was, says Mr. Brooks, "a very useful one, standing about 12 hands 2 inches, and in 1866 Moss Rose, for that was her name, was entered in a pony race at Malvern, and that was the celebrated jockey's first real race. He also rode her at Beckford, a well-known sporting rendezvous on the borders of Gloucestershire and Worcestershire. Moss Rose was a fractious little piece of goods, and always required careful steering ; on one occasion she jumped the ropes, we believe at Malvern, but Freddie made her repeat the performance back into the course, and then finished second".

The pony afterwards fell into the hands of old Harry Ayris, the well-known huntsman of the Berkeley Hounds, and she gave him a cropper ; subsequently she came back to Mr. R. Chapman at the Oaklands, and eventually went to London.

Freddy and Moss Rose became regular attendants at the district meets of the Cotswold Hounds, then hunted by the late Mr. Cregoe Colmore. The pony could jump stone walls almost as big as herself. After a good run Freddie was often in at the finish or thereabouts, and on more than one occasion he had the brush. It was, indeed, astonishing to see this weedy little boy on a pony leading the field far ahead of grown men on hundred-guinea hunters.

"Thus," says a writer in *Baily's Magazine*, "in this eminently sporting corner of old England, the rendezvous of the Fitzhardinge and Cotswold Hounds, young Archer took his first breathings and exercise in the saddle, and at a very youthful age was able to follow a pack of hounds over a country where stone walls are not infrequently the obtacles to be surmounted and the stiff red clay of the district often makes deep and heavy going in the arable. . . . Archer learned to sit a horse so well that when in the saddle he seemed to be part of this animal, or, as Dr. Oliver Wendell Holmes has it, to be merely an extension of the muscles of the steed.

"He frequently followed the hounds over the Cotswold

Hills, and was particularly clever with the dry stone walls in the neighbourhood of the Seven Springs, the source of the Thames, near Cheltenham."

This is the country described in Lindsay Gordon's "By Flood and Field," where Captain Nolan, of Balaclava fame, so distinguished himself.

I remember the lowering wintry morn
And the mist on the Cotswold Hills,
Where I once heard the blast of the huntsman's horn
Not far from the Severn Rills,
Jack Esdaile was there, and Hugh St. Clair,
Bob Chapman and Andrew Kerr,
And big George Griffiths on Devil-May-Care,
And Black Tom Oliver.

Colonel F. B. de Sales La Terrière wrote:

"My father and uncle were both prominent steeplechase riders in their young days, and old Billy Archer was a well-known professional steeplechase jockey, who had often ridden with them. When he took the inn at Prestbury he used to come out hunting on a cob and his two boys, Fred and Charlie used to come out on ponies. The two Owens, myself, and the two Archer boys were the small boys of the Cotswold Hunt, and used to shove along against each other. I think most of us were under 12 when I first remember. Everybody used to notice Fred's seat and his riding even at that early age.

"His riding career was stopped for a time by an accident out with the Cotswolds. He got jammed in a gateway, and a horse ridden by a huge man called Tom Potter lashed out and broke his leg. However, he mended all right, and I remember soon after that he rode his first race on a pony at a country meeting near Naunton Inn."

Fred's performances in the saddle naturally opened the eyes of his father and friends to the lad's abundant promise as a jockey, and with three or four training stables around, such as Weever's at Bourton, Holman's at Cheltenham, and Golby's at Northleach, it would be surprising if overtures were not made by one or another to secure the services of such a likely lightweight. Probably such were made, but more probably William Archer looked higher for his second son, having in

42

his eldest, William, one likely enough to follow in his own footsteps.

However, trade fell off at the King's Arms, Archer became hard pressed financially, and Charles went to William Reed's stable. There are several accounts as to how Fred's fate was sealed, and he was apprenticed to Mathew Dawson ; but there seems little doubt that Mr. William La Terrière first suggested that Fred should go to Mathew Dawson.

It was after a ruu with the hounds that William Archer and Fred were returning home when they met Mr. John Reed, the owner of the famous mare, Fantine. It is said of Fantine that they once sent her down from Stratford-on-Avon and walked her into Prestbury the day before the races in charge of a funny old countryman, and the people poked fun at him and Fantine as they came down the Evesham Road. But Fantine beat Mr. Marsh on Pickles and fourteen or fifteen others, and the old man spied some of the people watching the race who had laughed at him, and he turned round and said to them : "Well, and what do you think of my old mare now ?"

To return to the hunt. Mr. "Dick" de Sales La Terrière joined the party, and Mr. Reed invited all of them to the house to taste his famous cider. On arriving there, Mr. La Terrière dismounted, but Freddie and his father remained seated ; while having a chat, Mr. La Terrière said to Freddie's father : "What are you going to make of the boy ?" His father replied : "I think he would make a parson or a lawyer."

At this Freddie smiled, and Mr. La Terrière replied : "I think he would make a good jockey." Addressing Freddie, he said : "Would you like to be a jockey ?" Fred replied, "Yes, sir." Turning to Archer senior, Mr. La Terrière said : "If you like, I will write to my friend Mr. Mathew Dawson, of Newmarket, and see if he would take him." Mr. Archer agreed, and in a few days they received a reply to the effect that Mathew Dawson wished him to bring or send his boy to Newmarket. Freddie at first was reluctant to leave home, but afterwards consented to go with his father.

So a few days later the eleven-year-old child set out with William Archer for Newmarket.

43

CHAPTER IV

SEVERAL other sporting notabilities have been given credit for sending Fred Archer to Mr. Dawson. Mr. John Dawson says : "No doubt my uncle would have taken Archer on his father's recommendation alone. William Archer was himself a well-known steeplechase jockey. He had won the Grand National, which was quite enough to say as to his knowledge of horsemanship. Trainers get scores of letters about boys, it is true, and if a friend of Mathew Dawson's wrote to him, saying : 'There is a little boy down here in Cheltenham, a huntsman's son, or a jockey's' or what not, he would have as likely as not have written and said : 'Send him along, and I'll see what he can do.' All the same, boys are as thick as blackberries, and trainers are far from likely to write for them ; as a rule, they can get all they want without any trouble. William Archer's position in the world of sport was such that he could, as he would naturally, do the best he could for his son without any help from anybody, and he took him to my uncle, who was about at the top of his profession. There are always a lot of stories about racing matters, just as there were forty men in Newmarket and about five hundred in England who just escaped buying The Tetrarch as a yearling, only that another man did."

When William Archer took Fred to Heath House he stayed with Mr. Dawson for a week, and saw his son have a leg up with the other boys at headquarters the morning after his arrival.

This was in February, 1866. At the end of the week Mathew Dawson said to Fred's father : "He will do, Archer, you may leave him."

So, leaving Freddie behind him, Mr. Archer returned home,

most likely thinking he had given the hope of his family a good start off in the world.

Mr. Dawson seems to have been taken with the boy from the very first. Fred was apprenticed for the usual time—five years. The ordinary terms were a fiver for etceteras the first year, but Mr. Dawson said: "Well, I shall give him an extra sovereign. I like the look of his head." However, he seems to have given Fred not one, but two pounds extra.

At any rate, Archer was apprenticed, and the indentures read as follows:

THIS INDENTURE WITNESSETH THAT FREDERICK ARCHER now or late of Prestbury near Cheltenham in the County of Gloucester of the age of eleven years or thereabouts with the consent of his father William Archer of Prestbury aforesaid Innkeeper doth put himself apprentice to Mathew Dawson of Newmarket All Saints in the County of Cambridge Training Groom to learn his Art and with him after the manner of an apprentice to serve from the day of the date hereof until the full end and term of Five Years from thence next following to be fully completed and ended.

During which term the said apprentice his Master faithfully shall serve his secrets keep his lawful commands everywhere gladly obey he shall do no damage to his said Master nor see to be done of others but to his power shall tell or forthwith give warning to his said Master of the same he shall not waste the goods of his said Master or tend them unlawfully to any he shall not commit fornication nor contract matrimony during the said term he shall not play at cards or dice tables or any other unlawful games whereby his said Master may have any loss with his said goods or others during the said term, without licence from his said Master he shall neither buy nor sell he shall not haunt Taverns nor play-houses nor absent himself from his said Master's service day or night unlawfully. But in all things as a faithful apprentice he shall behave himself towards his said Master and all his during the said term and the said Mathew Dawson in consideration of the services of the same Fred Archer doth covenant with the said William Archer that he the said Mathew Dawson will pay unto the said Fred Archer the undermentioned wages the said term that is to say Seven Guineas for the First Year Nine Guineas for the Second Year Eleven Guineas for the third year and Thirteen Guineas for the Fourth and Fifth year respectively and his said Apprentice in the Art of a Jockey and Trainer of Racehorses which he useth by the best means that he can and shall teach and instruct or cause to be taught and instructed finding unto the said Apprentice sufficient meat drink and also hat coat and waistcoat in each year and lodging during the said term.

And the said William Archer doth hereby covenant with the said Mathew Dawson that he the said William Archer shall and will find and provide the said Frederick Archer with washing mending clothing

45

and all other necessaries during the said term except as aforesaid. And for the true performance of all and every the said Covenants and Agreements either of the said parties bindeth himself unto the other by these Presents In witness whereof the Parties above named to these Indentures interchangeable have put their hands and seals in the tenth day of February and in the thirty-first year of the Reign of our sovereign Lady Victoria by the Grace of God of the United Kingdom of Great Britain and Ireland, QUEEN defender of the Faith and in the Year of our Lord One Thousand Eight Hundred and Sixty-Eight.

Signed sealed and delivered by the above named Frederick Archer and Mathew Dawson in the presence of Richard Cole Clerk to Messrs. Kitchener and Fenn, Solicitors, Newmarket.

FREDERICK ARCHER.

The amount of money or the value of any other matter or thing given or agreed to be given with the Apprentice by William Archer by way of Premium must be truly inserted in words at length otherwise the Indenture will be void and double such amount or value forfeited.

Signed sealed and delivered by the above named William Archer in the presence of FREDERICK MARSHALL, Solicitor, Cheltenham.

When Archer became famous the indentures of his apprenticeship, framed and glazed, occupied one of the most conspicuous places in his sumptuous dwelling. He also, in later years, sent his master a copy of them, which Mathew Dawson acknowledged as follows :

46

June 2nd - 1886

My Dear Archer

Very many thanks for
the Indentures. I will keep them as a
souvenir of an event which has yielded
me an immense deal of profit as well as
pleasure.

I am Dear Archer
Ever faithfully yours

Th Dawson

The racing metropolis has a distinct atmosphere of its own. It is a place where horses live in considerable state, and other persons and things exist for their convenience. Whether for the first time you approach it from the windswept Heath or from the railway station, you realize that the town is unique and that hitherto you have missed a delightful experience.

On your right as you leave the Heath is the beautiful cemetery where, within sight of the winning-post of the old Cambridgeshire course, upon which the Whip and Challenge Cup are now run over, Fred Archer lies buried. Over the grave of himself, his wife and his little son is a beautiful white cross adorned with a cluster of roses, which he himself erected in memory of his wife, Nellie Rose Archer.

Near him lie Mathew and John Dawson and others of their family, and on the tombstones as you pass down to the gate are inscribed many names famous in the world of sport. Among these the grave of Captain Machell, Archer's intimate friend, is conspicuous. And nearer to the racecourse even than Archer lies Sir Daniel Cooper, the Australian millionaire, who loved the town so much that he desired to lie within sight of the course, and his grave was lined with his racing colours.

Some of the footpaths of Newmarket are made of cobblestones, with a strip of pavement up the centre. Of course there are inns. On the right is the Rutland Arms, one of the masterpieces of a well-known local architect, Mr. Clarke, the father of the famous racing judge of that name, who was so long in office. It is a beautiful red-brick building, with a large courtyard, which, with the High Street itself and the Jubilee Clock Tower at the end, formed one of the scenes of Cecil Raleigh's Drury Lane drama "The Whip". Behind the Clock Tower to the left are the Fordham Road and The Severals. The latter is a triangular piece of grass, facing one side of which stands Heath House, where Archer lived for so many years.

If you return along the High Street, with the Jubilee Tower at your back and the Rutland Arms on your left, you will find the Crown Hotel at your right hand. In the courtyard towards the end of 1873 Tom Oliver sat on a bench with death written on his face and the prophetic assurance in his heart

48

that he had trained a Derby winner. This was George Frederick; but Tom was dead ere that horse won in 1874.

Below is the Golden Hart, where Harry Morgan, the jockey, went to live when Fred Archer wanted his own rooms at Heath House. On the left-hand side are the Rous and other roads, and the steep Palace Street, named after Charles II's old palace, of which little remains but the foundations. It has been rebuilt into Palace House, the late Mr. Leopold de Rothschild's house. Near it is All Saints' Church, in which is a window to the memory of Archer's wife.

There is a bit of history connected both with Archer's village of Prestbury and Newmarket that is perhaps worth mentioning. The Honourable Berkeley Craven, Lord of the Manor of Prestbury, was allowed by his creditors to cross over from Paris to England, and to go to Newmarket for a month, in order, if possible, to retrieve his fortunes on the Heath.

This permission the witty spendthrift termed "The Jews' Passover". He shot himself after Bay Middleton won the Derby in 1836, as he would not face a settling-day at Tattersall's, though had he waited until after the Oaks he would have made up for his losses on the Derby.

Admiral Rous, of course, reigned in Newmarket for many years, and the memory of the racing dictator is still green in the town. Another old Newmarket celebrity, whose son and grandson both chronicled the doings of Fred Archer, was Mr. Wyndham Berkeley Portman, born June 4, 1804, died July 7, 1883. He was the third son of the late Mr. Portman of Bryanston, and consequently the brother of the then Viscount Portman. From 1840 until 1882 he lived at the Lower Hare Park, Newmarket. Mr. Portman had served in the Royal Navy, and commanded a gunboat at the Battle of Navarino. Although he never owned racehorses, he was for over thirty years a member of the Coffee Rooms, and for more than fifty years scarcely missed a Newmarket meeting. Throughout this period he was on intimate terms with the leading patrons of the Turf, and his old friend the Admiral frequently consulted him on all knotty points in connection with the sport they both loved. He was the father of the late Mr. Wyndham Portman and Mr. Seymour Portman Dalton, so well known in racing circles, and the former of whom found his true vocation as a brilliant and authentic writer on sport. He was a walking stud-book, a most genial man and capital company, and was nearly always at Tattersall's Sales. His obituary notice of Archer is one of the best bits of writing about the great jockey, written by one who knew him and the jockeys of a former generation.

His son, Mr. Arthur Portman, the owner of *Horse and Hound* and a well-known writer on racing subjects, has, together with the late Sir Willoughby Maycock, shown the greatest kindness in helping with the preparation of this book.

Newmarket first appears in history in the year 1227, but there is evidence that the vicinity of the town and Heath was inhabited by the ancient Britons in almost prehistoric times. The Rev. Dr. Dibden mentions that in this year a plague broke out in Exning, and the market was removed to the adjoining village, which thereafter received the name of New-market. The Devil's Dyke on the Heath is mentioned in the year 908. In the Norman period it was called St. Edmund's Dyke.

In 1453, Margaret of Anjou, Queen of Henry VI., was at headquarters, when she gave to two men whose stable was burnt down £3 6s. 8d.

In 1609, James I. was here, hunting and hawking with the Earl of Dunbar, who had married Catherine, daughter of Sir Alexander Gordon of Gicht. (Byron's mother was the last of the Gordons of Gicht, and Lindsay Gordon and he were distantly related.)

In March, 1613, the King, the Prince of Wales, Princess Elizabeth, and her fiancé, Frederick, Prince Palatine of the Rhine (the White King of Bohemia), came to Newmarket, and the Princess chose hunters and hounds to take away with her to her new home.

Judge Coke was disgraced here in 1616 for hinting that the King had caused the death of Prince Henry—a very un-courtierlike suggestion even for the good old times.

In the *Post and Paddock*, p. 10, we are told that in 1751 "two or three were still living who remembered how the Court turned back to London at the news of the Rye House Plot;

and how Nell Gwyn held her infant son out of the window as her royal lover passed down the palace gardens to his stables, and threatened to drop him down if he was not made a duke on the spot.

"Although the King had roasted little Sir Christopher Wren for thinking that the apartments at his hunting palace at Newmarket were quite high enough, there were none at Whitehall that he loved better. One day His Majesty might be 'seen among the elms at St. James's Park, chatting with Dryden about poetry', and on the next his arm was on Tom Durfey's shoulder, and he would be taking a second to his 'Phillida Phillida !' or 'To Horse, my brave boys of Newmarket ! To Horse !' The races have not degenerated since the Merrie Monarch and his wastrel crew crossed the threshold for the last time.

"A writer of Queen Anne's reign speaks of 'the great concourse of nobility and gentry on the Heath, all biting one another as much as was possible', and draws no very flattering contrast between them and the 'horse-coursers of Smithfield'.

"A hundred and thirty-four years after Francis, sixth Earl of Rutland, was nominated a Knight of the Garter at Newmarket, his descendant John Manners, Marquis of Granby, by his marriage with Lady Frances Leveson, became Lord of the Manor of Newmarket, and this property has been successively held by the Dukes of Rutland ever since."

The town of Newmarket is divided into two parishes—All Saints' and St. Mary's, the former in Chieveley Hundred, Cambridgeshire, the latter in Lodeford Hundred, Suffolk, the High Street dividing the two.

The Dawson family, of course, came to Newmarket from Scotland. Mathew was the third son of George Dawson, who was in his day the principal trainer in Scotland, and, besides many horses, he, like the patriarchs of old, trained successfully at Gullane most of his seventeen sons and daughters, all born, save the eldest, in a charmingly situated old house there.

"Gullane," says *The Druid* (in Scott and Sebright, p. 179 et seq.), "was once the Malton of Scotland, and half a dozen horses busy at their ๑ shaped work in the 'myres' served in

1861 to keep up a faint association with Lanercost, Inheritor, and Despot, those knights of the straw body and green sleeves who were once the presiding genii of the spot.

"The house where all the Dawsons were born and bred nestles at the foot of the hill on which stands the rude wooden lighthouse, keeping watch and ward over the German Ocean, and we could hardly wonder that I'Anson always kept his 'Caller Ou' impressions as the breezes fresh frae the Forth swept over us that July. On one side the yellow harvest fields of East Lothian were waving and Dirleton's Woods grew green and fair down to the very edge of the beach. Following the gently curving lines of creamy spray to the right, the eye rests on the Bass Rock, ever clangorous with sea-fowl and standing out blunt and bare from its wave-washed base, and the cone-like eminence of Berwick Law ; while the distant range of the Fife Hills takes us back to Johnny Walker and his 'dearies' before his View Halloo was heard at Wynnstay."

At the then headquarters of Scottish sportsmen Mr. Dawson trained for others beside his original employer. This was in the days when Mr. Ramsay was famous across the border.

"Mr. Ramsay hunted the Carnwath country as well as the three Lothians, and he did not scruple to give 1,500 guineas for Lanercost, 1,000 for The Doctor, and 850 for Inheritor." Then there were his coaches. "Like Ambo, who revelled over the Mostyn Mile, and Charity, the third great Liverpool Steeplechase winner, some of the best Gullane geldings took to the road at last. Wee Willie, Zoroaster, and Clym o' the Clough all came trotting out at the sound of the horn to take their turn in the fourteen-miles-an-hour 'Defiance' ; and Pyramid, who led out of Edinburgh when two bays and two greys cross-fashion was Mr. Ramsay's delight, worked himself stone blind in the cause. The old 'Ury lion' was roused once more in his lair, and horsing this crack coach from Lawrencekirk to Aberdeen, and driving it many a stage, was as great a boon to him as getting up his dog Billy's muscle for another fight or going through solemn pedestrian exercises for the same end with 'my friend Tom Cribb'."

Even the gravest Edinburgh professors liked to see the Ramsay coaches, with their rich brass-mounted harness and the scarlet and white hats when the dashing young owner was on the box, and Alick Cooke, Jim Kitchen, George Murray, and Jamie Campbell were the reigning favourites.

Soon after the death of George Dawson's famous son Mathew the following appeared in the *Illustrated Sporting and Dramatic News* of August 27, 1898 :

"Cramond Regatta being on about a week ago, we thought we would have a look at Barnton, a name ever to be associated in the annals of the British Turf with that genuine British sportsman the late Mr. Ramsay, the owner of Lanercost, Martha Lynn, the Scotch-bred Voltigeur, and numerous other grand racehorses. No doubt Dalmeny, which is just over the Cramond Water, can now show a better record as far as victory in the classic events goes, but if one meets with any old veteran about the coaching haunts of Edinburgh, wearing a square hat and his trousers drawn somewhat tight about his knees, he may be prepared to hear that there never was such a game owner of racehorses as Ramsay of Barnton, and never will be again, sir. Never, sir.

"Ramsay is as much of the past as the thoroughbreds he drove down the Queensferry Road in the mailcoach, and Barnton is being rapidly cut up into building sites and golfing greens for the wealthy lawyers of Edinburgh.

"The thought of Lanercost and the I'Ansons, with the notices of the death of Mr. Mathew Dawson, were the cause of a recent pilgrimage to Gullane, the birthplace of three of the famous training brothers, Mathew, John, and Joseph—Thomas Dawson, the elder brother, having been born at Bogside, Irvine, Ayrshire, in 1809, when George Dawson, the father, was still in the service of Lord Montgomerie. Gullane is, alas, no longer the Newmarket of Scotland, for training on the grand bit of turf on the Haddington shore of the Firth of Forth is entirely forbidden. The last time Mr. Mathew Dawson was in Scotland was to speak against the interdict, and he journeyed down to the old family home to see and chat with some of the old folks and have a last reverent look at his father's grave in the old kirkyard.

"Stamford Hall, in which Mathew Dawson first saw the

light, has changed since old Thomas Dawson disposed of the property to an Edinburgh commercial gentleman, and the old red-tiled stables have long since disappeared in which, seventy years ago, were trained for Lord Kelburne, Reviewer, which ran unplaced in 1827 for the St. Leger, the curiously named Purity, by Octavian out of Hellcat, who won the All-Aged Stakes at Doncaster the same year, and others. Around Goose Common, where the younger members of the racing stud were exercised till ready to be put into harder . work up on Gullane Moor by the sea, there are still a few old natives who remember the place when it was in every way entitled to be called the Newmarket of Scotland.

"Following the track of the horses as they used to go out to work we were soon on the old course, a bit of splendid turf now entirely monopolized by the golfer. Gullane Hill, from which trials were watched many a time in the old days, we found crowned with a perfect forest of Scotch thistles, most of them in full bloom, quite three feet high. The average home-rule Scotsman, who cannot stand the word England being applied to his country, would have gone mad at the sight. We could not help, however, under the circumstances, thinking them emblematic of the Dawson family, sturdy there against all encroachments and still rigid against the fierce blasts which blew in from the North Sea."

Not long before his own death, Mr. John Peart, private secretary and book-keeper to John Scott of Whitewall House, Malton, wrote a memoir of the Dawson family. In it he describes George Dawson as a most upright, skilful and industrious trainer, and also a rigid disciplinarian in the education of his many sons and daughters, whom he did not forget to make acquainted with that Scottish instrument of torture, the tawse. George Dawson certainly spoiled no son or stable-lad of his by flying in the face of Solomon's axiom. More than once in later days Mathew Dawson was heard to declare that he wished his father had had to govern his stable for a short time. George Dawson was most particular that his sons should write well, and it is said that once a friend showed the late Lord Granville four letters, one written by each of the four trainer brethren. Lord Granville gazed long and earnestly at the beautiful specimens of penmanship, and said : "Would that my father had had me taught to write like that."

Among George Dawson's patrons at Gullane were the eccentric Earl of Glasgow, then known as Lord Kelburne, Lord Montgomerie, until his death, Sir David Baird, Mr. Ramsay of Barnton, Sir James Boswell, Mr. Bell, and others.

Thomas Dawson was the eldest of George Dawson's children and was carefully brought up to his father's profession. As soon as he reached man's estate, he left home with his little brother John, and established himself first at Belleisle and afterwards at Brecongill, Middleham, Yorkshire. The fearsome-looking Highlander in Mr. John Dawson's garden at Newmarket once struck awe into the hearts of all beholders beside Tom Dawson's front door at Middleham. He stands on a rockery with stones and plants from Middleham, so, . Mr. Dawson says, his foot is, so to speak, on his native heath.

George Dawson's early death left John in his brother's charge, and the two worked together for nine years. Thomas Dawson became a power in the land in the days when the North-country stables well held their own with the stables south of the Trent, and when the rivalry between the two sections of the racing world, North and South, was at its height. He died in 1880, within a few months of his brother Joseph.

It was Joseph Dawson who, first of the Dawson family, took the road south to Newmarket, whither he was eventually followed by his brothers Mathew and John. Joseph first established himself at Ilsley, in Berkshire, whence he moved to Newmarket, having made up his mind that the town possessed advantages which could not be found elsewhere. He began, with Mr. Pryor as his chief patron, in hired stables close to Heath House, and then resolved to start an establishment of his own, which he did at Heath House itself ; but he moved into Bedford Lodge as soon as a new range of stabling was completed. It is said that under the roof of Bedford Lodge the question was once asked, "Who was Joseph Dawson ?"

Mathew Dawson had named James Waugh as his successor as private trainer to Mr. Merry, and moved into a "cosy place" opposite to St. Mary's Rectory, Newmarket, whence he moved into Heath House as soon as Joseph vacated it. From this time the brothers were never again separated, and John soon afterwards joined them in the racing metropolis, where in 1861 he took up his quarters at Warren House, as private trainer to Prince Batthyany, a connection which lasted for twenty-two years and came to a tragic ending on the afternoon that Archer won the Two Thousand Guineas on Galliard. Scarcely had Galliard, the son of Prince Batthyany's old favourite, Galopin, passed the post, the winner of a very close race, when Prince Batthyany staggered and feel on the steps of the Jockey Club stand and died almost immediately afterwards.

His devotion to everything that pertained to Galopin had always been so great that, when on the eve of the Derby the horse was seized with gripes in the night from drinking chilled water out of an artesian well, John Dawson was afraid to tell the Prince of the stable-boy's carelessness and Galopin's illness lest the shock should upset his very weak heart. Galopin was wrapped in blankets, recovered, and won the Derby.

Since the days when the attention of Joseph Dawson was favourably attracted to Newmarket the history of the little town in Cambridgeshire has undergone what virtually amounts to a revolution. When Mr. Dawson arrived at headquarters he found racing languishing there, and by Joseph Dawson and Godding that revolution was mainly inaugurated. The turning-point was reached when, in 1863, Godding won the Derby with Macaroni.

The spring of that year had been unusually dry, and the old prejudice against Newmarket as being a training-ground with adamantine gallops led to the removal of many favourites to other quarters. Undaunted by the fears of other trainers, Godding continued to send Macaroni along in his gallops, and was rewarded by a double triumph in the Derby and the Two Thousand.

It was just about this time that Joseph Dawson came to Newmarket. When he died, it was said that there had never been in Newmarket a trainer more beloved and respected. To his brother Mathew, his senior by a few years, his loss was simply irreparable. Their love for each other was wonderful, passing the love of brothers.

John Dawson was born on December 18, 1827, and was the last survivor of the famous quartette. Mathew clung longer to his profession than did his younger brother, who retired in 1900, although his love of the Turf remained, and he was to be seen at every Newmarket meeting watching the racing with longing eyes.

The first racehorse Mathew Dawson remembered was Mrs. Barnet, dam of Filho da Puta, the winner of the St. Leger of 1815. Mr. Dawson was once asked how long it was since he trained his first Derby winner. "My first runner—not winner, mind you—I trained in Scotland for Lord Glasgow, and thought I was certain to win, and I told Lord Glasgow so. It was Little Wonder's year, and my horse finished two hundred yards behind the last! You see, young men are apt to be over-confident."

Nothing was more interesting than to hear Mathew Dawson describe the incidents which befell him during his first long journey (now more than a century ago) from the Land o' Cakes to the South of England, in charge of Pathfinder. His journey was performed principally by road, as railways were then in their infancy. On their way southward the horse and his custodian stopped at Catterick Bridge, where Pathfinder, ridden by George Nelson, won a match for three hundred sovereigns against Mr. Meiklam's Remedy, ridden by Tommy Lye. George Nelson was the jockey in whom, by reason of his famous name connecting him with the sea, William IV., the Sailor King, took an interest and put him on the back of Fleur-de-lis when she won the Goodwood Cup in 1830, followed home by Zinganee and The Colonel, both of them, like the winner, the property of His Majesty. The King had inherited them from his brother, George IV., on the death of the latter in June, 1830. So little did William IV. care for racing that he invariably turned his back on the course when his horses were running.

Mathew won the Cumberland Plate with William le Gros as far back as 1843, and again in 1845 with Pythia for Mr. William Hope Johnstone. His first engagement on his own account was as private trainer to Lord Eglinton. At this time he married the devoted wife who was one of the good angels of Fred Archer's professional career.

When Lord Eglinton's horses were sent to Fobert, Mathew returned to his father for a time and then set up for himself at Lambourn, where he trained horses for Mr. (afterwards Sir John) Don. Wauchope and Lord John Scott. For the latter he won a fair number of races, but it was not until 1851 that he got a really good one in Lord John's Hobbie Noble, son of Pantaloon and Phryne, who ran away with the New Stakes in the first Exhibition year and also the July in the same season. Mathew Dawson was very fond of Lord John, and was never tired of telling anecdotes about him and about Mr. Wauchope, for whom in 1853 Mathew won his first classic, the Oaks, with Catherine Hayes by Lanercost. Dawson also trained The Riever and Morgan La Faye. In 1856, Cannobie ran third for the Derby, won by Ellington, trained by Thomas Dawson.

When Lord John Scott sold off his racing-stock, Mr. Merry, for whom Mat now trained at Russley Park, winning the Derby of 1860 with Thormanby, commissioned Dawson to buy Lord John's beautiful mares, including Phryne, Catherine Hayes, and Lady Lurewell.

At Heath House, a port-wine-coloured mansion, facing The Severals and backing on to Bury Hill, the famous trainer reigned for nearly twenty years, until he handed over the establishment to his nephew, George Dawson, and moved to Exning.

Once the late Mr. Tattersall was ill and he went down to Newmarket. He ought not to have gone at all, but he wanted to go, and so he would not ask his doctor's advice. Therefore it was not the fault of Newmarket that he was ill, but he recovered, and lived for about two years afterwards. While he was there, Mrs. Tattersall called to see Mathew Dawson who remarked that Newmarket was not a place fit for any human being to live in for six months of the year. Yet he had managed to live and prosper there for half a lifetime.

Mathew Dawson also trained for the then Dukes of Hamilton and Newcastle, the latter of whom owned Julius, Pace, and Speculum. Leonie did the Duke of Hamilton good service.

The year of Archer's apprenticeship, 1868, was a great year for Heath House, as nearly every horse in the stable won races of some sort. Julius, as a four-year-old, twice turned the St. Leger tables on Hermit and once on Achievement. In the preceding year he had been beaten a length and a head by Achievement and Hermit. In 1868, too, Mathew Dawson won the City and Suburban for the Duke of Newcastle with Speculum, carrying 6 stone 12 lb. This colt also won the Goodwood and Brighton Cups.

For the Duke of Hamilton the Heath House trainer won the Prendergast Stakes at Newmarket and had other successes. Leonie did splendidly, and Mathew also won many races of minor importance.

CHAPTER V

HEATH HOUSE was in every way a model training establishment. No boy was allowed to speak a sharp word to his horse. To use a stick was a criminal offence. Firmness and kindness were the means which had to be employed. At Heath House the moral welfare of the lads was as scrupulously cared for as were their domestic conditions. Long after Archer had become a famous jockey he had to join the other lads in the services held by a chaplain paid by Mrs. Dawson, and he often used to say in after-life how much he owed to Mrs. Dawson's care and kindness and teachings.

For his first few months away from his mother Fred was very miserable, and he used to send her most pathetic letters begging to come home. He was always delicate, and the elder boys bullied him, and Mrs. Archer was perfectly wretched and wanted to get him back. She would meet Mr. Ned Griffiths sometimes, and he would say: "Well, Mrs. Archer, and how's the boy getting on?" And she would tell him all her troubles and talk things over with him, and feel better about everything. But after a time she ceased to have unhappy letters. The elder boys left off bullying the strange little bundle of contradictions from Cheltenham—the sensitive, highly strung little boy who could jump the stiffest wall in the Cotswold country.

And yet Archer, so Mathew Dawson is said to have once told Mr. Cecil Raleigh, used to cry because he had to go out with the horses in the morning, to such a pitch of excitement did the prospect of the day's labours work up the highly wrought little creature who was long-sighted about danger. He united nerves with the iron nerve of a Spanish bullfighter; he took his life in his hands over the Cotswold country and round Tattenham Corner, and yet always preferred company in the dark.

Fred, during his five years' apprenticeship to Mathew Dawson, gave no trouble, apparently impressed with that immortal North-country proverb which ought to be written up in letters of gold over every racing-stable, and a good many less important institutions, "It's canny to say nowt," and he from childhood kept his eyes open and his mouth shut.

Of Archer's career as a stable-boy and unknown to fame there is really little to record except that from the first he conformed to the patriarchal maxim : "Whatsoever thy hand findeth to do, do it with all thy might." No act of insubordination or disobedience is recorded against him, and he set himself with a will to acquire the rudiments of the difficult art which was to lead him to fame and fortune. He thus by degrees mastered every point of good riding, that of finishing well costing him more trouble than all the others put together.

About a year or fifteen months after Fred went to Mr. Dawson's he came home for his holidays. Henry Parker was still one of the household at the King's Arms, and he said he could still see Freddie in a kind of tan-coloured stable suit, as he sat on the old black oak settle that stood by an old-fashioned fireplace they used to have in the kitchen. Fred recounted his experiences in the racing metropolis, and this news from headquarters was listened to with interest and excitement at the time.

It was very early in his apprenticeship, too, that Mr. William Villar saw Fred riding at an Agricultural Show held near the Oaklands, Cheltenham, where Bob Chapman lived, and the boy's feats of horsemanship amazed everyone. Bob Chapman was the "swell horsedealer", Lindsay Gordon's "hard riding Bob". The Cheltenham people said that King Edward used sometimes to come down when he was Prince of Wales and visit Bob Chapman at the Oaklands. Bob ran away with the daughter of a Colonel Hogg and married her. He was employed to pilot her out hunting. When remonstrated with, Bob replied, "Well, I took her out of a pig-sty into a stable."

61

In these holidays Fred hunted whenever he had the chance. Sometimes he borrowed Cecil Raleigh's pony, but oftener he rode Chow, the famous racing pony that old Billy Archer generally rode. Chow was by Hazard, dam by Olic, and stood about 13 hands, a perfect little wonder and the winner of three silver cups and several stakes and matches in various parts of the country.

Mr. Dawson was one of the kindest and most thoughtful of masters. He was likewise a good and observant judge of the riding of his apprentices, and had been a brilliant horseman himself in his young days. He soon began to notice the promise shown by Fred Archer, and used to say that it did not take him long to find out that he had discovered one of the greatest jockeys of all time.

The late Mr. John Corlett wrote:

"Our recollections of Archer go back beyond those of any sporting writer, and our first knowledge of him was stamped in a most peculiar manner on our memory. We were one morning on Newmarket Heath, when Mr. Mathew Dawson, pointing to a small boy on a bay horse, said: 'There is a little fellow I shall be able to make a jockey of. He wants "hands" at present, but he is the pluckiest lad I ever had; he will do anything.' Calling Archer out of the string, he said: 'My little man, dare you jump your horse into that field? Your father used to ride over fences, and I don't see why you shouldn't.' 'Yes, sir,' said the boy, touching his cap. He at once jumped his horse from the heath into the adjoining field and back again, and then took his place as before, a smile of satisfaction beaming over the broad genial face of the trainer."

We are told elsewhere that Archer was riding St. Pancras when he thus attracted The Master's attention.

In 1869, the year after Archer was apprenticed, Lord Falmouth resolved to link his racing fortunes with those of Mathew Dawson at Heath House. Up to that time Fortune had not smiled upon the Cornish peer, although John Scott had won him the Oaks with Queen Bertha. Had his lordship died in that year, his name would have gone down the stream of time as that of a man who owned racehorses for twenty years and won but two races which were worth recording—namely, the One Thousand of 1862 and the Oaks of 1863.

But from the time he sent his horses to Heath House his racing career was one long-sustained hymn of perpetual triumph. Just about this time Mathew Dawson's connection with the somewhat reckless Dukes of Hamilton and Newcastle ceased, and he had more room and more time to bestow upon his new patron. His new apprentice, too, was growing up ready to win for Lord Falmouth the greatest series of victories that the world has ever seen. The proximity of Archer was just luck, perhaps, but the choice of Mathew Dawson as a trainer was part of the wisdom which brought about much of Lord Falmouth's success as a breeder and owner of thoroughbreds.

Lord Falmouth was born on March 18, 1819, his father being John Evelyn, son of the third viscount. He was educated at Eton and Christchurch, called to the Bar in 1841, and married, in 1841, Baroness Le Despencer, of Mereworth Castle. He was one of the most popular, genial, and high-minded noblemen ever tried by the fiery furnace of the British Turf. He was one of the most generous of men, and so interested was he in sport that he spent several months of each year at Newmarket in studying his horses, and consulting with Mathew Dawson as to how they might best be prepared to meet their engagements.

The popular colours were first enrolled in the Racing Calendar in 1860, when "Mr. T. Valentine's" Silverhair (purchased as a yearling at Middle Park) won the Great Northern Handicap at Ripon, ridden by Egerton. In 1862, Queen Bertha made her début and won a great stake at Newmarket, and in the following year she won for Lord Falmouth his first Oaks, ridden by Aldcroft, after an extraordinary race with Manifold and Vivid. She also took the Ascot Triennial but was second to Lord Clifden for the St. Leger. In 1864, Lord Falmouth threw off his *nom de guerre*, and in that year was elected a member of the Jockey Club.

On the whole, his luck was provoking until he placed his horses under the care of Mathew Dawson. A great friendship, and even affection, sprang up between the pair, which lasted to the end of their lives. Meanwhile we find Lord

63

Falmouth in 1869, with Kingcraft as a two-year-old (he won the Derby in 1870), winning six races with 3,765 sovereigns, including the Chesterfield Stakes, at the July meeting.   With these successes, and with those of Stromboli, Gertrude, Atlantis, Lady Betty, Nightjar, etc., the Magpie colours soon became well known.   This was the time when Fred Webb first distinguished himself as a jockey.   Mathew Dawson was perhaps less successful for Mr. Naylor than for his other patrons.

Archer first supported silk at headquarters at the Second October Meeting in Cherie's Cesarewitch week in a handicap plate.   He had the mount on Honoria, but the mare was merely started to give Archer practice and make the running for Fred Webb, the stable's leading lightweight, on Lord Falmouth's Stromboli, a King Tom colt out of Hurricane, who won the race.   The coming luminary finished ingloriously last.

About this time William Archer visited Newmarket to see how his little boy was getting on and he took Fred to the sale of Mr. Naylor's horses.   Mrs. Willins, of Gorgate Hall, East Dereham, was there too.   She sometimes attended the Cheltenham Races, and Fred is even said to have ridden a pony of hers in an event previous to this time.   At any rate, this well-known patron of the Turf, in her somewhat mannish attire, was well known in Archer's village, as at nearly every race-meeting in the country.

William Archer pointed to his little son, and said to Mrs. Willins : "Here, madam, this is the one to ride over fences." Mrs. Willins took the hint, and went to ask Mathew Dawson's leave for Fred, a pigmy of under five stone, to ride a pony of hers, the well-known Maid of Trent, in a steeplechase at the featherweight of 4 stone 11 lb.   Years afterwards, and not long before his death, Fred Archer gleefully described to an interviewer how he "scored his first winning mount at Bangor prior to his successful début on the flat at Chesterfield."   This proves that Mrs. Willins, who ran horses on almost every course in the kingdom, was right when she claimed that Archer rode his first winner for her.   He afterwards, during his apprenticeship, rode two winners for the same lady at Rugby.

Mr. Dawson, with the keen eye of a sportsman had, as has been said, soon "spotted" the qualities of the lad, and gave him many chances of distinguishing himself in his profession, and Freddy showed his superiority over the other boys by his pluck in mounting any awkward kind of horse, and clinging to his seat when he got there. Allowed to ride in public, he secured his first win at crooked-spired Chesterfield. This first race won by Archer under Jockey Club rules took place on September 28, 1870. The trainer, Mr. John Peart of Malton, himself lifted his juvenile jockey into the saddle, and at the time of Archer's death he was still living to tell the tale.

The quiet little meeting at Chesterfield has long since dropped out of the list of fixtures. The Nursery Handicap which Archer won on Mr. Bradley's two-year-old was quite unimportant, but it was a beginning, and, though it did not look like it at the time, it was an exemplification of the saying that "small beginnings make great endings". His mount, Athol Daisy, was not a real "daisy-cutter", though he later won a few more plates ; but his fame will chiefly rest on being the first winning mount of the prince of modern horsemen. In this second year of Fred's apprenticeship he was put up on fifteen occasions, winning twice, and was no fewer than nine times second.

Consequently people began to take notice of Billy Archer's little boy. Maidment, the jockey, said that Jim Snowden was once about to ride in a race against Freddy Archer and looked contemptuously at the juvenile horseman, remarking to Maidment : "Is yon lad a 'Sune', or what ? Tha' tell me he can ride !"—meaning was he put up at such an early age because he was the son of a trainer or some notability.

At one period in the race Maidment was riding on the outside, Snowden in the middle, and Archer on the inside, and Snowden said to Archer : "Canst ride, m'lad ?" It was a well-run race, and Snowden beat Archer by a head. He turned to his crestfallen young opponent (for Archer at no time took defeat kindly) and said with scorn : "Tha told me tha couldst ride, lad. Tha cassn't ride for nuts !"

Even in after years Archer hated to be beaten, and once

after a race a friend said to him : "You look a trifle put out."

"Yes, and I feel what I look. And you'd perhaps be put out if you'd been riding against Fordham in that race. He was 'cluck-clucking' at his mount the whole of the way. I thought I had him beaten two or three times in the two miles. But, with his infernal 'cluck, cluck', he was always coming again. Still two hundred yards from home I supposed I had him dead-settled. 'I'll cluck, cluck you !' I thought, and at that instant he swoops on me and beats me easily. Yes, I do feel put out."

Mr. and Mrs. Mathew Dawson had no children of their own, and perhaps that made them extra fond of Fred. And he was just as devoted to them. He used in later days to say to his sister Alice : "There are no two men in the world I would sooner see come into my house than Lord Falmouth and Mathew Dawson." And they were the two men he had most to do with during his whole riding career.

"Everything," once said his sister Alice, "was changed for my father and mother when their brilliant son began to come to the front. Fred knew we were short of money, and he was a most generous and thoughtful little boy. At first he would send postal orders for a few shillings whenever he could spare them. Later it ran to 'fivers', and, of course, at last to big sums of money. Their hard times had never taught my father and mother economy, and they often ran up long bills, for the tradespeople always knew that they had Fred Archer at their back, and would trust them for large amounts.

"At last a long bill would come in, and then father and mother at once wrote off to Fred, and a cheque would come by return of post. And they always used up all the money as soon as Fred sent it, to pay off the whole bill ; they did not spend some of it on other things and pay the bill by instalments. But it always went on like that ; they always owed long bills, and Fred always paid them.

"Fred had a great deal of character. He was very gentle, but he took no liberties himself, and no one ever thought of taking one with him. His brothers and sisters, and indeed his whole family, looked up to him, and his servants, some of whom had been in the stable with him when he was an apprentice, were marvellously obedient.

"And yet he was always so quiet. There was never any ranting and raving. If a groom brought round a horse, Fred always looked it over, and if he saw anything wrong he would tell the man to take it back; the man would be off in a moment, and very soon back with everything all right. And the horse had to be round to the moment. Fred would rather be two minutes early than two minutes late. He got that from his grandfather, the old churchwarden, and certainly not from father; and mother soon dropped into father's unpunctual ways when she was married.

"Of course, some very untrue things were said about Fred. People have only to be celebrated in any way to get all sorts of tales told about them. Folks were always chaffing Fred about great ladies who admired him. There's that absurd cutting in the scrap-book saying that a sporting duchess proposed to Fred and he refused to marry her. He always said that the duchess was just like a good comrade to him, interested in the same things, and he took no notice when people told him he might be her second husband.

"One day, when I was putting some things straight in Fred's bedroom, I found a letter lying about from a lady of very high degree indeed, and she was writing and asking Fred why he was so cold to her and all that—a married lady too! Just then Fred came in and saw me with it in my hand.

"Fred said: 'Well, then, you must just forget all about it, as if you hadn't read it at all.' And I promised, and I never, of course, said anything about it in his lifetime, nor have I ever told who it was; but it just shows that Fred wasn't one to talk about people being silly over his riding. He had always associated with aristocratic people since he was quite a boy, and I think he had very good manners.

"Mother lived with us after father died. She and Fred were both of them wonderfully sympathetic people. Fred was always more of a listener than a talker, but you always felt you could tell him things, and it was the same with mother. I never minded things much when I had her to talk them over with. We used to tease her because she would sit reading some novel or the *Sportsman* at an age when we told her she

67

ought only to have sat and read the Bible. But she said :
'I can't be a hypocrite—I like the same things now I am old
that I liked when I was young ; and as for racing, it has been
my whole life !'

"Father never was a betting man, nor a card-player, but
he always let mother do exactly as she liked, and thought
everything she did was right too—and she loved a game of
cards to her dying day, and always liked to have a bet on
too. It must have been a proud day for her when she saw
her son of about nineteen win the Derby. Mother was very
charitable, and I don't think I ever heard her say anything
unkind about anybody. She always found some excuse for
people if we blamed them."

CHAPTER VI

IN 1871, Fordham and Maidment ran a dead heat for first place on the list of winning jockeys. Amongst the successes of the Heath House stable in this year were those of Queen's Messenger, who won every time he ran, including the Buckenham Stakes and the Clearwell, while Patriarch won the Ham Produce at Goodwood, and Noblesse was second to Hannah in the Oaks and third to her in the One Thousand. Archer's first mount in 1871 was in a handicap plate at the Craven Meeting. This and his subsequent doings are quite insignificant down nearly to the close of his indentures in 1872. In this season he had twenty-seven mounts, but was only successful in three races. That Archer framed to be an exceptionally fine horseman was noticed by some critics very early in his career.

"It first struck me," said "Vigilant" in the *Sportsman* of November 9, 1886, "that a great future was before him when he rode in an unimportant race ending at the Rowley winning-post, and I saw him gradually draw up to the horses in front of him, glance across at the judges' box, and, measuring his distance, make an effort that, if I remember rightly, just got him home first."

About this period young John Dawson went to live at Heath House with his uncle Mathew, and he had much that was interesting to say about Fred Archer, with whom he shared a sitting-room. He once said : "Of course, I know the sort of life he lived in the early days of his apprenticeship, for it was just the sort of life any other boy about a stable lived. Where he differed from the other boys of his day is that he became a jockey very early. In those days the jockeys were all middle-aged men, between thirty and

69

forty at any rate—bearded men one might almost say, only that it was the long side-whiskers that they wore.

"It was Tom French's death that started Archer off in the world. My uncle realized what a brilliant little boy he had in his stable, and when French died and Lord Falmouth thought that everything was at an end because he hadn't got a jockey, my uncle insisted on putting up Archer. Fred was riding at 6 stone 1 lb., in the same week as that in which he won the Two Thousand Guineas. That would be nothing in these days, but it was a most extraordinary thing then. Nowadays any little boy in knickerbockers may win the Derby. Why, there were two little boys knocking about a stable in Newmarket some years ago, riding everything they came across, and one day on the Heath a lady picked up one of the little creatures (J. Rieff) and kissed him, so the story goes. And he was quite a famous jockey!

"I first remember Fred Archer when he was beginning to get famous. He was a very nice-looking fellow, with sometimes, especially when he was wasting, a very sad expression. He was a very clever man, who, if he had been educated at Oxford or Cambridge, would have made his name in other professions. He was not like many other jockeys—nothing when he got out of the saddle. It was a pity he had not more education. But there, what are you to do? They come to us at about twelve or thirteen, and they are no use when they get to a certain weight.

"They have to learn to ride by the time they are up to about four stone, and it takes them most of their time, so there's not much left to be educated in. Fred and I were about the same age. My uncle didn't believe in the lads being out late at night, and he had sort of wire entanglements (I think some of them are left now) put up round Heath House. He forgot that you can neither keep boys in nor out if they want to be elsewhere. I used to walk home with Fred, and help him over the fence; he'd climb up the wire, rather helped than otherwise by it, and get in at his bedroom window. His old rooms are there now, just the same, on the right-hand side of Heath House.

"I don't say Fred was the greatest jockey that ever lived. Perhaps I think so, and another man would think differently.

Just as a lot of men think The Tetrarch the greatest horse that has ever run, and I think St. Simon has never been equalled. You can't compare the jockeys and horses of one generation with those of another, and say one is better or worse than another, because they have lived under such different conditions. Neither can you bring back all the men who fought with Tom Sayers and the rest, or all the old horses and jockeys that ran against the champions of old days, and thus you can't tell what they had to contend against. You can neither bring back the men nor their environment. Times change.

"But the remarkable thing about Archer was the attention he attracted. The King even may come down to Newmarket now, and less stir is made than when, for instance, Archer used to go to Manchester. I've seen the whole of the street blocked with carriages and people as far as you could see to watch for Archer as he came out of the Queen's Hotel and see him get into his cab and drive away.

"Of course, he came very much to the front in Newmarket. One thing he started was the Drag, which developed into the Newmarket Drag Hounds, and went on for many years after his death. It began in his getting a few of us to ride a sort of steeplechase across country, and anyone might be first who could.

"Mrs. Archer, Fred's mother, was a fine-looking woman. Perhaps Fred was not altogether like her, but he wasn't a bit like William Archer, who was a little, round sort of man. But Fred and his mother looked as if they came of aristocratic people, and Charlie did too. I don't know who she was, but she gave you that impression. Fred had rather a long, narrow face. He was rather tall, and it meant a fearful amount of wasting, and that's what indirectly caused his death.

"He was training down to ride a horse in the Cambridgeshire down here, and there was a lot of money on it. For people staked much larger sums in those days than they do now, and that meant perhaps that they stood to win £80,000 or £100,000 on the Cambridgeshire, mostly in the hands of one or two people, so that a great deal depended on Fred winning that race, and he had to get down to 8 stone 6 lb.

for it. He caught a chill on the top of all this wasting, and had no strength to throw it off. It turned to typhoid fever, and they had two or three nurses down and a lot of people about. But between them all he was allowed to do it. Anyone else might do a thing like that in a delirious state of high fever.

"A good many people at the time said it never ought to have happened; he ought to have been watched, and they oughtn't to have left him, or taken their eyes off him for one moment. It seemed so sad for such a brilliant young life as that to be cut off, quite one of the things that ought not to have happened. I think most of the people who were looking after him were thrown off their guard by not knowing that he had a revolver, and by not even thinking of the possibility of his doing anything of the sort."

Bells' Life of November 15, 1886, says : "When, just before staggering out of bed and firing the fatal shot, he put to his sister the question that will live in the pages of the future—'Are they coming ?'—the words referred to the expected arrival of the solicitors to alter some portions of his Will. This fact alone shows how cool was the man's brain up to the one tick of the clock, as may be said—and how unpremeditated the deed."

It is said that Fred Archer had a great fear of being buried alive, and this terror may have worked in his disordered brain, and made him think that as he was so ill that death seemed to be inevitable, he would himself make certain that he should not be buried before that event happened.

"The wasting," continued John Dawson, "was hard upon Fred. We would come in from riding, and the rest of us had lunch and he had a nap. He'd perhaps had a very light breakfast, and then nothing else. Of course, he was a very wonderful and unusual boy, who shot up like a rocket into fame when he was almost a child. But I dare say he was lucky to get with my uncle. Of course, he got a very thorough training, and good horses to ride—and riding, to a very great extent, depends on the sort of training a boy gets."

ARCHER'S PRINCIPAL WIN IN 1872

Cesarewitch Stakes.—Salvanos, 11 to 2.

CHAPTER VII

It was practically not until he was out of his apprenticeship that Archer really became famous, and not so much was heard of him in 1871 and 1872. In the latter year, however, Archer, who had no difficulty in going to scale at the minimum impost of 5 stone 7 lb., won the Casarewitch on Salvanos, who had that weight to carry.

In the October Handicap, Salvanos, a colt belonging to Mr. J. Radcliffe, had bolted, overpowering Chapman, his rider. This kind of accident rarely happened to Archer during his whole career, though it was his fate now and again to be up upon an incorrigible animal, that nobody else could do anything with, and which possibly succeeded in unseating him and bolting *without* him.

Even with this class of kittle cattle he sometimes did wonders. He made the savage Muley Edris win at two and three years old, and later on he overcame, with infinite patience, the vagaries of Tristan and Peter, notably in the latter's Hunt Cup victory of 1881.

When Salvanos bolted at the First October Meeting he looked very like the winner of the Newmarket October Handicap, and Mr. Dawson, who had already a very high idea of Archer's riding, substituted Fred in the Cesarewitch for the lightweight who had ridden the colt on the first occasion.

The result was justified, for Salvanos led the field down the Bushes Hill and was never headed, Archer simply sitting still and riding with all the confidence of a veteran. The owner, Mr. Radcliffe, was a pleasant, cheery man, whose fallen fortunes were for a time retrieved by his Cesarewitch victory, for prior to this he had gambled freely and lost

75

heavily.   It is said that the result of the Cesarewitch made him more reckless, and he was a big loser when Salvanos was badly beaten in the Cambridgeshire.

Archer's apprenticeship finished at the Christmas of 1872, and Dawson presented him with a gold watch inscribed: "For good conduct.—Mathew Dawson." With all the temptations which beset him, and which few could have withstood, Archer was always steady, and, showing his watch to a friend, he said: "I value this more than anything I have, and shall keep it as long as I live."

Although his successes up to this time had been very limited, yet they seem to have been won with great style and with cleverness.

Archer stepped into Webb's shoes as the stable lightweight, but it was the death of poor Tom French that gave him his great opportunity and the first real step to his future greatness. A more exemplary, well-conducted jockey than Tom French never lived, and he was a brilliant horseman. To one like Archer, so quick to learn, it must have been a great advantage to have such a man as French for a senior. The latter's death occurred in the summer of 1873, from consumption brought about by over-wasting. Next to Archer, who stood 5 ft. 8½ in. in his stockings, French was perhaps the tallest jockey ever seen.

Looking back to this past time, we cannot fail to notice a strange similarity in the closing scenes in the lives of these two famous horsemen. They both died at the same age—twenty-nine; both were identified with the same stable and were devotedly attached to its interests; both loved their profession and sacrificed themselves for it; both succumbed, in one form or another, to the trying effects of wasting. Alike, too, in physique, they resembled each other in style, the younger jockey, as so many of his races showed, having formed his style on that of his predecessor.

In September of this year Archer won the Ayr Gold Cup on Alaric for Mr. Houldsworth, who had claimed the horse in a selling race from Count Lagrange. This was a runaway win by ten lengths, and created some surprise, as the horse had been nearly last for the Ayrshire Handicap the day before, and the victory was no doubt due to the young jockey's trick of getting off well and making the most of his advantage.

Mr. Dawson always considered that Queen's Messenger was very unlucky in not winning the Derby of 1872, in which he could only finish third to Cremorne and Pell Mell, though he beat Joseph Dawson's favourite, Prince Charlie, who had finished four lengths in front of Queen's Messenger for the Guineas.

Maidment, the rider of that year's Derby winner, still lived in Newmarket, and his proudest boast seemed to me, *not* that he twice carried off the Blue Riband of the Turf, but that he first tried Emblem and Emblematic over hurdles, and his hints enabled George Stevens to win the Grand National with these two mares in successive years. It was worth going a long way to hear Maidment's dramatic account of Stevens getting ready to ride the second year, and asking in a hoarse and agonized whisper, "Can I win on sisters?" to which his guardian angel (Maidment) replied: "Of course you can. I could myself, and I'm not a steeplechase jockey."

The Lincoln Meeting of 1873 found Fred riding as a free lance and carrying Mr. Rufford's colours on Seringa. He did not win, and in riding Cobham for his own stable in the Handicap Archer had no better fortune. He went on to Liverpool and scored twice on Mr. Houldsworth's Woodcut, and next took the Nottingham Handicap with Sybarite and the Delapré Free Handicap at Northampton with the Vevette colt by Wamba. No sooner was the lad out of his articles than retainers came in right and left. Some of his supporters were Prince Batthyany and the Earls of Rosebery and Bradford. The last mentioned wrote to Archer on the occasion of his wedding:

"Weston Park, Shifnal.
"*February* 25, 1883.

"ARCHER,

"As one of your earliest employers, after your own stable—indeed, I believe the first, except Prince Batthyany— I must write to send you my congratulations and many good wishes for your happiness as a married man; and I send you a little present for your breakfast table, which I hope may be

useful. I hope I shall have a horse or two for you to ride
in the course of the season.

"I remain,

"Faithfully yours,

"BRADFORD."

In 1873, though he did not win any of the classic races, he
advanced rapidly to the front. He had no less than 419
mounts, winning on 107, Constable defeating him for first
place by three, having a record of 110 wins out of 397 mounts.

There was a severe contest between them as to who would
be at the top of the list, but Constable had a bit the best of it
at Warwick.

It was in this year that Tom French died, and a few years
later Archer lost Constable as a friend and companion.

The *Sporting Times* says Archer was apprenticed to Mr.
Dawson at a very fortunate time. Webb, who had been
riding lightweights for the stable, and had won the Cesarewitch
on Chérie, accumulated flesh very rapidly, and Archer was
just in time to take his place. A year or two later the death
of poor Tom French caused a still greater vacancy. It was
hardly anticipated that a lightweight would be made first
jockey to the most powerful stable in England, but such
proved to be the case.

It was the way Archer rode Andred that caused Lord
Falmouth to put on one side all the old-fashioned prejudices
against deadweight.

What confirmed him in this opinion, there can be no doubt,
was Archer's fortunate mount on Atlantic in the Two
Thousand Guineas.

Andred, it is notorious, won all his best races in the hands
of Archer.

ARCHER'S PRINCIPAL WINS IN 1874

WOODCOTE STAKES (EPSOM).—LADYLOVE, 10 to 1.
LINCOLNSHIRE HANDICAP.—TOMAHAWK, 14 to 1.
CLEARWELL STAKES.—C. by MACARONI—REPENTANCE,
10 to 1.
STEWARDS' CUP (GOODWOOD).—MODENA, 10 to 1.
TWO THOUSAND GUINEAS.—ATLANTIC, 10 to 1.

CHAPTER VIII

The next year, 1874, saw Archer fairly at the head of affairs with the magnificent total of 147 wins. Early in this year his lowest riding weight was 6 stone, but at the end of it he had gone up a lot in the scale, so, even after severe wasting, had to declare 3 lb., overweight when getting down to 6 st. 1 lb. for the Truth gelding in the Cesarewitch, a race in which many think he would have been successful but for the weakness from which he suffered in consequence of wasting. At any rate, he allowed the strength of that pocket Hercules, Glover, who had the mount on Lord Ailesbury's Aventurière, to turn the scale of riding against him.

The following story is worth relating as throwing an interesting light on how handicaps were made in those days.

Admiral Rous was the handicapper, and when he was in any difficulty he was in the habit of consulting his friend George Hodgman. The gelding by Wamba out of Truth belonged to Mr. Fred Swindell, who was, to say the least, rather "warm", and he had saved the horse for the Cesarewitch. So long-headed was Swindell that he even took the gelding away from his own trainer and sent him to Mathew Dawson twelve months beforehand, because he knew that by doing so he should make sure of Archer's services.

Admiral Rous and Hodgman happened to meet at Leamington, and the former produced his Cesarewitch handicap, which was then in the making. "What does this mean?" said Hodgman, pointing to the Truth gelding. "You have him in at all sorts of weights—7 stone 4 lb., 6 stone 12 lb., 6 stone 4lb., 6 stone, 5 stone 12 lb. What does it all mean?" The Admiral confessed he was in a quandary. Some people had told him it was "a rod in pickle", while others had

81

endeavoured to impress upon him that it was a rank bad horse, and he suggested that Hodgman should ask Swindell what sort of a horse he was.

"Now, Admiral, you really don't expect that that old fox would tell me anything ?" replied Hodgman, but all the same, he carried the message to Swindell, who rose to the occasion.

"Tell him," said Swindell, "that if he's got 6 stone on him he may scratch the damned horse. And further, tell him that he can have the brute for a hundred."

"Better make it two hundred," suggested a friend. "The old boy might take you at your word."

Hodgman returned to the Admiral, who on the strength of the message flung the Truth gelding into the Cesarewitch with 5 stone 12lb. Swindell kept out of the way of Hodgman for weeks, and, hearing nothing, the latter laid against the horse, thinking there was something wrong.

In the meantime Swindell had backed the horse to win £100,000, but, when eventually they did meet, he declared he had very little on and would only lay Hodgman nineteen "ponies", while he laid the Admiral twenty "ponies".

Both men knew they had been "done", and were correspondingly wild.

"I do hope he will be beaten," declared the Admiral; "but Mat Dawson says the race is as good as over."

This was one of Mr. Swindell's coups that did not come off; but there were others that did. However, Archer was not connected with these.

A writer in the *Newcastle Journal* for August 22, 1898, says :

"I have an idea that the largest sum Mathew Dawson ever stood to win was on the Truth gelding in the Cesarewitch, when he was beaten by a head by Adventurière. In this desperately contested finish Archer was so pressed to reach the weight that he rode without his shirt."

Archer's first appearance in 1874 was in the green jacket of Prince Batthyany at Lincoln, when he won the Brocklesby Stakes on Nightstar, and the next day achieved a far more important success by riding for Mr. Swindell—sometimes named "Lord Freddy"—and Mat Dawson, the handsome chesnut son of Thormanby, Tomahawk, in the Lincolnshire Handicap, and an immense sum was won thereby by Freddy

Swindell and the astute division who obeyed his suggestions and followed his clever manipulations.

Mat was remarkably sanguine as to the success of Tomahawk, and as with ruddy and beaming face he saddled his well-prepared pet, whose burnished coat even so early in the season exhibited manifest signs of the perfection of the trainer's art, he quietly remarked to a well-known patron of the Heath House celebrated stable : "It will take a good one to beat him to-day with only 6 stone 4 lb. on his back. In fact, unless there's something more than the ordinary, this year's Derby will be his."

Mat's instructions to Archer were : "Get well away, hold a good place, don't get shut in, and ride him tenderly."

Tenderly Archer did ride him, for his horse won with consummate ease in front of thirty-four others, and afterwards Tomahawk saw a short price for the Blue Riband of the Turf. He was, however, a difficult horse to train, not over and above a genuine stayer, and George Frederick, the winner, though coarse and heavy-looking, was by far and away in a superior class to the Lincoln Handicap winner.

Early in 1874 two Hungarian gentlemen, Messrs. Alexander and Hector Baltazzi, were forming a stud of racehorses in England. Mr. Alexander Baltazzi succeeded in winning the Derby of 1876 with Kisber. Hector Baltazzi, who raced under the name of Mr. Bruce, was a gentleman rider of some repute. Maidment, who won the Derby on Kisber, said that before the race Mr. Baltazzi said to him : "Why are you always so cool ? I am always like this." Maidment, a born mimic, was not content with imitating his foreign employer's accent ; you could see the Hungarian rise up before you with his trembling hands on the horse's reins.

"But I," said Maidment, "am just the same in the Derby as when I am riding in trials." Maidment added that Mr. Baltazzi on first seeing him ride exclaimed excitedly : "You *shall* ride for me !"

At the Epsom Summer Meeting, Archer took his first great two-year-old race, when Ladylove won the Woodcote Stakes.

At the three Newmarket meetings he won thirteen races, the majority being for Lord Falmouth and the principal one the Clearwell Stakes on the Repentance colt, while for both the Cesarewitch and the Criterion he was second. In the latter instance, Lord Falmouth won with Garterly Bell; but Ladylove, ridden by Archer, carried the proper colours.

Custance says, in his "Riding Recollections and Turf Stories" :

"Lord Lonsdale was a nobleman who raced purely for the sport. He rarely betted, and only had a 'pony' or a 'fifty' on a horse of his own in a big race to make presents with in case he won. His lordship was very fond of seeing his own colours when he came to Newmarket, and I well remember his making both Captain Machell and J. Cannon, who trained for him, very much annoyed because he would enter King Lud, whom they were specially training for the Alexandra Plate, in the Ditch Mile Handicap at the Newmarket Meeting of 1874.

"When the weights came out, King Lud was allotted 8 stone 10 lb. Andred, belonging to Lord Falmouth and ridden by Archer, had earned a penalty, bringing his weight up to 9 stone 3 lb. There were ten runners, and King Lud, who was always rather a gross colt, looked more like a mare in foal than a horse going to run. The layers offered long odds against him, though his price was returned as 100 to 1 against. Captain Machell, more out of bravado than anything else, took 100 to 3 at once.

"It was a good run race, and when we came to the cords, which they had at that time about two hundred yards from home, Archer looked like winning easily; but the Ditch Mile, finishing at the Bushes, is very severe. In fact, I always thought, and so did Fordham, that it wanted more running than the Rowley Mile. To my eyes, Archer took things rather easily, and left off riding. Seeing there was just a chance, I kept King Lud going, he being a real game 'un, and he came with a wet sail before Archer could set his horse going again, and won by a neck."

At Chester, Archer carried off only the Great Cheshire Stakes, a 6 to 1 chance, on Andred; but since Newmarket he had been gradually increasing his score in minor events. In 1874, for the only time in his life, Archer was suspended for fourteen days or thereabouts for disobedience at the post. He seemed much chagrined, but philosophically remarked, "Perhaps it serves me right." Poor Harry Constable chaffed his pal on his enforced days of idleness.

84

Thus, in 1874, Archer began his long career of great turf triumphs in the service of Lord Falmouth. His performance on Atlantic confirmed Lord Falmouth in his opinion that Archer was the natural and fitting successor of Tom French. This noble owner never swerved in the opinion which he had formed of young Archer, and the great jockey did yeoman service for the great owner who has been appropriately described as the greatest ornament the Turf has ever seen.

Indeed, Archer's last winning ride was on Lord Falmouth's Blanchland, in the Houghton Stakes at Newmarket, a fitting conclusion to his long and brilliant connection with the all-conquering black body, white sleeves and red cap. Archer achieved a list of triumphs such as will cause his name to be for ever associated with the great days of Lord Falmouth's career as an owner of horses. At that time such jockeys as Webb, Fordham, Chaloner, Custance, Tom Cannon, and John Osborne were riding, and it was no small thing for a man to come to the front in such company. That he did come through the crowd, however, is a matter of history.

From 1874, Archer's majority became overwhelming, varying from 150 to a third of that number over Charles Wood in 1880, because in that year Archer was savaged by Muley Edris and was out of the saddle a good deal of the season.

Lord Falmouth took a devoted interest in Archer when a boy, even securing the most remunerative investments for the jockey's early earnings. He was the first owner to pay Archer a yearly salary of £100, at which Fred was content to serve him to the day of his death, although tempted by fabulous offers from other quarters for the first claim on his services or second, third, or even fourth claims.

A noteworthy incident of Archer's career was the joint presentation with his old master, Mathew Dawson, of a handsome silver salver to Lord Falmouth, who told them that no gift or family heirloom at Tregothnan would ever be more valued or cherished.

Mr. John Corlett wrote in 1874 :

"There is no more hospitable man breathing than the Heath House trainer, and whether it is the Prince of Wales or the humblest visitor, he must, before leaving, pay a visit to the 'sanctum', hung round with portraits of Alice Hawthorn,

Eclipse, Kingcraft (with Lord Falmouth at his head), and, in fact, all the celebrities of bygone days.

"This year the stable has been overwhelmed by an embarrassment of riches, and at one time there were in it: Atlantic, Aquilo, Couronne de Fer, Tomahawk, Trent, and Leolinus, all of them Derby horses. With such cards to shuffle it may be imagined, if the trainer had been unscrupulous, what wealth would have poured into his pockets. The same was the case with the St. Leger. So thoroughly, however, had every horse his duty done by him, that in the Derby they went past the winning-post almost in a straight line. . . ."

Again, Mr. Corlett says: "Owing to the moral training he has received at Heath House, Archer, the best lightweight of the day, has been able to avoid those shoals and quicksands on which so many fashionable lightweights have been wrecked. . . . We doubt whether the Calendar furnished another instance of such races as the Two Thousand, One Thousand and Oaks having been won by so young a jockey. It is not our intention to weary our readers by following Archer through all his mounts. Nor do we mean to exalt him into a demi-god. Though he has won so many races, we cannot yet report him as being a really great horseman in the sense that Fordham is. He is often inclined to be in a hurry, and, though he is not so fond of taking up his whip as he used to be, he is still rather handy with it.

"A great recommendation to him is punctuality. When an owner has engaged him to ride, he has not to hunt all over the place at the last moment to find him. He is the first to present himself to the Clerk of the Scales, and he is never behindhand in taking up his place at the post. Nor is there that flashness about him that we see in so many of the light-weights. His position in a great measure he owes to the schooling he has received. Even when he was a fashionable jockey he had to attend with the other boys at the evening classes presided over by Mrs. Dawson. He has not forgotten his early training, and as he is a nice weight we see no reason why he should not be at the head of the winning jockeys for many a year to come."*

* Archer was premier jockey from the year 1874 until his death in 1886.
Footnote by Mr. A. F. B. Portman:
    Archer did not ride One Thousand or Oaks winner in 1874. He won these races on Spinaway in 1875; Two Thousand on Atlantic in 1874.

86

ARCHER'S PRINCIPAL WINS IN 1875

GREAT NORTHAMPTONSHIRE STAKES.—PEEPING TOM, 6 to 1
CHESTERFIELD STAKES (NEWMARKET).—SKYLARK, 4 to 1.
CLEARWELL STAKES.—FARNESE, 4 to 7.
STEWARDS' CUP (GOODWOOD).—TRAPPIST, 100 to 7.
YORKSHIRE OAKS.—SPINAWAY, 1 to 5.
CHAMPAGNE STAKES (DONCASTER).—FARNESE, 5 to 4.
LIVERPOOL AUTUMN CUP.—ACTIVITY, 25 to 1.
NOTTINGHAMSHIRE HANDICAP.—QUAIL, 7 to 1.
ONE THOUSAND GUINEAS.—SPINAWAY, 10 to 1.
THE OAKS.—SPINAWAY, 5 to 4.

In 1874, Archer had been premier jockey with 147 wins.
This year he held that position with 172 wins to his credit.

CHAPTER IX

In 1875, with Camballo, the property of Mr. Clare Vyner, Mathew Dawson won the Two Thousand Guineas, while with Lord Falmouth's Spinaway, destined to become the dam of Busybody, he won the One Thousand and the Oaks. The colt by Macaroni out of Repentance was third in the Derby, and Ladylove, the stable second string, was second to Spinaway in the Oaks. Farnese won the Champagne Stakes, the Ham Produce Stakes (which, with the Buckenham, were almost farmed at this period by Lord Falmouth), the Prince of Wales's Stakes at Goodwood, the Champagne at Doncaster, the Buckenham, and the Clearwell. Skylark, a son of Wheatear, won each of his four races, including the Chesterfield Stakes, at headquarters. It was in this year that Galopin, a horse trained by John Dawson, won the Derby.

During the winters of 1874 and 1875, Archer increased considerably in weight, and though a year previously he could manage 6 stone comfortably, and got so late as the Second October Meeting down to 6 stone 1 lb., for his memorable second on the Truth gelding for the Cesarewitch he could, at the commencement of the season, scale no less than 6 stone 12 lb., while at the end of it another 4 lb. was added to his minimum.

At the very outset of the season he was to the fore, and opened the ball at Lincoln with a victory on Bella in the Tathwell Stakes, and she was also ridden by him when winning the important Althorp Park Stakes, while, too, at Northampton he carried all before him, including the big handicap there on Peeping Tom. At all the principal meetings of the year, except Ascot, he had a good total of winners, but at the Royal Heath he was singularly unlucky, as he rode thirteen losers right off the reel, and scored during the whole meeting only one solitary win, upon Ladylove for the Three-Year-Old Triennial.

Among his chief successes, in addition to the above named, which helped to make his total one of celebrity in 1875, we have mentioned the One Thousand Guineas. Much of Archer's success he no doubt owed to Lord Falmouth, but it must not be forgotten that the latter always esteemed Archer very highly, and it is to Archer's credit that he gained and kept the friendship of that chivalrous and high-minded nobleman. Lord Falmouth's "I believe Archer" became an article in the creed of every racing man. Fred Archer always went down to Cheltenham in the winter for the hunting, though he often spent some of the season elsewhere, as, for instance, at Lord Wilton's.

Fred Webb had come to Mathew Dawson's about a year later than Archer, who was the younger of the two men. These great rivals were also the greatest of friends, and Webb often came home with Fred, and was well known round Andoversford.

Harry Morgan was at that time a brilliant lightweight in the stable, and he said, when talking in 1914 about Archer, that once when Fred was away for some time in Cheltenham he occupied his rooms. They were very nice ones, with lots of photographs about. When Archer came back, Morgan moved out and slept at the Golden Hart.

"Webb and Archer," he said, "were very quiet men in their ways, and didn't talk much. Archer would come round and have a couple of games of billiards in the room upstairs at the Rutland Arms and wouldn't say much. He was usually home about ten. He had a temper, though, and no mistake. You want to know what he got into tempers about? *About getting beaten in races!* He couldn't stand that. Really, the only thing he thought about was being always at the top of the tree. He and another jockey used to have words after the races. They were the best of friends at other times. I rode Isonomy in the Cambridgeshire, the best I ever rode, I think. I won the Cambridgeshire twice. One of the exciting races when Webb beat Archer was in the race for the Manchester Cup. When we were training we'd just have a lean chop and be off out for a long walk. Webb was the man for walking; he'd think nothing of walking to Cambridge and back. But Archer wasted by taking medicine and Turkish baths. Fred *did* like sweet stuff. He was a one for jam and cakes. In fact, for anything sweet.

"It often used to amuse me, as Archer got more and more famous, to see how people came and asked for plates off horses he rode, or for his whip. I can quite believe that there are nine of Eclipse's hoofs about. The lads gave away plates off any horse, and, as for whips, we often used one another's. Jockeys had much more chance of cheating about weights and such-like in our day than they have now, and I think some of the best of them did it as a matter of course. Fred Archer was very fond of hunting, but not so fond of it as his brother Charlie.

"Old Mr. Mathew Dawson always called me 'Morgie'. When I went to see him he would say in his Scotch sort of voice : 'Have a glass of port, Morgie?' And I'd say : 'No, thank you.' He'd say : 'Have a glass of sherry, then?' and perhaps I'd have one.

"I can't stand the silly names some people give to horses. I think Lord Falmouth chose the best names for his horses. Merry-go-Round and Spinaway and Lady Golightly—those are names one likes to think about. And Silvio. I call that a lovely name for a horse. I don't care to go up to the racecourse nowadays and see the boys riding, looking like monkeys on a stick. Danny Maher doesn't ride as short as the other modern jockeys. He found it didn't pay, and he rides fairly long.

"When Archer was married there was a lot of speechifying and an ox roasted on The Severals. I did not have any, but those who did said it was neither cooked nor raw, but something between."

Fordham this year won one of his cunning victories over Archer in the Ascot Derby. He fell behind, and Archer fell in and took up the running upon Spinaway, who was the favourite. Fordham came with a rush on the inside and won by three-quarters of a length.

"Lord Falmouth," says Sir George Chetwynd in his

"Reminiscences", refused to declare to win with Spinaway in the Newmarket Oaks. Archer was on Spinaway, and although he was not the Archer of a decade later, spectators might have supposed that he would have chosen the right one." Lord Falmouth also ran Ladylove. He told me that he and Mat Dawson (just before the race) disagreed about the merits of the two animals ; hence his letting each take her chance."

Cheltenham, at this time, although a great steeplechasing centre, was without a flat-race meeting until, in 1875, one was established for a year or two, after which it fell through and has not been revived. Fred Archer attended the first, which was held on the racecourse which is now the cemetery.

During this season Archer attended some of the other race meetings in his own West Country ; at the Worcester Summer Meeting he was in great form, and won four races right off the reel, including the principal handicap with Bassoon.

About this time the late Mr. Cyrus Faulkner Dobell, a younger brother of Sydney Dobell, the poet, was living at Whittington Manor, and remembered Archer's early hunting days, when, he said, it amazed him to see the little weedy boy on a small pony leading the whole field, far ahead of grown men on hundred-guinea hunters. At the time of which we are writing Mr. Dobell seems to have seen a good deal of Archer, and said :

"He was a very superior fellow to most jockeys, and dressed more like a curate than a jockey. I used to have long chats with him after a day's hunting as I rode home to Whittington and he rode to his father's inn at Andoversford, and he would tell me his thoughts and ideas about things in general, and he talked well. One's first impression of Archer would have been that he was a gentleman by birth, with a college education. I should have said that he read a good deal, and that, if he had not had much education, he had improved his mind later. People always used to say that Mrs. Archer must have had some good blood in her veins. She was a big, fine-looking woman, with handsome aquiline features, and I think it was from her that Archer got his *character* and partly his looks. At any rate, he was not one bit like his father, who was just a clever man and a very good steeplechase rider, an ordinary jockey, and nothing more.

"There were Haywards who kept the King's Arms before William Archer went there; very likely they were Mrs. Archer's people. Fred seems from the beginning to have asserted his own individuality, only in a quiet way. His neckties and pins and his clothes generally were all so quiet and unobtrusive, and, indeed, his ideas about many things were so refined. He was a very remarkable man. I always thought that, with proper advantages, he would have made a great general. His riding was marvellous, but no end of his success was due to his character, which, as I say, I think he got from his mother, to his wonderful knowledge of pace, and to his consummate understanding of horses.

"His judgment was so wonderful. As we rode home together I got to know a good deal about his thoughts and his tastes. He was good at other sports besides racing. I remember he told me that in his earlier days he hardly had to train at all; he managed to try and keep himself fit with hunting, etc. One day, out hunting on Leckhampton Hill, we were on the edge of a quarry and Archer rode along the top of the wall. I was on the safe part, and Archer was riding in front of me; I knew that the wall got narrower and narrower, and that eventually there wouldn't be foothold for the horse. I think I called to him—anyhow, I thought there was bound to be an accident. But Archer just rode quietly on, and when there was no longer any room for the horse he jumped down into the quarry. I held my breath and I thought, 'Well, this is the end of it all.' But he managed his horse so splendidly that he came down all right. He did it so quietly, too, as he did everything. There was no brag or showing off.

"I often say to people now, when they are talking about this method of riding with the jockeys' legs crouched up on their mounts' withers: 'Well, and did Tod Sloan and the rest ever show more ability than Archer did?' And Fred had such a good seat on a horse; he rode so gracefully. Of course, other people know more about Archer's character and riding than I do, but those were my impressions of him."

Fred Archer paid his first visit to France, "accompanied by another Gloucestershire jockey, Tommy Glover; and an old Cheltonian, then residing in Newmarket, also visited the French capital with them". From this time, up to his

93

death, Archer was frequently seen on French racecourses and won many victories there—as his nephew, Willie Pratt, has done since.

"The Hôtel de Nice," said Mr. Brooks, "a modest though thoroughly comfortable hostelry in the Place de la Bourse, Paris, lays claim to have extended its hospitality to the great jockey on his first visit to the Metropolis of France. It was during this stay that Archer rode his first French winner, on the day previous to the Grand Prix, on the two-year-old Argues, and it will show that the great luminary had not then shone in all its brilliancy when we state that, in spite of the small number of runners, Archer's mount was allowed to start at 6 to 1. The race was won in a canter, thanks to the advantage which Archer secured at the start over the other jockeys."

One of the onlookers never forgot the remark made after this excellent début by an eminent French sportsman, by whose side he happened to be standing in the "pesage" while the race was on : "Ma foi ! il monte rudement bien, ce gamin la. Qui est-ce ?" It is presumable that further acquaintance with Archer convinced the sportsman in question that his first appreciation of the "youngster's" merits was correct, for later on Archer rode, in this gentleman's colours, several good winners.

ARCHER'S PRINCIPAL WINS IN 1876

LIVERPOOL SPRING CUP.—LADY PATRICIA, 5 to 2.
CITY AND SUBURBAN.—THUNDER, 1,000 to 45.
GREAT CHESHIRE STAKES.—THUNDER, 2 to 1.
GOLD VASE (Ascot).—THUNDER, 2 to 1.
CHICHESTER STAKES (GOODWOOD).—MOUSQUETAIRE, 6 to 1.
PRINCE OF WALES'S STAKES (GOODWOOD).—MONACHUS, 2 to 1.
GREAT EBOR HANDICAP.—LILIAN, 3 to 1.
CHAMPAGNE STAKES (DONCASTER).—LADY GOLIGHTLY, 3 to 1.
CLEARWELL STAKES (NEWMARKET).—SILVIO, 5 to 4.
CESAREWITCH STAKES.—ROSEBERY, 100 to 14.
NEWMARKET DERBY.—SKYLARK, 2 to 1.

CHAPTER X

THIS brings the record down to 1876, and in this year Archer scored another wonderful feat and beat all records, his total successes amounting to 206. Poor Harry Constable was next on the list with but 74 wins, a great difference indeed!

In this year Skylark won half a dozen races, and a couple of two-year-olds brought valuable grist to the mill. These were Silvio, by Blair Athol out of Silverhair, and Lady Golightly, by King Tom out of Lady Coventry. The former won four out of his five races, and Lady Golightly won five out of eight. Farnese as a three-year-old became a roarer and was soon drafted out of the stable. Thunder, then the property of Mr. Clare Vyner, won the City and Suburban, carrying 9 stone 4 lb., the highest weight which had ever been borne successfully in the history of the race.

In this year, too, came Lilian's Ebor and Rosebery's Cesarewitch.

Custance says in his book of Reminiscences, after describing a race in 1874 (the Ditch Mile Handicap at Newmarket):

"I beat Archer over the same course in somewhat the same way. This was at the Newmarket Craven Meeting of 1876. Archer was riding a hot favourite in Great Tom, belonging to Lord Falmouth, for the Post Sweepstakes, and I was on Wild Tommy. Poor Fred was very wroth about this, as he thought he ought to have won both races. He certainly ought to have won the first, but I am not so sure about the second. At the Chester Meeting of 1876 I rode Lowlander, when he accomplished a great performance. This was in the Stewards' Cup, when Thunder (who had won the City and Suburban a fortnight previous with 9 stone 4 lb. on) and Lowlander were engaged at even weights over a mile and a quarter.

"This was out of Lowlander's course, and just the distance that Thunder had won the City and Suburban over. Archer said : 'I suppose you will be waiting and messing me about as usual, but I have some different goods to-morrow.' I really thought the same myself. There were only those two runners, and a deal of excitement was caused as they were both champions over their courses, although a mile was quite as much as Lowlander liked to travel. We started at the bottom of the Straight. Going past the post for the first time there is rather a sharp angle just beyond the winning-post, and Archer, who was making running, slipped his horse along as hard as he could for about two hundred yards. I had only to wait my time. I wasn't going after him there, especially as Lowlander was a big horse, over 16 hands 2 in., and with very sharp turns it would not do to bustle him. Still Lowlander was kept going at the same pace, without bustling him or getting him crosslegged, which Archer found had been the case with Thunder. He steadied his horse back to me, and presently he went off with another rush, yet came back again. As we neared the River Dee side of the course, Archer was rather perplexed what to do, as I had placed my horse right behind him, so that he could not really see what was going on. Mine was not a difficult race to ride, with one exception, which was to win at the winning-post and nowhere else, so my sole object was to keep Archer from knowing how my mount was going on by keeping right on his track, and just close enough to him not to strike against his horse's heels. About the distance Archer was looking for me again, but could not see me. Apparently he did not really know what to do. Luckily for me, instead of catching hold of Thunder's head and sending him straight home, he waited for one run. Fortunately I got this first, and won by little less than half a length."

ARCHER'S PRINCIPAL WINS IN 1877

EARL SPENCER'S PLATE.—CŒRULEUS, 5 to 1.
CITY AND SUBURBAN.—JULIUS CÆSAR, 8 to 1.
THE DERBY.—SILVIO, 100 to 9.
EPSOM CUP.—HESPER, 9 to 2.
ASCOT DERBY.—SILVIO, 2 to 1.
GOLD VASE (ASCOT).—SKYLARK, 4 to 1.
CHICHESTER STAKES (GOODWOOD).—MOUSQUETAIRE, 8 to 11.
PRINCE OF WALES'S STAKES (GOODWOOD).—CHILDERIC. No
   betting on the race.
DE WARRENNE HANDICAP.—MOUSQUETAIRE, 4 to 6.
ASTLEY STAKES (LEWES).—REDWING, 5 to 2.
YORK CUP.—SKYLARK, Evens.
ST. LEGER.—SILVIO, 65 to 40.
GREAT EASTERN HANDICAP.—THE MANDARIN, 100 to 9.
CLEARWELL STAKES.—JANNETTE, 1 to 10.
NEWMARKET OAKS.—LADY GOLIGHTLY, 6 to 4.
CRITERION STAKES.—JANNETTE, Evens.

In 1877 Archer headed the list of winning jockeys with
218 wins.

CHAPTER XI

IN 1877 Archer drew further ahead of his compeers, and scored 218 victories out of 596 rides, which was so far his best average.

This unprecedented score included his maiden Derby and St. Leger, both on Lord Falmouth's Silvio, in addition to which he rode the winners of the City and Suburban, Clearwell, Prendergast, Criterion, and Ascot Gold Vase. In the City and Suburban he scored for Mr. Gee on Julius Cæsar.

Mrs. Pratt said that it was a proud day for her mother when she saw her young son of twenty win the Derby. A correspondent wrote to "Diogenes", of the *Cheltenham Examiner* :

"In Silvio's year I stood by the refreshment stand while the Derby was being run, and I noticed a middle-aged couple watching the race close by me. After it was won by Silvio ridden by Fred Archer, there were the couple—man and wife —waiting to congratulate their son, the winning jockey, as he rode back to the paddock receiving the ovation of the crowd. Mrs. Archer was naturally excited. She clapped her hands and shed tears of joy, for she had been for years the careful guardian of the lad. She sobbed audibly as Freddy, with the flush of victory on his face, waved his recognition of her happiness. When he came out of the weighing-room and 'all right' was called out, she folded him in her arms and kissed him fondly. Archer *père* was not demonstrative at all. Like old Weller, he kept his feelings under control, and only chuckled. Presently, however, he spoke. 'I knew our boy would do it,' he said, and he went into the refreshment booth to celebrate his knowledge."

A French writer told in the *Figaro* how, in 1877, Archer,

who had pulled off the Derby with Lord Falmouth's Silvio, was in the stalls of a theatre with a friend. Lionel Brough, "the Christian of the London stage", who never lost a chance of a good gag, had to say : "I will fly to—such and such a place—as quick as thought," but recognizing the favourite jockey among the audience, Brough exclaimed : "I'll go faster than Freddy Archer !" Immediately all eyes were fixed on the celebrated Freddy, and cheers burst out from all parts of the house. Freddy could not stand this fire of glances and coloured up until his face was redder than the cap he had worn the day before when steering Silvio to victory on Epsom Downs.

On one occasion the Hon. John Boscawen was with Archer, and said that, "No king could have had a greater reception."

Although Mathew Dawson had already captured more than one Derby and others of the classic races, it was not until 1877 that he was able to add the great Northern race as a laurel to his crown. Silvio had been third in the Two Thousand Guineas and had won the Derby, and with eleven opponents in the St. Leger he became a very hot order, 13 to 8 being the best offer.

Lord Falmouth's second string, Lady Golightly, was, however, well backed at 4 to 1, and for nothing else was there any very large demand. As, indeed, might have been expected for they were, taken altogether, but a sorry lot. It is true Manœuvre was beaten by the mare by a head only for second place, but that by no means represents the difference between them ; for, barring accidents, she would have left Lord Bradford's filly far enough behind if she had not actually beaten Silvio. But Archer, who rode the horse, no doubt had a long pull in jockeyship over old Jack Morris, who steered the mare, and while Fred, with consummate ability, kept clear of all scrimmages, Morris got sadly interfered with at one part of the race, being nearly knocked down by either Sheldrake or Zucchero or both of them ; and towards the finish when she was coming like great guns, running through her field like the real good racehorse that she was, who that was present will ever forget the eager, anxious look of Archer as he turned his head to look where she was, or how he then rode like a veritable demon to place as wide a gap as possible between Silvio and his stable companion? For there is no doubt he had a well-grounded fear of her, and had no intention of coming to close quarters if it might be avoided. As it was, he won by three lengths, and Mathew Dawson was congratulated on winning his first St. Leger, occupying also the second place.

Mr. T. S. Townend, the well-known journalist (of the *Melbourne Argus*, etc.), was a North-countryman, and used often at the time of the races to stay with relatives near Doncaster. He said he often used to meet Archer at their house, which was just a pleasant walk out of the town.

Mr. William Villar saw many of Archer's great races, and amongst them Silvio's St. Leger at Doncaster. "I think," he remarked, "that there has never been such a horseman as Archer. I don't believe that any of the present-day jockeys could touch him. He was such a finished horseman, and, more than that, he rode with his head, and was a very clever rider with heaps of judgment. When I took that horse I have a picture of—Spark by Flash-in-the-Pan—to Manchester, and he won the Great Foal Stakes, Fred and Charlie Archer were there, and Fred said, 'Here comes my farmer friend,' and backed my horse and introduced me to a lot of people. We were all in a party that day. Of course, that race was only a small affair.'"

Archer seems always to have been more than pleased to meet any of his old friends among the Cotswold farmers, whether they were descended from Marshals of France, like the Villars, or otherwise. It mattered not to him if his friends had become celebrities themselves, had stayed as they were, or had sunk into insignificance. Archer's genius for friendship was equal to all demands made on it.

Mr. Cecil Raleigh wrote: "I think that the memory of Prestbury used to come back to Archer's mind whenever he met me, for he always went out of his way to do me any service he could.

"His sittings to Carlo Pellegrini, and the appearance of the famous cartoon in *Vanity Fair*, were the result of a chance meeting in Regent Street, when these things were arranged. I walked along the pavement with Mr. Thomas Gibson Bowles on one side of me and Fred Archer, whom I had just introduced to him, on the other, hoping that I should meet a lot of people that I knew, and saying to myself, 'This is fame!' "

ARCHER'S PRINCIPAL WINS IN 1878

PRINCE OF WALES'S CUP (LIVERPOOL).—HESPER, 3 to 1.
GREAT CHESHIRE HANDICAP.—WOODLANDS, 4 to 5.
THE OAKS.—JANNETTE, 65 to 40.
EPSOM GOLD CUP.—HAMPTON, 3 to 1.
ROYAL HUNT CUP.—JULIUS CÆSAR, 10 to 1.
CORONATION STAKES.—REDWING, 8 to 1.
ALL-AGED STAKES (ASCOT).—TRAPPIST, 2 to 5.
ROUS MEMORIAL STAKES.—PETRARCH, 5 to 4.
WOKINGHAM STAKES.—TRAPPIST, 7 to 2.
CHESTERFIELD STAKES.—LEAP YEAR, 7 to 1.
RICHMOND STAKES.—WHEEL OF FORTUNE, 2 to 1.
PRINCE OF WALES'S STAKES (YORK).—WHEEL OF FORTUNE, 6 to 5.
YORK CUP.—LADY GOLIGHTLY, 4 to 9.
CHAMPAGNE STAKES (DONCASTER).—CHARIBERT, 5 to 4.
THE ST. LEGER.—JANNETTE, 5 to 2.
ALEXANDRA PLATE (DONCASTER).—DALHAM, 5 to 6.
PARK HILL STAKES (DONCASTER).—JANNETTE, 1 to 4.
GREAT EASTERN HANDICAP.—HACKTHORPE, 5 to 2.
CHAMPION STAKES (NEWMARKET).—JANNETTE, 4 to 6.
NEWMARKET OAKS.—JANNETTE, 1 to 2.
PRENDERGAST STAKES.—LEAP YEAR, 5 to 6.
DEWHURST PLATE.—WHEEL OF FORTUNE, 1 to 2.
FREE HANDICAP (NEWMARKET).—LORD CLIVE, 4 to 7.
JOCKEY CLUB CUP.—SILVIO, 5 to 4.

Archer headed the list with 229 wins.

CHAPTER XII

FRED ARCHER had a great year, for he rode 229 winners, and he won his second St. Leger in succession on Jannette, who also carried off the Oaks. He won the Jockey Club Cup on Silvio, and several of the big two-year-old races on Wheel of Fortune.

It was this year that George Fordham returned to the racecourse after over two years' absence. Tom Jennings gave him his first mount in the Bushes Handicap on a horse called Pardon, belonging to Count Lagrange, at the Newmarket Craven Meeting of 1878. Fordham would not mount in the Birdcage, as no one hated flattery more than he did. He went down the course with Harry Custance to the Ditch Mile starting-post, and he got into the saddle about half-way down.

He seemed all right at first, but just before he got to the starting-post his spirits failed him, and he said : "Cus, I wish I hadn't got up. Look at those kids ; I don't know one of 'em." There were several smaller boys, and only Archer of the older ones riding.

Custance replied : "My dear George, don't you trouble about that. They will soon know you when you get alongside of them, especially at the finish."

In the end Archer won on Advance, and Fordham was second, beaten three lengths, so the judge said. It struck Custance that Fordham did not exert himself much in this race, which he attributed to his being rather weak and out of condition. Afterwards he went to him and said : "Why, you didn't have half a go !"

He answered with a knowing wink : "You didn't think I was going to let him (Archer) beat me by a neck the first time I rode, which he would have done !"

Custance went to Mr. Jennings and told him what Fordham had said, and asked him if he would run Pardon in the Bretby Plate, only the second race after the Bushes Handicap. He said, "Certainly," and it is pleasing to be able to say that Pardon won this time. No one could have received a greater ovation than George Fordham did on his return to weigh in that day, and he soon regained his old form and rode as well as ever.

After Archer's death a story was told that in the autumn of this year, when Archer went to Chelmsford to ride a horse for his brother Charles, a fortune-teller crossed his right hand with a bit of silver with which he had presented her, and foretold his death by that hand. These were indeed prophetic words, if the story is true.

It was in 1878 the first of the two great tragedies of their lives befell William Archer and his wife. At that time they had left the King's Arms and kept the Andoversford Hotel. On the first day of the Cheltenham Steeplechases an accident took place in front of the house, and a farmer, Mr. Charles Wood, was killed. The following morning, as William Archer the younger was leaving for the steeplechases, he said : "Let us draw down the blinds out of respect for the poor fellow who is dead."

On that very day, and while the inquest was being held in his own home on the body of the farmer, young William Archer, himself fatally injured, was being carried from the steeplechase course.

It is said that poor Wood's death had greatly affected young William Archer, who had driven by the scene of the accident on his way home to the Andoversford Inn. Although Mr. Wood's body had been removed the road was stained with blood, and the sight so affected William, who, like his brother Fred, had a sensitive and highly strung nature, that he told his father he did not think he could ride on the morrow.

William Archer the elder, however, is said to have insisted that his son should fulfil his engagement. Indeed, he had no real excuse for refusing to do so, and young William, finding his fears ridiculed, went down to ride next day, after, as has been related, pulling the blinds down. Young William is said not to have been nearly so good a jockey as the rest of his family, though on no other occasion did he show any distaste for riding.

The race in which he took part was a selling hurdle race of £5 each. There were only three runners, these being Mr. Quartley's Neptune, aged, J. Jarvis; Mr. Palmer's Woodcote, aged, C. Archer; Mr. Thomas's Salvanie, 4 years, W. Archer, jun.

Salvanie, when just opposite the grandstand, stumbled at a jump, threw his rider heavily, and fell upon him with his entire weight. Taking place in full view of the spectators, the accident evoked a cry of horror, and so quietly did the injured man lie that the gravest fears were entertained.

The fears were more than justified by the examination of the surgeons. Young Archer was taken to the residence of Captain Cotton, and there he remained unconscious until an early hour on the following Saturday, when he died, his recovery having from the first been hopeless.

In the Cheltenham Grand Annual Steeplechase Handicap of this year Lord Marcus Beresford was second on Captain Paget's Pilgrim's Progress, while the winner, Duellist, was ridden by Charlie Archer—the third of William Archer's sons.

A writer in the *World*, May 28, 1879, thus describes Heath House, where Archer received his training from the famous Mathew Dawson:

"Quiet at night, at least for several years past, Newmarket is especially delightful as the shades descend upon Sunday. All is clean and neat—and stillest, neatest of all, is Heath House. The trees are daintily pruned, there is a spice of primness in the fresh gravel, of trimness in the accuracy with which the flower-beds are planned, of severity in the high polish of the brass-work on the door. There is nothing of the horse, horsey about this side at least of Heath House, and as the sound of a hymn, sung by youthful voices, catches the ear of the visitor he marvels whether the tales he has heard of Newmarket can be true. No sooner, however, does he cross Mat Dawson's threshold than he recognizes that he is in a dwelling where the merits of the noble animal, very useful to man, are thoroughly appreciated.

"Passing by a neat rack of whips, above which lies the famous whisk constructed of the tail of Thormanby, who won the Derby in a year of 'clinkers', he enters Mr. Dawson's sanctum, with every inch of wallpaper covered with portraits of famous racehorses, and finds ensconced in comfortable armchairs the master of Heath House and his friend Mr. Harry Hall, by whose pencil most of the portraits of this equine Valhalla have been wrought. To them enters presently a tall, slender young man of some 22 years. His general costume is, like his manner, exceedingly quiet and unassuming. There is nothing horsey in his raiment, in the fashion of his dark hair, nor does he wear a scarf tied in a coaching fold with the almost inevitable fox-tusk pin, the place of this eminently sporting article of costume being filled by a sailor's knot. Nor is Fred Archer afflicted with the Newmarket air, the five to two carriage of the head so offensive in the successful lightweights of the old plunging days. It is odd that really great jockeys never wear a jaunty air, preferring to leave that sort of thing to the featherweights suddenly lifted to fame by the winning of a few handicaps.

"As he enters, dressed in a suit of dark clothes, relieved only by the chain which holds the magnificent watch presented to him by Mr. Dawson when he was out of his time, with his overcoat thrown back and his billy-cock hat held in his left hand, Fred Archer might easily be taken for the rising young clerk in a thriving bank dropped in to take his chief's orders on some important business. Success appears to have steadied him rather than unsettled him, and nothing is more pleasant than to witness the deferential air of the most successful jockey of the day towards his former mentor and present friend and part employer.

"That it may not be thought that Fred Archer's quiet and modest demeanour is dwelt on over-much, it may be well to mention that his present income, entirely his own, for he is out of his apprenticeship some four or five years, is about as great as that of a Queen's Counsel in mid-career, of a special surgeon, of any kind of a Royal Academician, barring perhaps five, and almost half as great as that of an Italian tenor singer. It is quickly earned, without long delays, expectations or disappointments, for when it is put in his charge it is not long before the event is decided. His great causes depend on the application within the space of a minute of his nice judgment of pace ; of his successful operations on the display of consummate nerve and courage in tearing down a perilous declivity and hugging the rails of an awkward turn ; and his great pictures are dashed in with a single stroke, as when he drove Jannette through the leading pair at Doncaster ; his sensational effect when he brings an outsider like Charibert to the front and makes mincemeat of his field. A very large income, the unbounded confidence of employers and of the public, might help to turn less ordinary heads just arrived at legal manhood ; but Fred Archer quietly goes his own way, and studies diligently to improve in his calling.

"It is about eleven years since his father brought Fred Archer to Mat Dawson's to launch him in his career,"

ARCHER'S PRINCIPAL WINS IN 1879

CITY AND SUBURBAN.—PAROLE, 4 to 1.
GREAT METROPOLITAN.—PAROLE, 2 to 5.
ESHER STAKES (SANDOWN).—THE MANDARIN, 8 to 1.
TWO THOUSAND GUINEAS.—CHARIBERT, 25 to 1.
ONE THOUSAND GUINEAS.—WHEEL OF FORTUNE, 40 to 75.
GREAT CHESHIRE HANDICAP (CHESTER).—PAROLE, 9 to 2.
THE OAKS (EPSOM).—WHEEL OF FORTUNE, 1 to 3.
PRINCE OF WALES'S STAKES (ASCOT).—WHEEL OF FORTUNE,
    4 to 6.
KEMPTON PARK CUP.—MASTER KILDARE, 5 to 4.
RICHMOND STAKES (GOODWOOD).—BEND OR, 4 to 7.
STEWARDS' CUP (BRIGHTON).—ADVANCE, 2 to 1.
YORKSHIRE OAKS.—WHEEL OF FORTUNE, 1 to 3.
PRINCE OF WALES'S STAKES (YORK).—BEND OR, 1 to 2.
ALEXANDRA PLATE (DONCASTER).—MASTER KILDARE,
    100 to 30.
PORTLAND PLATE (DONCASTER).—HACKTHORPE, 9 to 2.
ROUS MEMORIAL (NEWMARKET).—BEND OR, 2 to 5.
NEWMARKET OAKS.—WHIRLWIND, 4 to 6.
GREAT SAPLING STAKES (SANDOWN).—FIRE KING, 100 to 30.
JOCKEY CLUB CUP.—JANNETTE, 8 to 1.
LIVERPOOL AUTUMN CUP.—MASTER KILDARE, 100 to 8.

In 1879 Archer headed the list of winning jockeys with
197 wins.

CHAPTER XIII

In 1879, 197 wins showed a falling off. One reason for this was the increasing weight of the Cheltenham horseman, his lowest scale during the season being 8 stone 7lb., while Lord Falmouth was scarcely so successful as usual in the weight-for-age races. Archer's connection with the Russley, Bedford Lodge, and Stanton Stables, however, made up for this deficiency, and he became more popular than ever.

In 1878 Wheel of Fortune and Peter (Sir John Astley's best horse, then owned by General Peel) had made their début together in the Richmond Stakes, which the mare won easily. Archer in the same year was successful with her in the Prince of Wales's Stakes (Yorkshire) and the Dewhurst Plate.

Sir George Chetwynd wrote of her performance in 1879 : "Wheel of Fortune in the One Thousand won easily from a bad lot of mares, though she would have beaten with almost equal ease a lot that were far above the average, for she was a great horse, and doubtless the best mare Lord Falmouth ever owned." Of the Oaks, Sir George went on to say : "Wheel of Fortune made hacks of her opponents in the Oaks, as she did later on at Ascot in the Prince of Wales's Stakes."

The mention of Wheel of Fortune always brings up the eternal question of which was the best racehorse.

In an interview published in the *Illustrated Sporting and Dramatic News* of March 22, 1884, "Rapier" and Archer, at the time of Lord Falmouth's sale, discuss some of his horses and also the wonderful St. Simon. It is interesting, though we are dealing with the year 1879, to see what Archer thought of Wheel of Fortune. "Rapier" writes :

" 'How about your race on St. Simon against Tom Cannon

on Duke of Richmond ?' I inquired of Archer. 'It's interesting, because the question is by how much St. Simon is the best three-year-old in training ; for I suppose there's no doubt about his being so by a long way. Tom Cannon tells me he wasn't beaten quite so easily as people seem to think in the match at the Kempton Meeting, and that 6 stone 7 lb. might have made all the difference.'

" 'I know Tom thinks that, but I won very easy—very easy indeed,' replied Archer. 'I don't suppose 12 lb. would quite bring them together—at least St. Simon would beat him. There's no better judge of horses than Tom Cannon, but I think St. Simon is a good deal better than he supposes. Mr. Dawson thinks that St. Simon is the best colt he ever saw.'

" 'That's saying a good deal !' I said. 'There have been some good ones at Heath House. What do you think the best you ever rode ?'

" 'Well, St. Simon, I suppose,' Archer replied, 'but Wheel of Fortune was a wonderfully fine mare. I don't think I was ever on a better. She must have been good, too. In the spring of 1879 we tried Wheel of Fortune at weight for age against the Leger winners of the two years before, Silvio and Jannette, and Wheel of Fortune won in a canter. That was good enough to go on.'

" 'Good enough to make the One Thousand a certainty, unlike so many of those uncertainties that don't come off ?' I answered.

" 'Yes, and there's a good two-year-old at Heath House now, out of Wheel of Fortune, that ought to fetch a long price at the sale. A real good one, I should think ; but she's only been cantering about, hasn't been tried, so we don't really know what she can do, though she looks like galloping.'

" 'This sale is rather a painful subject for you, I'm afraid ?'

" 'Yes, you may be sure that I'm sorry to think I am parting from the Wheel of Fortune jacket. I have ridden for Lord Falmouth for eleven years, and there has never been a wrong word. I owe most of my success to having been able to ride his horses with such confidence, knowing that if I did make a mistake coming a bit too soon, or a bit too late, there would be no complaint, and his lordship would be sure I had ridden to the best of my ability. I'm certain that many races are thrown away through jockeys not having enough confidence in their masters and being afraid to tell them what really happened in a race.'

" 'What do you think Busybody will fetch ?' I inquired. 'She must be about the pick of the basket in spite of the rest.'

" 'Mr. Dawson thinks she won't go under £8,000 or £10,000, and that Harvester ought to fetch well over £5,000. He's improved very much, Harvester has—grown into a wonderfully nice colt. That's what Mr. Dawson puts them down at—£15,000—guineas, I should say—for the pair.' "

People were always asking Fred Archer which was the best animal he ever rode, and although towards the end of his life he would say St. Simon, he always introduced Wheel of Fortune into the conversation, and anyone could see she was the horse of his heart. Mathew Dawson, too, always had a sneaking affection for Catherine Hayes, his early love, though in St. Simon's day he gave a whole-hearted allegiance to that wonderful horse.

The *Sporting Times* of November 26, 1886, says :

"In the *Morning Post* of Monday last, 'Pavo' states that, meeting Archer at the house of a nobleman on the night before the Oaks, he took the opportunity of asking him which was the best horse he had ever ridden, and the reply was : 'Wheel of Fortune,' and this after he had won the Derby on Ormonde. That Archer did say this we well believe, as we have heard him say the same thing. In the list, however, that he sent us some time afterwards, on our asking him his opinion of the ten best horses of the century, he gave only four, viz., Wheel of Fortune, St. Simon, Barcaldine, and Bend Or, and in reply to the question, Which was absolutely the best horse he ever knew ?, we see that his reply was 'St. Simon'.

"Mathew Dawson had achieved his first classic triumph in the Oaks with Catherine Hayes by Lanercost, Sir John Don Wauchope's charming filly, whom he always considered to be the best of her sex he ever trained, not even excepting that wonderful *multum in parvo*, Wheel of Fortune, whom Archer looked upon as the best he ever rode until St. Simon came on the scene. Whatever Mr. Dawson may at one time have thought about Julius, he afterwards expressed the opinion that not only was St. Simon the best horse he had ever trained, but the best he had ever seen, and Archer expressed the same opinion, highly as he had up till then thought of Wheel of Fortune."

The late Mr. Tattersall was once watching Mat Dawson's horses out at exercise. Archer was on St. Simon, and suddenly the horse bolted away with his rider and almost got out of control altogether, in which case it would have been a bad job. This was probably when he was a two-year-old, as Archer never rode the Duke of Portland's colt after that year.* St. Simon had won all his races, and now Archer had touched him with a spur for the first time. He could win easily without ever needing a spur, but now, Mr. Tattersall said, he never saw a horse run so fast in his life.

When the splendid old Squire Fletcher of Shipton Oliffe, whom they called "The King of the Cotswolds", went to stay with Archer, the jockey made him have a ride on St. Simon so that he could say he had been on the back of such a famous horse.

Mr. Portman writes :

"Of course the horse in the Heath House Stable, both in 1883 and 1884, was the never-beaten St. Simon, much the greatest racer that Dawson ever had under his care, and probably about the best the world has ever produced.

"Fred Archer, who had ridden both St. Simon and Ormonde, told me not long before his death in 1886 that he was sure St. Simon would have beaten the other celebrity and Triple Crown hero ; but had Prince Batthyany lived, St. Simon would never have had the opportunity of figuring among the select few who can claim that distinction, for the only big three-year-old event he had been entered for was the Two Thousand Guineas."

The Duke of Portland very kindly allowed me to use some reminiscences in "The Life of Mathew Dawson" (Witherbys), from which I quote the following :

"As all the engagements of St. Simon had become void owing to the death of Prince Batthyany, I entered him for

* Archer won for the Duke of Portland, on Langwell, Oct. of 1884.

two races at Goodwood, the Halnaker Stakes, and the Maiden Plate, and a few days before the Goodwood Races I went to Newmarket and we gave St. Simon a gallop, which he won by a short head ; though if Archer, who rode him, had allowed him to do so he might have won by fifty yards. The gallop was on the five furlongs course. St. Simon . . . won his two engagements at Goodwood with the greatest ease.

"The Duke of Westminster, at this meeting, ran a two-year-old colt called Bushey, who won the Richmond Stakes, and whose name was subsequently changed to Duke of Richmond. . . .

"As Duke of Richmond was not entered for any of the three-year-old races there was no chance of his meeting St. Simon unless a match between them could be arranged. They were undoubtedly the best two-year-olds of the season . . . and a match was made between them for £500, to be run over the Bretby Stakes Course at Newmarket at the ensuing Houghton Meeting. . . . We had great fun over this match, and when the day arrived there was considerable excitement. I remember that several ladies of the family of my friend the Duke of Westminster accompanied him to the races, and they were all covered with yellow flowers and bows, the Duke's colours. Naturally, we had chaff about it, as I, being a younger and unmarried man, had no lady supporters decked out with my black and white colours.

"I heard John Porter, the trainer to Duke of Richmond, give the following instruction to Tom Cannon : 'Jump off, Tom, and cut the beggar's throat from the very commencement.' I told Mat what I had heard, and he immediately said to Archer, who was standing by : 'Archer, you heard what His Grace said was the order given to Cannon. You will be so good as to do the same, and I have no doot, mon, you will do it with success.' The flag fell, and St. Simon was quite fifty yards ahead of his antagonist before he had gone a quarter of a mile. Archer then dropped his hands, allowed the Duke of Richmond to come much closer, and eventually won by three-quarters of a length. The first to congratulate me were the Duke of Westminster and the members of his family. I noticed that there was not quite as much yellow showing then as before the race."

A match in which the then Prince of Wales was interested was one of the events of that year, and recalling it long afterwards, Sir Beaumont Dixie, writing to his cousin, the late Sir Willoughby Maycock, said :

"Poppleton Court, York.
"*June* 13, 1914.

"My Dear Willoughby,

"Thanks for yours received yesterday. Yes, I was pretty good pals with Freddy Archer in the seventies and early eighties, and when he always used to ride for me when he could do the weight, but in the matter of personal anecdotes of him I am afraid I cannot help you. You see, he died in November, 1886. This is a very long time to remember anything particularly. He rode my horse Kismet in my memorable match with Markey Beresford's Caramel in '79—T. Cannon up, for £500 a side, Rous Course, and won in a canter, and before the race he said he could d—n well carry the other! The match was made after dinner with H.R.H., and I wanted it to be for a thousand ; but he stopped it and said it must not be for more than a monkey, and so, of course, this was the sum run for.

"I was very much about with Freddy, and he used to dine with me, a sardine and half a glass of the boy being his lunch for fear of increasing weight. You will, of course, remember he was a terribly hard swearer, and a terror to all other Jocks ; but then he was a spoilt child and could do exactly as he pleased! If your acquaintance does not know it by any chance, when compiling his life, the Derby of 1880 should not be forgotten, won by the most wonderful superhuman effort. Freddy beat Robert the Devil, Charlie Brewer the bookie's horse, trained by Blanton, a head on the post on Bend Or, and never was such horsemanship ever seen ; for Freddy fairly lifted Bend Or the last few strides past the post, and Rossiter's surprise was a treat to watch when, as he thought, he could win easily. I was there and saw the race, and shall never forget it, nor will those either who were present.

"I was in Edinburgh last week to attend the wedding of my younger son, a Commander in the Navy, and it all went off splendidly. I knew you were 'Sir Willoughby', and the old name sounds very nice I think. With kind remembrances to your wife,

"Yours ever,
"Beaumont Dixie.

"P.S.—A very old pal of mine has written to say Solly Joel told him to back Bluestone for Hunt Cup! 15th Hussars, my old regiment, coming to York in October, so shall have a grand time of it."

"Archer," wrote Sir George Chetwynd in his "Reminiscences", "rode an extraordinary race on Master Kildare in the Liverpool Cup. He had been easily beaten in the Great Tom Stakes at Lincoln the week before, and therefore started comparatively friendless. The horse was in action as the flag fell, and Archer, seizing on his advantage, must have been ten lengths in front for the first half-mile, which obliged all the other jockeys to ride to catch him. He judiciously eased his horse after this, and coming again at the distance, won cleverly by half a length from Lord Hartington's strapping mare Rylstone. This race was won entirely by Archer's cleverness in profiting by the start he was fortunate enough to obtain, and by his tact in making so skilful a use of the advantage."

A French poet wrote a sonnet, "En l'honneur du Master Kildare, monté par le célèbre jockey, Fred Archer, vainqueur au Liverpool Autumn Cup," of which the first lines run as follows :

> Si, d'un coursier brillant sur l'arène poudreuse,
> Ma muse en cet instant veut suivre les exploits
> Et chanter sur son lutte les glorieux émois,
> Nul ne se prête mieux à cette idée heureuse
> Que le Master Kildare à l'œil vif, pénétrant
> Dont tous louent la vigueur, la forme et le talent.

FRED ARCHER'S PRINCIPAL WINS IN 1880

LIVERPOOL SPRING CUP.—ADVANCE, 9 to 4.
CITY AND SUBURBAN.—MASTER KILDARE, 9 to 2.
WOODCOTE STAKES (EPSOM).—ANGELINA, evens.
THE DERBY.—BEND OR, 2 to 1.
RICHMOND STAKES (GOODWOOD).—BAL GAL, 4 to 1.
ROUS MEMORIAL STAKES (GOODWOOD).—BAL GAL, 1 to 10.
NASSAU STAKES (GOODWOOD).—MURIEL, 3 to 1.
CONVIVIAL STAKES (YORK).—THECLA, 3 to 1.
PRINCE OF WALES'S STAKES (YORK).—BAL GAL, 1 to 2.
CHAMPAGNE STAKES (DONCASTER).—BAL GAL, 4 to 9.
DONCASTER STAKES.—APOLLO, 10 to 11.
ROUS MEMORIAL (NEWMARKET).—BAL GAL, 1 to 6.
CLEARWELL STAKES (NEWMARKET).—BAL GAL, 1 to 6.
NEWMARKET OAKS.—MURIEL, 100 to 30.
DEWHURST PLATE (NEWMARKET).—BAL GAL, 3 to 1.
FRENCH DERBY.—BEAUMINET, 2 to 5.

He headed the list of winning jockeys with 120 wins.

As the result of Muley Edris having savaged him, Archer was out of the saddle between Epsom and Goodwood in 1880, and by dint of walking exercise he managed to keep his weight down.

CHAPTER XIV

ARCHER steered Bal Gal to victory in the Richmond Stakes at the Goodwood gathering, and rode his second Dewhurst Plate winner in Bal Gal in splendid style, Lord Falmouth's filly defeating Mr. L. de Rothschild's Brag after a great struggle by a neck. This year he was second for the Lincolnshire Handicap, on Placida, to Rosy Cross, but was not very fortunate in the big handicaps. Archer won this year the Prix du Jockey Club (French Derby) on Mr. Lefevre's Beauminet.

Melton's Derby has sometimes been described as "Archer's masterpiece", and not without reason. Melton belonged to Lord Hastings, whose title was created by Edward I. in 1290, so that it was one of the oldest families in the kingdom. From 1391 to 1841 it was in abeyance, but then it was revived in favour of Sir Jacob Astley. The owner of Melton was born in 1857, and reached the title through the death of his brother in 1875.

In 1880 he married one of the pretty daughters of Lord Suffield, having, by the advice of Captain Machell, become associated with the turf some three years previously. From the time of her marriage, Lady Hastings took the greatest interest in racing because her husband was so fond of it. At first Lord Hastings's horses were under the care of Joe Cannon and were managed by Captain Machell, but he later sent them to Mathew Dawson, and they did equally well from the first with him. Breadfinder and Master Kildare were amongst the earlier bearers of his colours, and one of the latter's victories has been recorded in the last chapter.

Almost in his noviciate Lord Hastings played a somewhat conspicuous part, his pretty "eau de nil ; crimson belt and cap" on several occasions, both before and after an important race, having been the observed of all observers. This Lord Hastings must in no way be confounded with the Marquess of Hastings, the victim of Hermit, Danebury, and plunging, and the registered owner of the scarlet and white hoops.

In 1880, Master Kildare, ridden by Archer, won the City and Suburban, and at that time he was a very good horse.

Mr. G. Parker wrote :

MASTER KILDARE

Winner of the City and Suburban

April 22, 1880

Owned by Lord Hastings. *Trained by* M. Dawson

Epsom Spring ! What golden memories came unbidden at
  thy name—
Memories of thy once great stronghold, "metropolitan" of
  fame ;
But thy cherished source of greatness to a rival soon gave
  way,
And the "City" at thy gathering long has held the pride
  of sway.
With its string of gallant warriors, bringing fame to horse
  and man,
To the time of doughty Thunder, who in weighty armour
  ran.
Epsom now again invites us—welcome in the name of
  Spring.
Haste we then into the presence of the Champions of the
  Ring.
In the lists appears a champion, with a bright untarnished
  shield,
And a massive weight of armour—Aintree's hero in the field.
There's a foeman to oppose him, who is first upon the scroll
Of the last great "City's" record—true and gallant game
  Parole ;

Westbourne's ready to confront him in the mighty Kings-
clere's cause,
While a host of other champions meet with partisan's applause.
One-and-twenty steeds are prancing, eager for the coming
fray !
Rider knights are now preparing skill and courage to display.

Now McGeorge has placed his forces—now his signal bids
them speed.
But too eager is our hero, in the fight he's first to lead ;
Soon his gallant knight has checked him, guides him with
unerring hand
Through the ranks of straggling warriors, for a final effort
grand.
Numbers in the field are yielding, as they now descend the
hill,
Till the son of brave Lord Ronald finds a match in Leoville.
Lake's and Archer's skill is vieing, but a Naylor's hopes have
fled,
While the banner borne by Master for Lord Hastings gleams
ahead.

"That time when Archer won the City and Suburban,"
said an old friend of Archer's, "I went with Archer and
several others back to London and spent part of the evening
with them at the Golden Cross Hotel, by Charing Cross
station. I said to Archer : 'I have to get home ; do you
know of anything for Sandown to-morrow ?' Fred said :
'I should back Vegetarian.' Now, Cradle was a hot favourite
at one to two, and most people had backed him. On the way
home I was talking to some men in the train and I said to
them : 'I should back Vegetarian for the Esher Stakes
to-morrow, as I have it from Mr. Archer.' I don't know if
they backed him, but I didn't. I had won on Master Kildare
and I thought I would be content with that. But the others
who had been with us at the hotel went down with Archer
to Sandown, which I wasn't able to do, and all backed
Cradle, and so lost."
"One evening after Lichfield Races," said the same friend
of Archer's, "we were standing on the platform of the station,

waiting for the train to take us to Manchester, when a not very prepossessing man came up to Archer and asked him to help him to get his ticket. Archer put his hand in his waist-coat pocket and handed him half a sovereign. The man looked at it and said : 'What's the use of that to take a ticket to Manchester ?' 'Oh,' said Fred, 'let me look at it ; what did I give you ?' The man held the half-sovereign between his fingers to show him, and Fred calmly took it and replaced it in his pocket, saying, 'Thank you.' You can imagine the chagrin of the man when he found what he'd lost through his greediness and impudence.

"Once at Ascot, the special first-class, directly after the last race, was waiting at the platform all ready to start, full up with dukes, lords, ambassadors, Members of Parliament and all the élite of the fashionable world, impatient to be off, everyone asking guards and porters why we tarried. 'Waiting for two gentlemen,' was the reply. Imagine the consterna-tion when Archer and Constable, sauntering along leisurely, entered the train, which was immediately despatched on its journey.

"One morning we were having breakfast in the coffee-room of the Queen's Hotel, Manchester, when Fred sauntered in. Of course, everybody asked him to sit down and have some breakfast with us. 'No thanks,' he said, 'I had mine an hour ago.' 'What did you have, Fred ?' 'Oh, a table-spoonful of hot castor oil and half an orange. That will have to last me till dinner-time.'

"I was much amused once at Leicester. I was talking to Fred outside the weighing-room about ordinary topics of the day, and, leaving him, went towards the grandstand, and was pounced upon by a man with whom I had a slight acquaint-ance. 'What did he tell you ?' 'Who ?' I said. 'Why, Archer, of course.' 'Oh,' I said, 'we were not talking about racing.' 'Good heavens,' he said, 'fancy a man on speaking terms with Archer, and not asking him what he fancied ! I wish I knew him ; I'd get him to mark my card every day.' 'I'll get him to mark mine now, if it would please you,' I said, 'and you can see him do it, and see it after he's marked it.' 'Do,' says he, 'and I'll never forget your kindness.' So I hastened up to Archer again. 'Fred,' I said, 'mark my card, telling him the reason. He laughed, took out his pencil, and marked four horses out of the seven races. I took it back to my aquaintance and said he could keep it if he'd give me his.

"Of course, I pretty well knew Archer had marked four horses he was going to ride himself, and, as luck would have it, not one of the four won, much, I fear, to the pecuniary loss of my acquaintance, for he was very far from hilarious when I saw him in the evening, and hardly deigned to acknowledge my 'Good evening'.

"A trainer friend of mine had a run of bad luck that seemed endless once, and a friend of his said to him : 'You'll never win another race until you get Archer to ride for you and break the spell.' 'Wish I could,' said he, 'but Archer don't care to ride unless he thinks he has a thundering good chance to win, and my lot are so dead out of form he'd laugh at me for asking him.' 'Shall I ask him ?' I said. 'He'd do a little to oblige me.' 'Wish you would,' says my friend. 'It might have a good result.'

"Well, next time he was running a horse I asked Fred if he'd ride it, and he said yes, he would, if he was not obliged to ride for someone else in the same race, and he'd let me know in good time. That was about 8 a.m., and at 10, Soloman, his valet, came round to my lodgings to say Mr. Archer had sent him to say he'd ride Wasp Nest for us. And sure enough, to our great joy, he won easily, and at 4 to 1, too. That proved the end of my trainer friend's misfortunes.

"Sometimes I have known Archer to have a run of awfully bad luck himself. Once I knew him ride thirty-three losers right off the reel, and, as many followers of racing only backed his mounts, and that at an increased stake every time he lost, you can imagine what a dreadful time they had, I amongst the number. And when the spell was broken, it was a seven to four on chance that did it ; but few of his followers had been able to weather the gale. Those that were did not forget to cheer, you can vouch.

"One good trait in Archer was that he was always out to win, and his followers knew that. Whatever the price in the ring, Archer was trying if the owner and trainer were not ;

and I remember what a fury he was in once at Newmarket on dismounting from one he at least fancied had been run for market purposes. I saw Archer ride some thousands of races, but two will always remain in my mind as the extremes of good and bad. The best was Dutch Oven in the Leger ; the worst was Galliard in the Derby.

"I often wonder if Archer had been spared would he have adopted the crouch seat and where he would have put his long legs to do it. Personally, I don't like the crouch seat, and think it at the bottom of the jostling, bumping, crossing and unfair riding one sees on racecourses at the present time. Like most old men, I don't think jockeys of the present day can be compared to Archer, Wood, Tom Cannon, Fordham, Custance, Goater and others of my youth, but acknowledge that, as far as owners and trainers are concerned, the present will compare favourably with the old days for honourable dealing and horses being run for their engagements."

> Which shall the wreath of glory claim ?
> If speed make Valentino's chance
> And Fortune eye Bend Or askance,
> Well might you blindly seek his name.
> Mayhap Fate's box when shaken throws
> Robert, or what the Devil knows.
> — "Orange Blossom" in *Bell's Life*, May 22, 1886.

Most people who knew Archer well and saw his many victories acknowledge that he had three great days in his life : his wins in the Manchester Cup on Valour and on Bend Or and on Melton in the Derby.

And this despite the fact that Mr. Richard Marsh, when asked to write down a few exciting tales about Archer, remarked :

"Why, his life was one long excitement !"

Mr. Nat Gould, too, said that when one began to write about Archer the difficulty was to know when to stop. This is especially the case with regard to the Derby of 1880.

Bend Or's Derby was preceded by an event which nearly had a tragic ending.

Archer had ridden a savage horse called Muley Edris, and he gave him some severe thrashings, which the horse did not forget. On May 1 Archer rode Muley Edris in a gallop on Newmarket Heath, and after dismounting threw the reins on his arms while he adjusted one of the "dolls" which were numerous on the Heath.

Suddenly Muley Edris grabbed Archer by the arm and, lifting him right off the ground, commenced to carry him away.

The savage beast had not gone far, however, when he dropped the unfortunate jockey and knelt on him. Archer was as near death as possible, but good fortune did not desert him, for one of the hind legs of the horse slipped from under him, and he rolled over. Muley Edris was soon up on his legs again, and, possibly frightened at the fall, bolted across the Heath.

The muscles of Archer's arm were terribly lacerated, and for many weeks it was done up in plaster of Paris, and Archer not only could not ride, but became very fearful as to whether he would ever have his arm restored. Lord Falmouth and Mr. John Boscawen were on the Heath at the time of Archer's mishap, and they took the injured man to a doctor, and afterwards Lord Falmouth took him to the best men in London, but no one seemed able to do anything for him.

"Thormanby" says, in "Kings of the Turf", that after Lord Falmouth's horse had bitten Archer "he was advised to see Sir James Paget, the eminent surgeon, who bound up the wound. Fred then requested to know how long it would take to heal. 'Oh, I think in three or four weeks you will be all right,' said Sir James. 'But shall I be fit for the Derby ?' Archer queried. 'Yes, I think you may go to the Derby.' 'But you don't quite understand me, I think, Sir James,' Archer persisted. 'I mean shall I be fit to ride ?' 'Better drive—better drive,' the surgeon replied. Rather taken aback by this very innocent and unexpected reply, Archer had to explain ; 'I fear, sir, you scarcely realize who I am !' 'No,' said the surgeon, politely referring to the patient's visiting-card, 'I see I have the honour of receiving Mr. Archer, but——' 'Well, Sir James, I suppose I may tell you, then, that what you are in your profession I am in mine,' and then he proceeded to tell him what that profession was.

"The famous surgeon, on learning the status of his visitor, was at once greatly interested, and asked him many questions, among others what would be his loss supposing he were unable to fulfil his Derby engagement. To which Archer replied: 'About £2,000.' His average income he stated (if no mistake has been made) to be about £8,000, to which Sir James is said to have replied: 'You may well say that what I am in my profession you are in yours. I only wish that my profession were half as profitable as yours."

At last, one day when he was fretting his heart out down at home in Cheltenham, while his chances of the Derby and of topping the list of winning jockeys grew smaller every day, Archer poured out his grief to Bob Chapman. When he heard that all the London doctors could not put Archer together again, so well, or so badly, had the savage Muley Edris done his work, then Chapman bethought himself of Hutton. Now Hutton was a bone-setter—in the eyes of the faculty a "quack". But Archer, although he had not come to the end of his own and Lord Falmouth's resources, had yet spent a good deal of time and money on physicians, and he listened when Bob Chapman discoursed on the genius of this irregular, if effective, surgeon. The result was that he went to Hutton, who cured him, as he had done his predecessor, Fred Webb.

Mr. John Dawson once said: "We don't get so very excited about racing, or not often, for it's so in the ordinary course of things for us to see races. The most exciting races I ever saw were when Archer won the Derby on Bend Or and the Manchester Cup on Valour. Not long before the Derby a horse down here had bitten Archer's arm very badly, and Fred went up from Cheltenham (he was down there at home, for he could do nothing) to one swagger specialist after another to get his arm treated. Lord Falmouth was seeing after him then, and he got the very best advice; but nothing seemed to do it any good. Have you heard of Hutton, the bone-setter? Fred went to him, and he got him well enough to ride in next to no time.

"Fred Webb could tell you of a yet more wonderful cure than that even—his own. He had been to all sorts of doctors for a fearfully bad arm, and at last he went to Hutton with it. He had his coat over the well arm, for he was quite incapable of taking it off himself to show his arm to the bone-setter, or of dressing himself afterwards. Hutton just stripped the bandages down off his arm and pulled it out straight and back and straight and back again. He hurt him a good deal, but something had been out of place, and Hutton had worked it into place again. Webb put on his coat himself and went out clothed and in his right mind, leaving the bandages behind. But before he went he asked Hutton what his charge would be, and Hutton said : 'Oh, that's all right ; we'll have a bottle of champagne on it !' Of course, he'd have charged about £50 to other people, but they're like that in the profession—among racing folk.

"Of course, the doctors were wild with Hutton and called him a quack and so on. And no doubt he made mistakes sometimes, but don't the doctors ? A man like that rises up now and again—perhaps once in a generation. They aren't trained for it or educated. Yes, I suppose it's a sort of instinct, but anyhow, Hutton saved Fred's career for him."

It was a long time before his arm got really well, and while he had it in a sling he and C. Morbey went to church one Sunday, and, curiously enough, the psalm for the day was the 32nd, which contains the following : "Be ye not as the horse or as the mule, which have no understanding, whose mouth must be held in with bit and bridle lest they come near unto thee." Both jockeys could not help smiling.

At a time when Lord Falmouth did not look like having a horse fit to run in the Derby, Archer promised in that event to ride for the Duke of Westminster, and he was very anxious to do so. His arm had not recovered when he weighed out for Bend Or, and he had to wear a pad in the palm of his hand and a piece of iron up the arm, and when, in the excitement of the race, he forgot and raised his arm to use the whip it fell helpless. He won the Derby with one arm, and he came round Tattenham Corner so close to the rails that he had to lift his near leg along the horse's shoulder to prevent it being crushed.

When the horses got well into the straight the white jacket and blue belt of Robert the Devil was so far in front that his victory seemed assured, but Archer sat down and rode with one arm as if for his life. Gradually the space between the two horses lessened, the bookmakers' cries of "10 to 1 on Robert the Devil" suddenly ceased, and there was a look of surprise and alarm on the face of Rossiter when he heard the thundering hoofs of Bend Or so close to his side.

Rossiter flurriedly got up his whip, but two strides from the post Robert the Devil was still in front. Then Archer made one of those last-stride efforts for which he was famous, and with arm and legs he seemed almost to lift Bend Or that shade in front on the post which makes all the difference.

So close to the judge was he when he made his effort that those in the ring laid as much as 5 to 1 that he had not got up, while those on the stands agreed with the judge that he had been successful. The hoisting of No. 7 was the signal for an outburst of cheering the like of which had never prior to that day been heard at Epsom.

It is a strange coincidence that Archer shot himself in later years, while Rossiter was found one night in the Plantation near the Bury Hill at Newmarket with his throat cut, but fortunately he recovered and afterwards did well in Roumania.

As the race was run, many people thought that Rossiter should have won, but Archer as he was returning to scale heard a bystander making some severe aspersions on the riding of Robert the Devil, and Archer turned on him, saying sharply: "Don't say it; it isn't true. The lad rode as well as any lad could, but met a better horse."

Some weeks after the Derby was over a rumour spread in racing circles that Bend Or might be disqualified, not only for the Derby but for all the races he had won. After a time the matter took actual shape, for Mr. Charles Brewer, the owner of Robert the Devil, and Charles Blanton laid a formal objection with the Epsom Stewards and Messrs. Weatherby, their complaint being couched:

"We do hereby object to the stakes payable to the winner

of the said race being paid to his Grace the Duke of Westminster as the owner of the chestnut colt which was entered for and ran first in the said race in the name of Bend Or by Doncaster out of Rouge Rose, upon the ground that the last-named horse was not the horse which he was represented to be, either in the entry or at the time of the race, and we further claim payment of the said stakes to us as the owners of the first-named horse, Robert the Devil, which ran second in the said race."

The Epsom Stewards who inquired into the matter were Mr. W. G. Craven, Mr. James Lowther, and Lord Calthorp (acting for Sir G. Chetwynd). The case for the appellant was based on statements of a stud groom, who had been discharged from Eaton, his son, and two other employees at the Duke of Westminster's stud. Their evidence was to the effect that Bend Or was really Tadcaster, by Doncaster—Clemence, and that the two colts got mixed up when transferred from Eaton to Newmarket and from the latter place to Russley. The book of the stud groom showed that no markings had been entered opposite the name of Bend Or, but then there were numerous other omissions.

The inquiry was a long one, and eventually the Stewards gave the following decision : "We, as Stewards of Epsom, unanimously decide that the chestnut colt Bend Or, which came in first for the Derby of 1880, is by Doncaster out of Rouge Rose, and the objection lodged by Messrs. Brewer and Blanton is overruled."

The decision was a very popular one, but some years later there was a rumour that Mr. Lowther, as the result of further information which was brought to his knowledge, formed the opinion that he and the other Stewards had made a mistake, though one does not imagine that there was any real doubt in the matter.

The late Cecil Raleigh lived at Epsom for eighteen years and saw eighteen Derbys. He wrote to me that Mathew Dawson once told him how Fred Archer as a little boy used to get so worked up that he would cry when he had to go out with the horses. "He wasn't a coward," added Mr. Raleigh, "no one could call him that. He had an iron nerve and yet he was very highly strung and a bundle of nerves. I remember in the Derby on Bend Or how he came round the bend—as he would often—with about five horses in front of him, with his teeth set and simply shaking with excitement and sometimes swearing all the way. Indeed, he would sometimes drive the younger lads out of his way in a race by swearing hard at them. You could hear him if you were near enough! 'Brr, brr. Get out of the way you — young scoundrels. Brr— brr, etc.' In that Derby on Bend Or he was actually over the rails. That was the Derby in which he beat Robert the Devil, whose jockey, poor Arthur Rossiter, cut his throat soon after. He really ought to have won, but Archer was too good for him. A year after they had a match over the Derby course, the same two horses and weight for age, and again Bend Or won. I remember King Edward was there—then Prince of Wales—and he said to Marsh, 'What's your fancy?' and Marsh said, 'I think I prefer the Derby winner, sir, over his own course.' "

People say that the late Duke of Westminster said to a would-be American purchaser, "There is not enough money in the great American Republic to buy Bend Or."

The Duke wrote to Archer on October 27, 1881 : "Since I wrote, both Peck and Porter advise putting Bend Or out of training—which will be a great disappointment to me, as I had looked forward to another year with him, but in this case please consider my last letter as unwritten."

ARCHER'S PRINCIPAL WINS IN 1881

BROCKLESBY STAKES (LINCOLN).—BELLE LURETTE, 5 to 1.
CITY AND SUBURBAN.—BEND OR, 100 to 8.
GREAT CHESHIRE HANDICAP.—POST OBIT, 4 to 7.
WOODCOTE STAKES (EPSOM).—DUNMORE, 11 to 8.
EPSOM STAKES.—PETRONEL, 13 to 8.
THE DERBY.—IROQUOIS, 11 to 2.
EPSOM GOLD CUP.—BEND OR, 6 to 4.
MANCHESTER CUP.—VALOUR, 25 to 1.
PRINCE OF WALES'S STAKES (ASCOT).—IROQUOIS, 4 to 5.
ROYAL HUNT CUP (ASCOT).—PETER, 100 to 30.
HARDWICKE STAKES (ASCOT).—PETER, 5 to 4.
RICHMOND STAKES.—DUTCH OVEN, 6 to 1.
SUSSEX STAKES (GOODWOOD).—LIMESTONE, 6 to 4.
ROUS MEMORIAL (GOODWOOD).—DUTCH OVEN, 100 to 30.
CHAMPION FOAL STAKES (DERBY).—DUTCH OVEN, 7 to 4
GREAT YORKSHIRE HANDICAP.—PETRONEL, 2 to 1.
ST. LEGER.—IROQUOIS, 2 to 1.
PORTLAND PLATE.—MOWERINA, 100 to 8.
ALEXANDRA PLATE (DONCASTER).—SWORD DANCE, 9 to 4.
PARK HILL STAKES (DONCASTER).—BAL GAL, 4 to 6.
DONCASTER CUP.—PETRONEL, 4 to 11.
ROUS MEMORIAL (NEWMARKET).—DUTCH OVEN, 2 to 5.
CLEARWELL STAKES (NEWMARKET). — DUTCH OVEN,
  1 to 3.
CHAMPION STAKES (NEWMARKET).—BEND OR, 4 to 6.
DEWHURST PLATE.—DUTCH OVEN, 1 TO 3.

Archer headed the record with 220.

CHAPTER XV

ARCHER was in great form in 1881, and beat his own record of 1880 by nearly a score of wins, while he still was nearly a dozen behind his total in 1878. He began this year's victories with an old friend, Tower and Sword, at Lincoln, and from that time onwards, throughout the season, race after race fell to his lot, the Derby and St. Leger on Iroquois being among the number.

Added to these triumphs he left Robert the Devil in an easy manner in the Epsom Cup on Bend Or, steering him also in the City and Suburban and in the Champion Stakes. In this year also took place one of his most sensational wins, that on Peter in the Royal Hunt Cup ; and the outside price landed at Manchester on Valour. It is not many riders who can boast of carrying off all the four principal races of a St. Leger week, but Archer accomplished this on Petronel, Iroquois, and Mowerina, the first-named winning the Great Yorkshire Stakes and the Cup, Iroquois the St. Leger, and Mowerina the Portland Plate.

Early in 1881 Mathew Dawson took Archer into partnership in the training establishment at Heath House, where the famous jockey had begun his apprenticeship not so very many years before as a small boy, and it was one of Archer's best years from the point of view of the big races he was successful in.

This was the year Archer scored his sensational Manchester Cup victory on Valour. For months Sir John Astley had coveted Peter, a five-year-old by Hermit out of Lady Masham, and borrowing £2,500 from a friend he bought the horse, whom he regarded "as the best horse of his day, if not of any other", for £6,300.

Soon afterwards Sir John met Archer, who promised to ride Peter in the Royal Hunt Cup, but a small happening changed the whole course of events. One morning when Peter was out at exercise, and had gone wonderfully well in a mile and a half gallop, Sir John dropped across Sherrard, who had the management of the horses at Belford Lodge, and asked him to let Peter go round the Lime-kilns with Foxhall, who was then a three-year-old, and was being trained for the Grand Prix.

Peter cut down the Yankee in easy style, and when the riders were weighed after the morning's work it was found that Foxhall had been in receipt of two stone and a half.

Plans were changed, and it was decided to run Peter in the Manchester Cup, but the fates were working overtime against Sir John Astley. It is one of the unwritten laws of racing that an owner shall avail himself of the services of the stable jockey if he is a good rider, and Sir John told C. Wood he would have the mount on Peter in the Manchester Cup.

A week before the race Sir John was at Kempton, and as Archer went out to ride in a race he handed Sir John a letter, saying, "This will interest you, Sir John. I will ride Peter if you wish."

The letter was from Captain Machell, and it read : 'If you will ride Valour in the Manchester Cup I will run him, if not I shall not send him to Manchester."

When Archer returned he asked : "What answer shall I send the Captain ?" and Sir John told him that on no account would he take the stable jockey off his horse, that he could ride Valour, and sarcastically added : "What chance had Valour to beat Peter at 4lb. ?"

There is no doubt that Sir John did the proper thing in putting up Wood, but it cost him dearly, for Peter was beaten a neck by Valour, and the former's owner lost £12,000. Valour started at 25 to 1, but it was only Archer's wonderful jockeyship that won the day.

He knew that Valour could not really stay a mile and three-quarters, so he rode the race in twice, driving him for the best part of a mile, and then easing him. In the straight he brought him again for the second race, as it were, and just got up on the post.

The late Mr. Nat Gould gave me leave to use what he had written about Archer, and said : "I shall probably be able to send you something about him ; the difficulty is to know where to stop." He wrote :

"It was at Eagle Farm Racecourse, Brisbane, Queensland, at a meeting of the Queensland Turf Club, that I first heard of Fred Archer's lamented death. Bad news travels quickly, and the cable was not long in flashing the sad intelligence over those thousands of miles separating the Mother Country from Australia. It cast quite a gloom over the meeting, and it was with bated breath the question was asked : 'Have you heard of Fred Archer's death ?' It was a high tribute to the great jockey's fame that his death should cause such a widespread feeling of sorrow in such a far-off part of the world as Brisbane.

"In glancing over the late Sir John Astley's 'Fifty Years of my Life'—I had already read it—I opened it at a page where he describes how Peter lost the Manchester Cup when Valour beat him. I remember the race well, and as it was not often that a long price about Archer could be obtained, the following incidents may not be uninteresting. At that time I was residing at Newark in Notts, and went into McGeorge's Hotel a day or two before the race. I was under the impression at the time that Archer would ride Peter in the Manchester Cup. The late Mr. Tom McGeorge— what racing man does not remember that prince of starters ? —was a great friend of Archer's, who occasionally stayed with him at his residence near Newark. Young James McGeorge was at the time a stripling, and I often met him there. Then the Manchester Cup cropped up, and I said I supposed Archer would ride Peter. 'No,' said James McGeorge, 'Wood rides him ; Archer will ride Valour for Captain Machell.' I had backed Valour in the Lincolnshire Handicap and was desirous of getting my money back on him, but as he was generally regarded as more of a miler than anything else, I did not fancy he had much chance of lasting a Manchester Cup.

"However, I went to the meeting, and about the first man I saw in the paddock was Archer. Then I hunted up Valour and had a look at the horse, who seemed well enough for anything. Peter was a hot favourite, and according to Sir John Astley's book the genial baronet put a lot of money on him. 'Here, 25 to 1 Archer,' sang out a bookmaker whose lungs did credit to him. These were not the sort of odds a backer of Archer generally obtained, and it showed that the ring at all events did not think Valour had too much chance. Such a price was too tempting for me and, although I had a 'fiver' on Peter and thought the race a good thing for him, I took 25 to 1 about Valour which an accommodating man laid me, smiling as he put the 'ready' in his capacious pocket.

"I shall never forget that race. It was, in my humble opinion, one of the best races Archer ever rode. Charles Wood was a jockey ready for any emergency, but on this occasion he was fairly outridden. Archer evidently knew the sort of horse he had under him, and, to use a slang term, he 'kidded' Valour all the way. If Valour could for a few minutes have been gifted with the talking powers of that celebrated ass of Balaam's I fancy he would have delivered himself as follows :

" 'I thought it was a mile race, at the furthest. Archer rode me at the start at a good pace, and as we neared the end of a mile he set me going again, and I was in for another sprint, which rather astonished me. I could not understand running two races one after the other. I won both. You see, it was just my distance.'

"As I watched the race it suddenly dawned upon me what Archer was up to, and I thought it the cleverest piece of work I had ever seen.

"Knowing Valour did not care much for the Manchester Cup distance, Archer rode the first part of the race as though it was a mile. Then he gave Valour a rest but kept him well up, and when they came to the straight it was a race! Wood seemed to have the race won on Peter, but Archer on Valour still kept going. The Demon rode for his life, and I never saw a horse finish as Valour did. Peter was just beaten, and through sheer good riding on Archer's part. That Peter was a better horse than Valour I do not think anyone would deny. It was a genuine case of 'the riding did it'. Even the backers of the other jockeys could not help cheering Fred as he came to weigh in. I have had many a wager about Archer, but not at such a long price as I got about Valour in the Manchester Cup."

Again, Mr. Gould says :

"Valour's Manchester Cup was remarkable. Peter, owned by Sir John Astley, was a hot favourite and Wood had the mount. Valour's course was supposed to be a mile, and Peter was probably at his best over a similar distance. Valour was not put down as a probable starter on the morning of the race, or, if he was, had the 'doubtful' star in front of his name. I went from Newark to see this race, and had reason for going, as I had received a hint from a most exceptional quarter that Valour would run, also that Peter would win. In the paddock Fred Archer was standing, for a wonder, alone.

" 'Got any chance on Valour ?' I asked.

"For a moment Archer looked at me with a peculiar twinkle in his eyes, and said something to this effect :

" 'He's got a chance, especially as I know he's well.'

"He rode a wonderful race in snatches. He sent Valour along for a mile, and then eased him a bit ; when they were fairly going along in the straight he rode the horse again. Wood seemed to have the race in hand on Peter, but he reckoned without his formidable rival, and it must have been a surprise for him when he saw Valour's head alongside. It was a desperate race, but Archer's magnificent finish just did the trick, and he got Valour's head in front of Peter's at the end. I remember a friend of mine standing close to me, who had backed Peter, exclaimed : 'He'd win on a donkey !'

"The first time I met Archer was in the Saracen's Head at Lincoln. I had seen him ride many times. I fancy it was the year Rosy Cross won the Lincoln Handicap, or may be Touchet—it was one of them.

"I am writing nearly all the racing from memory. Somehow Archer seemed to fascinate people ; I know he did me. Perhaps it was the glamour of his wonderful riding, yet I think it was his personality. He had a kind, gentlemanly manner, though he could speak sharply at times. His face was most expressive, generally with a smile on it when he met a friend. He was tall for a jockey—about 5 ft. 9 in. I should think.

"Although he was thin he did not look it. His strength was great, but he had to waste to keep down his weight. He had wonderful eyes. At first they seemed languid, especially when the lids fell over them as he was thinking ; but once he became interested there came into them a smouldering fire which illuminated his face. He almost talked with his eyes, they were so expressive—at least I found them so.

"He had a voice that mated with them, for there was a slumbering power in it, a subdued strength, will, determination, a not-to-be-beaten tone, but it was never harsh or jarring, even when raised.

"A kinder-hearted man never lived than Fred Archer. That some people misunderstood him I know, but who has not been misunderstood at one time or another ? How much he gave away will never be known, for he did good actions in secret.

"I believe he was fond of money, but only for the power it gave him of doing as he wished. Sometimes he was silent, reserved, and then a different expression was on his face.

"That he was a thinker I am sure, and not only about racing. Many a poor man has had cause to bless Fred Archer's name. I recollect on one occasion a broken-down old fellow, who had been racing for years, said to me : 'If it hadn't been for him,' pointing to the jockey, 'I'd have been dead before now.' I asked how this would have happened.

" 'I was awful bad, and I met him as he was coming off the Heath one morning. He pulled up, looked at me, and asked if I was ever ill.

" 'I told him. He rode on. An hour or two later a letter came round for me, and in it was a ten-pound note. That first put me on my legs and I rested a bit. He's a good 'un, is Fred—a good 'un.' "

"Archer was born at Cheltenham on January 11, 1857, so that he was nearly a year older than myself. He married Miss Nellie Dawson, daughter of John Dawson on January 31, 1883, and when she died on November 8, 1884, it nearly broke his heart.

144

"He was left with one child, a girl, and I saw her riding on Newmarket Heath, with Mrs. Chaloner I think, not many years ago. Archer's father rode Little Charley in the Grand National in 1858, and his brother Charles, who trains at Newmarket, also rode races. Another brother, William, was killed at Cheltenham in 1878.

"From the photographs of Fred Archer and Charlie Archer it will be seen that there is a great likeness between them. Charles Archer named a horse after me, and as a flat racer it was a failure. He wrote telling me he was sorry the horse had turned out so badly, for he named him Nat Gould because I knew his brother well. Nat Gould, however, when put over the sticks, made amends; he must have won about forty events of one kind or another.

"What a rider Fred Archer was! Shall we ever see such another? I doubt it. Look at the list of jockeys when he was riding and compare his winning mounts with those of the jockeys of to-day. He got the cream of the riding, but not all of it, for in his day there were such past masters of the art as Tom Cannon, George Fordham, John Osborne, Charles Wood and others against him. The year I left for Sydney—1884—he rode 241 winners; in 1885, 246; in 1876, 1877, and 1878 he rode over 200 winners each season. From 1876 to 1885 he was only twice under the 200. He had a tremendous number of mounts in a year, and if ever a man deserved them, he did.

"One of his best races, in my opinion, was when he won the City and Suburban on Master Kildare. He rode Melton, Master Kildare's son, when he won the Derby. Master Kildare was a good horse. When Leoville, who was receiving 2 stone from Master Kildare, came down the hill it looked odds on Archer being beaten. He handled Master Kildare with consummate skill and won on the post by a head; it was a magnificent piece of horsemanship and he was cheered to the echo.

"This race was a foretaste of what he was to do later on in the Derby, and when he went out on Bend Or no doubt hundreds of people recollected how he got Master Kildare home a couple of months before.

Only a short time previously Archer had been savaged

by Muley Edris, and bitten in the arm so badly that he could only ride with one arm in the Derby.

"This was a Derby to be remembered. Robert the Devil, on whom Rossiter had the mount, was leading, and it looked a pound to a hayseed on him winning. Archer, however, came creeping up on Bend Or and stride by stride gained on the leader.

"It was a glorious struggle, but the jockeys were unequal. Rossiter was no match for Fred Archer. When Archer drew level Rossiter seemed paralysed; he sat still, then moved, but did not help his mount at all.

"Probably it was the knowledge of what Archer could do that frightened him, and small wonder at it. His finishing powers frightened better men than Rossiter. Bend Or drew level; they were together for a moment, then, like a flash, they were past the post, and the Duke of Westminster's famous horse had won. Bend Or was always at his best over Epsom course. Robert the Devil had his revenge in the St. Leger, when that grand horseman, Tom Cannon, had the mount. Bend Or was favourite at odds of 11 to 8 on, but must have been fifteen to twenty lengths behind Robert, and finished nearer last than first. It was an awful day. Rain came down in torrents, the course was a sea of mud, the riders were soaked and so was the crowd, and the jockeys were allowed to draw about a couple of pounds overweight on account of the dirt on their jackets.

"Tom Cannon's colours were sky blue and white, so it may easily be imagined how they looked.

"Next year Bend Or won the City and Suburban, carrying 9 stone, giving Foxhall 2 stone 6 lb. What sort of a performance was this, when we consider what Foxhall did afterwards, landing the Cesarewitch and the Cambridgeshire double? Fred Archer always regarded Bend Or as one of the best he ever rode, probably he was *the* best. I had a double event bet over the Derby and St. Leger when Iroquois won, but it did not amount to much.

"I also took 2 to 1 against the field for the St. Leger, Iroquois and Peregrine, the latter being soon after scratched; so I only had the American going for me. During the St. Leger week Iroquois went up and down in the betting like a cork, and some people in Newark were lucky enough to get 6 to 1 about the 2 to 1 chance.

"Iroquois was a good horse, but not in the same street as Bend Or. There was a fog covering the course during the race, and going over the brow of the hill the favourite was last, but he got into his field near the rifle-butts. Lucy Glitters, a pretty good mare, led into the straight, Jim Snowden riding her. When Archer called upon Iroquois the result was never in doubt, and he beat Tom Cannon on Mr. F. Gretton's Geologist, with Lucy Glitters third.

"Newark was handy for Doncaster Races, and I was often over the famous moor. I shall never forget Dutch Oven's St. Leger. She started at 40 to 1 and beat Geheimniss and Shotover, all three mares. When the news came we made merry for the rest of the day. Racing took place at Nottingham on the Forest when I was there at Newark; a peculiar place it was, shaped like an egg, all on the bend, with a sharp turn at the ends.

"I once saw Archer, Wood, and George Baird ride a tremendous race there, and Baird just won.

"George Baird (Mr. Abington) was a fine horseman, but he was wild, and did not take care of himself, and so he came to an early end. He would go from the south to the north to ride in a race, for he was passionately fond of it—and he could ride and no mistake. He had a style something like Archer's, although he had not the latter's skill.

"Fred Archer had marvellous hands, wonderful judgment of pace, and knew exactly what his opponents were doing in a race. His finishes were powerful. He seemed to wrap his legs round a horse and fairly lift him forward. When St. Blaise won the Derby there were a good many people who differed from Judge Clarke and said Highland Chief ought to have got the race. Galliard, ridden by Archer, and Highland Chief were neck and neck at the Bell, but neither of them could catch St. Blaise, on whom Wood had the mount. There was a lot of talk over this race at the time, and Archer was blamed for the defeat of Galliard. Many said he rode a bad race on him; some went even farther than that. It is surprising how the loss of a little money influences the opinions of some people. The fact of the matter was that Galliard lost ground coming down the hill, owing to being a heavy-shouldered horse, and could not make it up again. No one with an ounce of sense would ever for a moment suspect Fred Archer of throwing away a Derby, or any other race, if he could help it. He was too fond of winning, and it was his ambition to be always at the head of the jockey list. No man who ever threw his leg across a horse rode with a greater determination to win if possible than Fred Archer. . . . St. Simon first appeared at Goodwood in 1883, when he won the Halnaker Stakes and Maiden Plate easy.

"I have a shoe of St. Simon's, given me by Mr. Ernest Day, who brought Carbine over from Australia. . . .

"Wood and Archer were once supposed to be the head of a jockey ring. I do not believe it for a moment. Charles Wood is alive and, I am glad to say, well, and as good a jockey as ever one need wish to see he was in those days.

"He can speak for himself, and I am sure would bear me out when I say that neither he nor Fred Archer ever had anything to do with a jockey ring if there was one. . . .

"Archer was indignant at such accusations, and well he might be. The public—I mean the public who back horses —are not altogether fools, and they would not have stuck to Archer as they did if they were not perfectly certain that he rode to win. It is ridiculous to suppose for a moment that the jockeys at the head of their profession would do such a thing. Probably there were jockeys who backed Archer's and Charlie Wood's mounts because they were perfectly certain they would beat their own. . . . The idea of leading jockeys pulling horses on their own account is laughable.

"The Eagle Farm Racing Club has the big meeting of the Queensland Turf Club. It cast a gloom over the gathering when one heard whispers of 'Archer's dead', 'Archer's shot himself', 'Poor Fred!' We were 15,000 miles away, and yet Archer's death caused quite a sensation. There were men, like myself, who had seen him ride. One or two of us had known him, and we talked over the sadness utterly regardless of racing. Fred Archer seemed to be a personality even on this far-away Queensland course.

148

"Wasting . . . did it—not his own hand. I never go near Newmarket without looking into the graveyard on the Heath, within sound of the morning gallops, and I stand before Archer's grave and think over the past. If ever a man was done to death by his profession he was. No man could have stood such a strain. There he lies in peace. I sometimes wonder if he can still hear the sounds on the Heath and see the jockeys go to their work. I wonder. Who knows ? Perhaps he can."

"I dare say," said one of the greatest authorities on racing matters, in 1914, "that if you have been talking to Mr. Portman he has told you that Archer was not a bookies' jockey, and that one reason why he said he always wanted to win was to get the better of the bookmakers. Anyhow, his main object was always to win and he would do most things to attain it.

"If a man had a likely horse and Archer couldn't get the mount on it, he would tell the owner it was no good and dissuade him from running it if he could, while he took care himself to be on a horse that *could* win. He would shout at the other jockeys and swear at them and frighten them out of his way. He would win by almost any means in his power. Robert Peck told me that before the Derby of 1881 Archer went to him and asked him to give him the mount on Peregrine. Peck said he didn't see how he could as he had arranged for Webb to ride him. Archer then said : 'Well, give Webb a thousand and put me up.' Peck said it was rather a temptation, and it would have paid him well to give Webb the thousand pounds. But he didn't do it. Webb had to waste a good deal to do the weight and he was so weak and done up that Peck said he felt if he could have put a lemon squash in his mouth the last few strides he would have won. I don't see it would matter to publish this, for I don't think Webb ever pretends that he could rival Archer, and besides, he has given up riding.

"Archer was not only a wonderful rider : he had a wonderful brain, and as he rode in a race he always knew what all the other jockeys and horses were doing and what they were capable of doing. Webb is not easy to gets things out of.

149

Peck has told me that you would get more out of Archer about a race in five minutes than you would out of Webb in a whole afternoon.

"Archer was always *scheming* how to win. And he was a man who could win in a canter from a large field of horses where other jockeys would have lost. But when a man *can* do it it is a sight to see. Fordham was generally able to get the better of Archer on the Newmarket course; he knew it like a book and all the ins and outs of it. Archer would look round, and there was Fordham, who was too clever for him. Whether or not Archer or Fordham was the better jockey, Fordham was the one one would prefer to have on a horse if one wanted him to win races later on. Archer was very handy with whip and spur, and often a horse he won a hard race on never did any more racing afterwards. If any amount of flogging would help to win, Archer would be very unmerciful to his horse.

"Archer, of course, kept ahead of all the other jockeys for thirteen years. The nearest approach to his record has been, I think, Morny Cannon's, who could be riding now, and successfully, if he had chosen to take to the American style of riding and to march with the times. But he never really cared about riding. Although he was so brilliant, his heart was not in it. He would far rather go out boating any day, or watch a cricket march, than ride."

Bend Or beat Robert the Devil again in 1881 in the Epsom Gold Cup, and Archer was always of the opinion that the former was a better horse. In the discussion on the Derby a friend said to him : "I feel sure that Rossiter ought to have beaten you, and that he threw away the race by looking round to see what you were doing, instead of sitting down and riding his horse."

"Well," replied Archer, "it was not wise of him to turn round, perhaps, but you must remember this : I had to ride my horse with one hand that day. I hadn't long begun to ride again, and I couldn't use one arm at all. If I had been all right and fit to finish, and if I had had the use of both arms, I should have won very much easier, so it isn't safe to judge by the race for the Derby."

It is true that Robert the Devil turned the tables on Bend

Or in the St. Leger, but that was a terrible day, for rain fell in torrents, and the jockeys on returning were allowed to weigh in at 2 lb. overweight.

What kind of a horse Bend Or was is shown by the fact that he won the City and Suburban with 9 stone, giving Foxhall 2 stone 6 lb., and the American horse later won both the Cesarewitch and the Cambridgeshire, besides the Grand Prix de Paris.

Mr. Pierre Lorillard, a millionaire tobacco merchant, sent Iroquois and other yearlings over to this country in 1879, accompanied by their trainer, Jacob Pincus. F. Grey Griswold was in England, looking after things for Mr. Lorillard at the time when Archer rode Iroquois, and saw a good deal of the great jockey. He gave his impressions of him to an American interviewer after Archer's death, as did Sir Roderick Cameron, a well-known patron of sport, widely celebrated in America as the importer of Leamington, the famous sire of Iroquois. This was not the first of the numerous American invasions, Ten Broeck coming in the 'fifties, and then M. Sanford, whose Brown Prince ran second to Charmant for the Two Thousand Guineas of 1877.

As Mr. James R. Keene also sent some horses over, American methods—the very early morning gallops and the time test—soon became common here.

Iroquois was not fit when Peregrine beat him in a trot in the Two Thousand Guineas, and the latter colt was made a strong favourite for the Derby. One person who did not think it was the odds was Archer, and when he could not ride Peregrine he begged of Pincus to be allowed to ride Iroquois, and naturally the American trainer was only too pleased to accept the offer.

The story of the race is soon told. When Fred Webb asked Peregrine to challenge the leaders he swerved away from the rails. That was one of the openings Archer loved, and he promptly took the inside position. The two were soon clear, but Iroquois was the better horse, and the struggle between them was soon over.

The scenes in America were most enthusiastic when the code word, "Iropertow", which meant Iroquois I, Peregrine 2, Town Guard 3, was flashed across the Atlantic cable. Business was suspended in Wall Street and on the Stock Exchange, while the cheering was loud and long. It was even suggested that a bronze statue of Iroquois should be erected in a public park in New York. Poets let their pens run, and one wrote before the race :

Flushed red are American faces !
    Hurrah ! for old Leamington's son :
You'll show the Pale Briton how races
    Across the Atlantic are won.
Dash on as if life was at venture,
    And news shall unloosen the cork
From seas of champagne at Newmarket
    And oceans of "fizz" at New York !

It is said that on the day after the Derby Archer was coming out of the weighing-room when a total stranger walked up to him and said : "Mr. Archer, if you will let me take you over to the States and exhibit you for two months I will give you £10,000 before you start." Archer refused, but he little knew under what sad circumstances he would visit New York three years later.

The victory of Iroquois in the Derby and the St. Leger made Archer as popular in America as he was in England —a fact which he discovered when he visited the former country in 1884.

Archer received many congratulations, but one he perhaps appreciated most was from his old vicar at Prestbury village, the Rev. J. Baghot De la Bere, who wrote :

"Prestbury Vicarage.
"Cheltenham.
"*June* 5, 1881.

"MY DEAR ARCHER,

"At a time when you are receiving the congratulations not only of all England but of all America as well, it seems unnecessary for me to write and add to the number.

"But you might suppose me to know nothing and to care little about it ; the first may be true, but not the last, for I take, and have taken all along, the greatest interest in your wonderful career, great skill and ability, receiving such a reward in the way of success as I should suppose is without precedent. And I write now to offer you my warmest congratulations on the past and my best wishes for the future; and, coming from one who has known you all your life, and your mother and her father all my life, they may not be unwelcome to you even at such a time of universal congratulation.

"Three years ago I asked your mother if she would give me your *carte de visite* photograph with your autograph at the bottom, but at that time of trouble I dare say she forgot all about it. If you have one by you, and when you have time would send it me, I should value it much.

"When you next come to Prestbury I hope you will call and see me and that I shall be at home.

"Believe me, with all good wishes.

"Very sincerely yours.

"J. BAGHOT DE LA BERE."

Archer also won the St. Leger on Iroquois, who returned to America in 1883, after winning the Stockbridge Cup, and went to the stud.

The picture of Iroquois was sent specially for this book by a friend in America to Lieut.-Col. E. D. Miller, C.B.E., D.S.O.

There is no doubt that Archer's keen desire to win at all costs made him a bit of a bully on the racecourse, and some of the jockeys were rather afraid of him and his tongue, for he could, and did, swear during a race. There was one man, however, who was not afraid of him, and that was George Fordham. He was a wonderful jockey, and Archer could not give him any start.

Archer and Fordham had many tussles, and the former did not always get the best of it. Once, it is said, he had the bad taste to hector Fordham at the post in a race for the Royal Hunt Cup.

"You have taken a liberty with me, *Mister* Archer," Fordham said, "and I will teach you to act differently. I may not do it now. I shall probably wait until you are on something that you fancy yourself about. You must not take a liberty with George."

The right moment came. Archer was on the crack

mount Silvio. Fordham was riding in the same race, and he made the running. Archer came up on Silvio and called out, "Pull on one side!" but Fordham did nothing of the kind. He thought he saw some better going in the middle of the course, and he went for it.

There was no room for any objection, but by these tactics he most effectively prevented Archer from winning. "I do not think Archer will ever take a liberty with George again," quietly remarked Fordham as he dismounted.

On another occasion Fordham was riding Brag at Newmarket for Mr. Leopold de Rothschild, against Reputation, with Archer in the saddle. As Archer was going out of the Birdcage a friend said to him, "Fred, mind the 'Old Demon' don't do it again!" He had beaten Archer three times that week already. Archer replied: "I will be halfway home before the Old Gentleman knows where he is!" Reputation was a very quick horse off the mark, and Custance, who overheard what Archer said, jumped on his hack at once, knowing that George was walking on foot to the post, caught him up, and told him what he had heard Archer say. Fordham simply smiled and said, "All right."

Custance says he never saw anyone get into such a muddle as poor Fred did on that occasion. He was giving a stone away to a horse that had a fine turn of speed, and he had only one chance, to wait and come with one run near the winning-post. However, through Fordham "kidding" him that he had the best of the start, Archer made too much use of his horse with the worst of the weight. Instead of being half-way home, Reputation tired, and Fordham got up on the post and won by a neck. Poor Archer told Custance that he could always make out what every other jockey was doing, but he never could understand what Fordham was up to.

After Archer's death Rapier, in the *Illustrated Sporting and Dramatic News* of November 27, 1886, quoted from a letter from the late Duke of Beaufort:

"About poor Archer, he was strong on all points as a jockey. He had wonderful good judgment, quickness to seize an opportunity, or patience to wait for one if he was shut in and could not get through. Every now and then he made a mistake, no doubt, but he always said that he had done so and would speak of it : and he made fewer mistakes than any jockey I ever saw.

"He was quite equal to Sam Chifney, Jem Robinson, Frank Butler, Nat Flatman, Bill Scott, Alfred Day, G. Edwards, Tom Chaloner, Custance, French, Aldcroft, Sam Rogers, George Fordham, Tom Cannon, the poor fellow Constable, who died a few years since, or any other jockey I ever saw, and superior to most of them.

"There were several horses no one else could win upon.

"His race on my colt, Belisarius II, at Newmarket, on Friday, October 29, when he beat Grandison and Devil's Hoof, was a masterpiece of riding. That horse never galloped as he did that day, and probably never will again ; but Archer only hit him once and never spurred him. Lord Strathnairn would not win with anyone else. I have seen him often win when I felt sure no one else could have done so.

"I cannot specify the particular races without looking over the Racing Calendar. I fancy Bend Or's Derby was as good a race as ever he rode.

"One remark I lately read about him in a newspaper is a calumny. He was described as a most merciless rider. Now he seldom hit a horse, and never rode with rowels to his spurs. The only horse I ever saw him punish severely was Whipper In, and he was an idle horse that would not go without it.

"I do not remember when he first rode for me, but he won the Doncaster Cup and Great Yorkshire Stakes for me in 1881 on Petronel, neither of which races he had ever won before. I am not sure whether he had ridden for me before he rode Petronel. He came out with my hounds in the February of 1880 and asked me to let him ride Petronel in the Two Thousand, but I had asked Fordham, and he had promised if Mr. Crawfurd did not want him."

"Fred Archer and I," said the late Mr. Joseph Davis, "were great friends since he was quite a boy at Mathew Dawson's. Added to the fact that he was a good natural rider, he was an attractive lad with gentle and attractive manners, and that went a long way in influencing owners of horses to employ him. He was nice-looking, with blue-grey eyes, though his rather prominent teeth spoilt his looks a little. He was always a great man with the ladies and especially a great favourite with the aristocratic ones, owing to his good manners. He always rode for me when he could ride the weight. I had a very good horse, Strathavon, a selling-plater who won many races. I bought him from Sir Daniel Cooper—he previously belonged to Christophers, the secretary of Tattersall's—and Archer first rode him for me in 1881. Whenever Archer was a bit down on his luck he would come to me and say, 'Pull out the old grey and break the ice for me,' when I would enter Strathavon for a selling race.

"On one occasion he had been riding at Newmarket Races, quite out of luck. He asked me to enter Strathavon in a selling race at Kempton Park to break his spell of bad luck, which I did, although I was unable to back him. I entered Strathavon, but had to bet £1,500 to £600 on him. I always gave Archer £50 for winning a race for me, and I did so now; but later on he came back and said, 'I won't take your £50. I said, 'Nonsense. Take it. I won on the race; in fact, after buying the horse, I was £80 to the good.' But he said, 'No, I won't, but I'll have a suit of clothes.' So he came round to my rooms the following morning and we went together and ordered the new suit, and I made him have an overcoat too. The same morning I drove him to Kempton, and we had to go over Waterloo Bridge. There was a toll-gate there then, and I had to stop my phaeton to pay the toll. It was three-halfpence, I think; and Archer said: 'Let me pay this time—you paid the last!'

"Archer was called 'The Tinman', because he was saving with his money. *Mind* being called 'The Tinman!' Not he! He didn't mind *anything*. He was careful, it is true, but he could be very generous—especially to jockeys down on their luck; he would often give away a fiver in a quiet sort of way. He was very popular with all racing men, and he would just as soon talk to any poor man as to the aristocracy. He was not a great talker, but when you got him to yourself then he would talk.

"Chiefly about racing, though. He hadn't a great deal

156

to say on other subiects. Everyone liked to be with him; he certainly had *very* taking manners.

"I have no letters from him, for he didn't write very well, and he never wrote any letters himself if he could help it. I often wrote his letters for him.

"The people in the crowd used to say things to Archer sometimes at race-meetings. But he always had an answer ready—he was very good at repartee. I remember once he came to me very indignant after losing a race at Epsom. A man who had backed his mount shouted to him as he came off the course: 'You old yard of gelatine—you never tried a yard!' There were appropriate adjectives, too, of course.

"Archer married a very pretty little girl, Miss Dawson. I got up a subscription amongst Fred's racing friends and we gave him a silver dinner-service. He was very pleased with it, of course, and made a speech about three words long, saying that he thanked us all, and me especially. About a month after his wedding they were staying at the Albion Hotel, Brighton, and he wanted to give a dinner to several of his racing friends. He asked me to order it. I did, and the bill was over £100. I ordered a nice dinner and wines and suchlike. Fred came to me with the bill in his hand and he said: 'You have been pretty extravagant, but it was a good dinner.'

"No, I don't think Archer could possibly have won the Derby on Galliard. Could you put a heart into a horse to win a race if he hadn't got one?

"The last week at Brighton, just before Archer's death, we were all down there together at the Albion Hotel— Fred, Captain Pringle, Captain Bowling, Mr. F. Tudor, and J. D. Fred seemed down on his luck because he hadn't been winning, and I said: 'Look here—I'll take you £100 to 1 that you win all the races you ride in to-day.' He replied: 'That's a bet!' and he won three races—all he rode in—and the fourth he couldn't ride the weight, so Fordham had the mount and won. The name of the last horse Archer ever rode was Tommy Tittlemouse. Fred was getting ill down there and said he felt bad.

"But we all thought he was just depressed because he

hadn't won up till then for about a fortnight. I have always regretted very much that I didn't go home with him. Captain Bowling, I think, talked sanctimoniously to him instead of cheering him up. I don't think he would have shot himself if I had been there. You won't get much out of jockeys about Archer. They have their own little secrets which they keep to themselves."

If Archer had a catlike affection for old places, he had certainly a godlike or doglike faculty for friendship. He always drifted down to share his joys and sorrows with his own family and his old friends in Cheltenham. He came there for some of the hunting season, though he often spent a part of it elsewhere, sometimes with Lord Wilton.

Mr. Richard Marsh said that he and Archer were great friends and that he was a most fascinating man and a great favourite with the ladies. He spoke of his wonderful courage and skill as a jockey, and went on to say : "Archer was a great man to hounds, and one little thing that happened out hunting amused me very much. He was following a man down to a fence who fell, and while he was on the ground Archer jumped dangerously close to him. The man was extremely angry and told Archer he had no business to follow so closely. Archer was very much hurt, and told the man so, and added, 'I was not within two lengths of you when your horse took off'—thinking that, as in racing, it was a very big margin."

Archer's greatest friend from his youth up had been Herbert Mills, a well-known Cheltenham corn merchant. He very often kept his horses at Mr. Mills's house, and the two were almost inseparable whenever Archer came to Cheltenham. Besides which Herbert Mills was often at Newmarket, and, as he was very fond of racing, went about with Archer to many race-meetings. His son, Mr. Wyndham Mills, says :

"Father went to school at Hygeia House, opposite to the King's Arms, which William Archer kept. I dare say that's where he and Fred Archer began to be so friendly. I was only thirteen when Archer died, and father and mother were very strict with us and kept us out of the way of grown-ups, and especially of sporting people. And then those sort of racing men go about by themselves, and usually don't want a lot of children hanging round them and learning about their affairs. My chief recollection of Mr. Archer is of his giving me unlimited half-sovereigns and sovereigns, and sometimes even fivers. A connection of mine has in her possession a blank cheque of Archer's which he gave to my father when he went to America. He wanted father to go with him, but he didn't. Captain Bowling went. Archer said to my father : 'You may want money or be in difficulties while I am away, and, if you are, you will be able to fill in this.' But father didn't, and when Fred came back, father gave the cheque to him. Fred returned it to him, and said : 'You'd better kept it as a curiosity, for there aren't many of my pals that I could give a blank cheque to and they'd give it me back. Archer mean ? Yes, he was mean— but not to those whom he knew and trusted. He knew only too well how many people were hanging round him just to sponge upon him. And you know it's a saying that a Gloucestershire man gives nothing away but what he doesn't want.

"I was away a good deal, and so, although he was constantly at my father's house in the High Street, I didn't see so much of Archer as one would have expected—considering how inseparable he and my father were. I remember one simple little thing about him. He was very fond of blackberry jam, and when he came to tea he would often say ; 'Well, Mrs. Mills, and have you got any of your blackberry jam to-day ?' I remember one week-end, when I had gone up from school to stay at Falmouth House, we were playing one of those spelling games with letters. Fred came into the dining-room where we were all playing— his wife and mother and the rest—and he said he'd play, and he soon beat us all.

"You know there's a big yard at the Andoversford Inn. One night when I was there there were a bull-terrier and a bull-dog fighting in the yard. The other men who were there said : 'Let them alone, it's dangerous to touch them.' But Fred went up and separated them. I have thought since that it was a small instance of the tremendous nerve he showed when he was riding.

"You know, too, that there is a little trout stream down at the back of the inn. Freddy Pratt and I were always fishing in it, and never, of course, caught anything. One day by a fluke Freddy stuck in the end of one of those bamboo fishing-rods that pull out, and it stuck in the fin of a trout, and he pulled it out.

"We went up in triumph to the house with it, but his Uncle Fred utterly refused to believe that he had caught it. He said, 'Oh, the two of you together are a bit *too* much.' He thought we had got the trout from somewhere else and were just making it up.

"Father was a very reserved man. When mother died it simply broke his heart. Nobody could get him out of himself—he had no spirit left, and moped and wouldn't talk about his trouble, and at last it killed him. So I never remember his talking much about Archer. I think it was their very reservedness that drew the two men together. Each knew that the other wouldn't talk about his affairs."

Henry Parker was still living in Prestbury, and was there when this was written, up by Queen's Wood, when Archer had been in his grave this many and many a year.

"When Freddie was a great man," said this old friend and servant, "he never forgot me, and always spoke to me, whoever he was with, when he rode through the village, and he would often chuck me half a sovereign.

"Once, in 1881, when he came down for the hunting season and stayed at the Andoversford Inn, I went up there and valeted him. One day, when I was brushing his things, Mr. Archer said, 'You can take that suit away.' I was pleased with it. It was a lovely fine coat and waistcoat of fine Melton cloth, with 'F.A.' engraved on the buttons. I'm sorry I've lost them all now.

"His friend Mr. Jennings came down with him that year. I remember Mr. Jennings had a monkey, and it would be in and out all the time, among the saddles and harness.

"One day Fred was out in the harness-room and I remember he reached down one of his hunting-saddles and said : 'Rather different to the one I ride Bal Gal with !' "

ARCHER'S PRINCIPAL WINS IN 1882

ALTHORP PARK STAKES (NORTHAMPTON).—ALFONSO, 9 to 2.
DEE STAKES (CHESTER).—WHIPPER IN, 3 to 1.
PAYNE STAKES (NEWMARKET).—DEAD HEAT. LITTLE
    SISTER, 7 to 1.
WOODCOTE STAKES (EPSOM).—BEAU BRUMMEL, 8 to 1.
ROYAL STAKES (EPSOM.)—LIMESTONE, 2 to 1.
EPSOM GOLD CUP.—TRISTAN, 1 to 3.
ASCOT STAKES.—RETREAT, 5 to 2.
ST. JAMES'S PALACE STAKES (ASCOT).—BATTLEFIELD, 4 to 1.
ROUS MEMORIAL (ASCOT).—RETREAT, 8 to 13.
JULY CUP (NEWMARKET).—TRISTAN, 4 to 6.
MOLYNEUX CUP (LIVERPOOL).—MOWERINA, 10 to 11.
INTERNATIONAL TWO-YEAR-OLD PLATE (KEMPTON).—ROOK-
    ERY, 4 to 9.
ROYAL STAKES (SANDOWN).—SUTLER, 65 to 40.
PRIORY STAKES (LEWES).—POLARIS, 1 to 3.
LEWES HANDICAP.—FORTISSIMO, evens.
YORKSHIRE OAKS.—DUTCH OVEN, 4 to 9.
PRINCE OF WALES'S STAKES (YORK).—GALLIARD, 8 to 15.
THE ST. LEGER.—DUTCH OVEN, 40 to 1.
ALEXANDRA PLATE (DONCASTER).—SUTLER, 6 to 4.
MANCHESTER AUTUMN HANDICAP.—FRIAR RUSH, 7 to 2.
GREAT FOAL STAKES (NEWMARKET). — DUTCH OVEN,
    10 to 11
HOPEFUL STAKES (NEWMARKET).—BEAU BRUMMEL, 11 to 2.
CHAMPION STAKES (NEWMARKET).—TRISTAN, 2 to 1.
GRAND PRIZE OF PARIS.—BRUCE, 1 to 3.
CHESTERFIELD STAKES (NEWMARKET).—GALLIARD, 4 to 6.

CHAPTER XVI

In 1882 Archer's record of wins fell ten short of his return for the previous year, viz., 210, and his most important victory was perhaps that of landing the St. Leger for Lord Falmouth on the despised Dutch Oven, who started at the remunerative price of 40 to 1. A short time previously she had been hopelessly beaten at York, and so much controversy was caused that it is worth repeating an account of the race which was written at the time.

"Though Jannette gave Mathew his second St. Leger victory, it was reserved for another mare in the same ownership to supply one of the most sensational St. Legers he or any other owner ever had to do with.

"Dutch Oven, as a two-year-old, won nine of the twelve races she contested, among them some of the most important two-year-old races of the year, and she beat very many of the best of her time, giving promise of a brilliant three-year-old career. This promise, however, was not borne out in the earlier part of it. In 1882 before the Leger she ran more or less badly in the Derby, the Sussex Stakes at Goodwood, and the Great Yorkshire Stakes.

"At Goodwood she was a bad third to such moderate horses as Comte Alfred and Battlefield, so altogether there was little hope for her in the St. Leger, where she was fated to meet that wonderfully speedy mare Geheimniss (on whom 13 to 8 was laid), Shotover (winner of the Derby) and other good horses making up a field of fourteen. Dutch Oven naturally was a rank outsider, 40 to 1 being her S.P., but a longer price might have been obtained without much difficulty.

"Dutch Oven got away with a start, but Archer pulled her back and Actress went in front, making the pace a cracker, with Balliol close behind her. These, followed by Fenelon, Dutch Oven, Marden, and Sachem the favourite in Ben Loates's hands, lying close up and going well.

"In this order they went out of sight, and when they came again into view there had been but little change. Indeed, there was not much alteration until they approached the post half a mile from home, the favourite still going like a steam-engine and inspiring the layers of odds with a confidence which was increased when Actress and Fenelon retired, having shot their bolt, and Lord Stamford's beautiful mare rushed to the front and looked like having an easy victory.

"At this point Archer called on Dutch Oven, and she soon passed them on the whip-hand side and went in pursuit of Geheimniss, who sailed along to the accompaniment of excited plaudits from her backers until she reached the stand, having everything now well beaten save Shotover and Dutch Oven.

"Archer now passed Shotover and challenged the favourite, and the onlookers were surprised to see him get on terms. The struggle became short, for Geheimniss had come to the end of her tether and had hardly a kick left in her, whereas Dutch Oven stayed on and won by a length and a half from the Oaks winner amidst a scene of breathless excitement."

There was a lot of talk after the race, and Mathew Dawson, Lord Falmouth, and Archer received numerous letters accusing them of almost every crime under the sun. As far as Dawson was concerned, he had backed the mare at long odds, but after the York exploit he laid £1,000 to £20 against her.

Against Archer it was alleged that he had ridden the mare in her other races with a view to his own profit in the St. Leger. There was no evidence whatever to support this assertion beyond the astonishing victory of the mare, and after the death of Archer it was stated on the best authority that Archer did all he knew to get out of the Dutch Oven mount, and that when the mare was sent to Doncaster it was not with the intention of running her for the St. Leger, for which Archer did not believe she had a chance.

He had been offered £1,000 to ride Geheimniss, and was desirious of having the mount. Lord Falmouth ran Dutch Oven solely out of consideration for his trainer, who had backed her for £100 and naturally wanted a run for his money, no matter how hopeless the chance might seem.

Archer, as has been said, had fallen in love with Miss Helen Rose Dawson, daughter of Mr. John Dawson, and niece of his old master, whose partner he had become. Ever since he had first been apprenticed Archer had lived with Mr. Mathew Dawson at Heath House, still content with two rooms overlooking the stableyard, the furniture of which was subsequently in the house of Mr. Dawson's old house-keeper.

While Fred was courting Miss Dawson he used to walk up to Warren House and go back to Heath House very late in the evening. One night he was followed from Mr. John Dawson's gate by an enormous dog which growled ominously. Fred was afraid to quicken his steps, and equally afraid of being attacked by the huge creature, so he tried cajolery and remarked frequently to his pursuer, "Good dog ! Poor fellow !" and suchlike soothing remarks, to which the animal responded with, "Br-r-r . . . ." This went on as he walked the whole distance, and Archer was very glad to shut Mr. Mathew Dawson's gate on his dogged adversary.

Archer's brother-in-law, Mr. John Dawson, read through the proofs of this book. He wrote : "I have not made many alterations in your copy. To me it is amazing how you have collected all the information about poor Fred Archer and delineated his character. If I may say so, I think you have rather over emphasized his use of bad language. I knew him intimately and I was a great deal in his company, and very seldom heard him make use of any.

"Mrs. Archer, senior, I have always thought one of the most aristocratic-looking women I have ever met. She had such an easy poise of manner and so much charm.

"Poor Fred was a very clever, shrewd fellow, and in addition to his brilliant genius as a rider he would sit for hours working out how best to win a big race under various conditions.

"I can't help smiling at your asking if he was *careful*. It's the last thing he ever was. Well, yes, of course, in the sense of keeping his eyes open. His eyes were always very wide open ; certainly no one ever had more chance of getting bad accidents. But *careful*! The word did not exist in his riding vocabulary. Never was anyone less so. Riding at Manchester, when he won the Cup on Valour, he rode so close to the rails that they caught his foot and ripped his boot open from the heel to the toe. He finished the race and came limping and hobbling in to be weighed, put on some more boots, and rode another race—and the same thing happened again! *Careful?* I should say not!

"They say—I can't say I saw it myself, though I saw the race—that he came down the hill at Tattenham Corner with one leg over the rail.

"I don't know much about that missing list of wins, but I don't think one year would matter much in his biography."

Fred now built himself a princely residence in Newmarket on the Ely Road. It was called Falmouth House, and Lord Falmouth took the greatest interest in it and helped Archer with the plans. He had always given his jockey advice since the earliest days, had invested his earnings for him, given him legal advice, and in every way been most kind to him, and Fred sometimes told his sister, as has been said, that there were no two men whom he would rather see coming to his house than Lord Falmouth and Mathew Dawson. "And that speaks well for Fred," said Mrs. Pratt, "because they are the two men he had most to do with—at least during his professional career—and he had never had an angry word with either of them."

Miss Dawson is said by everyone who knew her to have been a pretty and very charming girl, and it looked as if Archer had nothing left to pray for.

Early in the New Year Archer was married, and one of the first to congratulate him was his old vicar, who wrote :

"I called at Andoversford on Tuesday last, hoping I might have seen you and offered you my congratulations and best wishes on the occasion of your approaching marriage. I found you had left the day before. I therefore write these few lines to say how sincerely I wish you every

166

happiness. I have watched your career of wonderful success with great interest, and my hope is that you will retire from the saddle with all your honours upon you, and before your health has suffered."

Prestbury is not next door to Andoversford, and the kindly vicar had taken a good deal of trouble in order that he might personally congratulate Archer. This kindness and interest literally followed Archer to his grave, and was never slackened when the clouds of religious persecution had darkened Prestbury village and driven out this good man from his home and parish.

Here, too, one notices the first note of fear and warning as to the possible results should Archer continue his suicidal policy of wasting. And this warning came, not from any of his racing patrons, but from the clergyman who confessed that he knew little or nothing about racing, and who only saw Archer as a rule in the hunting season, when he was not starving to any appreciable extent.

Yet love is not always blind, nor was it in this instance, and one can call by no other name the brooding tenderness with which Archer's vicar watched over his young parishioner's career. Doubtless his clear eyes saw, too, that amid much earthly dross there was a vein of pure gold in the character of the premier jockey. The spoilt child of fortune, with almost every earthly gift, it seemed to most men that this world had little more to offer to Archer. For his great desire was to be at the head of the list of winning jockeys, and this had been given to him, and almost everything else that he could wish for had been poured out before him most lavishly.

Still, in this glorious prospect, Mr. De la Bere seems to have seen

> One speck of dark appear
> In that bright heaven of blue.

On the eve of Archer's wedding one of the boys who had hunted with Fred among the Cotswold Hills, and who had at one time lived in Prestbury, sat down to wish his old friend good fortune. This was also a great horseman, and fated, like Archer, and like his own brother, Roddy Owen, to die young.   He wrote :

"FRED,
   "I wish you every happiness and the usual luck."
                                    "HUGH OWEN."

Some of Archer's friends wrote to him just before and some of them just after his wedding—but few, if any, seem to have forgotten him, and the following letters speak for themselves :

                              "Red House, Newmarket.
                                   "*January* 28, 1883.
"MY DEAR ARCHER,
      "Before sending you the accompanying tankard, Mrs. Ker Seymer and I have drunk your health out of it and that of your bride, and though it might make you a pound or two overweight to empty the tankard yourself, it is not half big enough to contain our cordial good wishes for the happiness of your marriage.
      "I hope it will please you, and that you will receive it as a token of my regard for you, and of the interest with which I shall always watch your career.
                              "Yours faithfully,
                                   "E. KER SEYMER."

                              "Babraham, Cambridge.
"ARCHER,
      "I send herewith a pair of candlesticks, which I hope you will accept as a wedding gift from me.   I am glad to take the opportunity of your approaching marriage to offer you my sincere wishes for your happiness and prosperity. You have well merited all the success you have achieved, and I have every hope you may be as successful in your future life as you have been in the past.
                              "Yours truly,
                                   "CADOGAN."

"MY DEAR ARCHER,

"I could not come to Newmarket last week, but hope to be there next week and see the painter and your picture. Will you kindly give this little present to Mrs. Archer? I hope she will accept it as a wedding present, if not too late.

"Yours truly,
"C. CH. KINSKY."

"12, Charlemont Row, St. James's."

"With Sir Henry Hawkins's compliments, and every good wish to Mr. and Mrs. Fred Archer."

January 29, 1883.

"MY DEAR ARCHER,

"As I hear you are going to be married, I send you a remembrance, which I am sure you will accept with my best wishes for your future happiness.

"Yours,
"Vienna." "COUNT FESTETICS."

"Tregothnan, Probus,
"Cornwall.
"February 4, 1883.

"DEAR ARCHER,

"I write a few lines to wish you all the joy in the world on your marriage. You must both of you be heartily glad all the fag and turmoil of the ceremony is over, and that you are now able to settle down together in quietness. May you long enjoy a prosperous and happy life. I was glad to hear that my wedding present arrived in time—for the fact is, just as I was about some time ago to send you one, I discovered your other friends had ordered the very same things I had fetched over as being most likely to be useful to you. I was not able, therefore, to have what I sent engraved, so when we next meet you must tell me what you would like put upon them and I will have it done.

"Perhaps you may have more of them and you may wish to change them for others. With repeated kindest wishes and best regards to Mrs. Archer,

"I remain,
"Faithfully yours,
"FALMOUTH."

"Jockey Club Rooms,
"Newmarket.

"DEAR ARCHER,
"I send herewith a little wedding present, rather late, but as I was not in London all the winter I was unable to get it for you, as I should like to have done, at the time of your marriage. I could not think of anything for yourself that you have not got already, so I am in hopes I shall please you equally by sending your wife a small ornament. Kindly ask Mrs. Archer to excuse my sending her a present without having made her acquaintance, and tell her I shall be much pleased if she will accept it with my best wishes for both your future happiness. I cannot wish you greater luck than that your married life may be as happy as mine is,
"Your sincere friend,
"LASCELLES."

"Telegraph Truro,
"Tregothnan, Probus.

"DEAR ARCHER,
"I had not an opportunity to choose you a wedding present until I came through London a day or two ago, but I have desired Messrs. Lambert to send you a pair of silver hand candlesticks, which please accept with my best wishes for the future happiness of Mrs. Archer and yourself.
"Believe me,
"Yours very truly,
"*February* 22, 1883."   "HUGH BOSCAWEN."

170

For weeks beforehand Archer's wedding was the one talk of Newmarket, which, as the day drew near, was in a state of simmering excitement. It was not merely his riding, but by dint of his magnetic personality he had become one of the most prominent men in the town. Excursions were run from many of the surrounding villages and towns, and the church was packed an hour before the ceremony.

Among the relatives and wedding guests who had seats in the chancel were: Mr. and Mrs. Mathew Dawson, Mr. Charles Archer and Mrs. Archer, sen., Mr. George Dawson, Mr. John Dawson, jun., Mr. and Mrs. T. S. Dawson, Mr. and Mrs. John Porter, Miss Tait, Mr. Archer, senr., and Mrs. C. Archer, Mr. and Mrs. F. Bates, Mr. and Mrs. Sutherland, Mr. and Mrs. J. Cartwright, Dr. and Mrs. Wright, Messrs. Davis and Smith, Mr. and Mrs. Wells, Mr. and Mrs. Aldcroft, and Mr. and Mrs. King.

The crowd outside the church attained to unheard-of proportions, and overflowed, lining each side of the road, to the back of the Rutland Arms, where the bridal carriages were expected to pass. The ringing cheers of these announced to the people in the church the arrival of the bridegroom and his best man, Mr. T. Jennings, jun. "Freddy", on alighting from his carriage, bowed and smiled his acknowledgments, and there was perhaps never a wedding where the bridegroom attracted so much attention, and that in spite of the prettiness and popularity of the bride. There were five groomsmen who followed Archer and Mr. Jennings into the church, Messrs. John and George Dawson, H. J. Newman, A. Briggs, and W. Manning.

After a few false alarms, a hush of eager expectation heralded the coming of the fair and charming little bride as she entered, leaning on the arm of her father, Mr. John Dawson. All eyes, of course, were turned on her as she passed up the aisle to stand near the bridegroom. She wore a lovely satin dress trimmed with Venetian lace, and wore by way of ornaments the bridegroom's lucky diamond horseshoe (poor little bride and poor bridegroom, never did horseshoe play so false a part—if by luck we mean length of days) and Prince Batthyany's magnificent bracelet.

The bridesmaids were Miss Annie Bland Dawson (sister of

the bride) and the Misses Rose Saunders, Aggie Saunders, and Harriet Briggs, who wore coral silk gowns and also the diamond-and-pearl bracelets which were the bridegroom's presents to them.

Archer and his bride as they emerged from the church were received with showers of rice and with loud and continuous cheering, which was taken up by the long lines of onlookers at the back of the Rutland Arms, deafening plaudits following the course of the bridal party.

The bells of the Parish Churches of All Saints' and St. Mary's rang out merry peals throughout the rest of the day. Telegrams came in shoals from Archer's friends and patrons, and from those members of the racing fraternity in general who had not been able to come to the wedding.

Mr. and Mrs. Fred Archer managed to give the crowd the slip when they went away, as the special railway carriage reserved for them had been shunted on to the upper Newmarket siding, and the ordinary four o'clock train from Newmarket to London, by which they were to travel, was backed on to it. A number of the guests who had been at the breakfast saw the bride and bridegroom off at the station. At Cambridge Mr. and Mrs. Archer received a characteristically demonstrative ovation.

Mrs. John Dawson gave a ball in the evening at the Rutland Arms, and all the 80 stable lads employed by Messrs. Mathew Dawson and Charles Archer were entertained to an excellent supper in the long room at the back of The Wagon and Horses Hotel. Great festivities were held on The Severals, where Lord Hastings's ox was roasted and eaten, and the day concluded with an ascent of balloons and a firework display.

The skin and hoofs of the bullock were made by Mr. Howlett, taxidermist, of High Street, Newmarket, into inkstands and snuff-boxes as souvenirs of the day, and Archer sent one of these to Lord Hastings, who wrote from Warren House, Newmarket:

"Yesterday I found a parcel on my table, and, inquiring as to where it came from, I was informed that Howlett had left it as a present from you. On opening it I found a charming candlestick mounted on the bullock's foot. I am indeed proud to accept this, and do thank you most sincerely for the handsome gift."

The honeymoon was spent at Torquay, where the following was written :

"Sutherland Tower,
"Torquay.

"Dear Mr. Archer,

"I am so sorry not to have seen you, and I should have been so glad to have the pleasure of making Mrs. Archer's acquaintance. Will you tell her this from me. The Duchess of Sutherland kindly took me to call on you, and I should have liked you to see her cobs, one of which, 'King Cole', is quite a sight. I hope you have had a very happy time in this lovely place ; and that you both have such a bright life before you.

"Yours very truly,

"February 8."   "Georgie Sumner."

Lord Courtenay sent two telegrams suggesting that he should come and see Fred and his wife if still in Torquay, and asking them over to Powderham Castle.

Mr. and Mrs. Archer returned to the costly house which he had built. Archer always regretted building such a big place, and more especially as it was in a very exposed position, and the contents were notoriously valuable. A burglary committed at Jewitt's made him nervous, and it was then he furbished up and loaded the fatal revolver which had been presented to him after Sterling won the Liverpool Cup.

Mrs. Pratt said : "I wasn't at Fred's wedding ; it was just when one of the boys was born. Soon afterwards, when I was in London, Nellie wrote to me to meet her at Blanchards Restaurant ; in Bond Street, isn't it ? I thought she was so pretty. She *was* very young, and she only looked about sixteen ; a little slim thing. I liked her so much then and I always liked her. I went to stay with them at Falmouth House, and took little Fred with me. I think Fred was very pleased with the boy. Falmouth House was beautifully furnished and a lovely place altogether.

"Indeed, it was all rather like a fairy tale. You see, Fred

173

just went to the Dawsons' as an apprentice boy, and he ended up by marrying his master's niece. When he was about twelve, the younger Dawson children would go out to parties, and sometimes their father or uncle, knowing that Fred was not a common sort of little boy, would say 'Just walk down there with Miss Nellie, or Master So-and-So'; or 'Go down and fetch them.' And he would put his hand in his pocket and give Fred a shilling. They were quite little children then—a good deal younger than Fred.

"The Dawsons were great people in Newmarket. There was a lot going on, and they were thought much of, even by the great people who lived round there, and, of course, in a way it seemed a great thing for Fred to marry Nellie. They say someone once remarked to Mrs. Mathew Dawson that Nellie's people might have looked higher for her. She and Mathew Dawson had no children, and they thought the world of Fred. Mrs. Mathew fired up and said very sharply, 'A princess might have aspired to marry Fred.' After that no more was said.

"Well, at the time when I went to Falmouth House with little Fred, Fred said, 'You may as well leave the boy behind.' I replied, 'But he's only come for a few days; he's just brought his best clothes and a few things besides.' Fred said, 'Never mind, we'll see to that. I'll write and get some things sent down.' He then said to the boy, 'You'd like to stay on, wouldn't you, Freddy?' And Fred, childlike, said, 'Yes.' For the next two years he never came home except on a visit. They kept him there altogether. His Auntie Nellie was so kind to him. She was not a bit selfish, like some young girls just married, and she had come from such a big house where she had had everything done for her. But she took such a lot of trouble with little Fred. She would always be so particular that he was clean and tidy, and would make him wash his hands when he got grubby, as boys will. She had little parties of other boys and girls—the trainers' sons and suchlike—for him, and did everything she could to amuse him and make him happy. Every night she heard him say his prayers. Little Fred, in a way, had a better time than his brothers and sisters, and he has seen a good deal of the world since."

174

Mrs. John Dawson has some letters written to her by Mrs. Fred Archer about little Fred. Once he got lost on the way back from school—whether intentionally or otherwise history does not relate—and Mrs. Archer wrote a note to her sister-in-law saying, 'Fred and I are very anxious about him.' Another time she wrote that she should be very glad for him to come to Mrs. Dawson's little party and that she should want to know if he was a good boy.

Mrs. Pratt continued : "I remember Geheimniss, that mare mentioned in the scrap-book. Fred was riding her in the Goodwood Stewards' Cup once when I was staying at Falmouth House. He was so sure of winning that he said, 'Look here, I'll put you on 100 to 8 about Geheimniss.' He and nearly everyone else felt so sure about the race that I felt quite hopeful of taking quite a large sum of money home with me—and it was needed, I can tell you. When Fred had gone off to the race-meeting, I asked my sister-in-law, 'Do you think Fred *will* win ?' Nellie said, 'Oh yes, I think he is sure to, he is so very confident about it. Indeed, I should say you can feel as if the money was already in your pocket.' I did ; but by and by came a telegram from Fred : 'Wood beat me by a head.' So that was the end of my hopes.

"Of course, when you feel sure of a horse is the time to put a large sum of money on him if you ever intend to do it. My brother Charlie had a thousand pounds on a horse once ; it was Highland Chief, one of Lord Ellesmere's that he had trained. They were all so certain of him winning. I saw that race, and the first three horses were so close together that you could have covered them with a sheet. The judge said St. Blaise had won, but lots of people thought Highland Chief had, and still think so to this day. Lord Ellesmere said, 'Well, I always hoped to win a Derby, and I believe I really won this one.' Of course, Charlie lost his thousand pounds, but he would have won a good many thousands if Highland Chief had won the race.

"Captain Bowling had been an officer in the Army, and he lived in rooms in Jermyn Street. He was a good deal older than Fred, but they became great friends, and there was always a room for Captain Bowling when he came to

Falmouth House. He was like a lot of Army men—very fond of arranging and getting things up. At last he drifted into living almost entirely at Falmouth House and managing everything. Indeed, some unkind person said to Fred once, 'Let's see, Captain Bowling, he's your butler, isn't he?' But Captain Bowling had plenty of money of his own; it was just that he had got fond of Fred, and wanted an occupation. He belonged to a firm of solicitors—Bowling and Creagh—and Mr. Creagh was the family solicitor after Mr. Jessop. Captain Bowling was a very pleasant man and was kind to my little Fred when he lived with his uncle; he used to drill him. His mother lived down by Merthyr, in Wales, and after Fred's death my sister stayed six months with Mrs. Bowling, who introduced her to a lot of nice people. My sister said it was such a rest after the turmoil and trouble she went through at the time of Fred's death. Captain Bowling himself died not long after Fred. I should think it might have been a year. I remember my sister was staying with me when she heard of his death, and she was very much upset about it, following so close on Fred's death.

"If Captain Bowling had been alive he could have told you a lot about Fred. He owned a lot of horses, and at one time he owned Paradox, who was known at first as the something-or-other colt, and was called Paradox later on. He sold him to the Duke of Westminster, who sold the colt to Cloete after his Middle Park failure."

ARCHER'S PRINCIPAL WINS IN 1883

CRAVEN STAKES (NEWMARKET).—GRANDMASTER, 2 to 1.
TWO THOUSAND GUINEAS.—GALLIARD, 9 to 2.
WHITSUNTIDE PLATE (MANCHESTER).—BELINDA, 9 to 4.
EPSOM STAKES.—BARCALDINE, 8 to 11.
PRINCE OF WALES'S STAKES (ASCOT).—GALLIARD, 9 to 4.
ST. JAMES'S PALACE STAKES (ASCOT).—GALLIARD, 1 to 7.
ALEXANDRA PLATE (ASCOT).—FAUGH-A-BALLAGH, 11 to 10.
WOKINGHAM STAKES (ASCOT).—DESPAIR, 5 to 1.
NORTHUMBERLAND PLATE.—BARCALDINE, 11 to 2.
NATIONAL BREEDERS' STAKES (SANDOWN).—REPRIEVE, 2 to 5.
MOLECOMB STAKES (GOODWOOD).—LA TRAPPE, 20 to 1.
FINDON STAKES (GOODWOOD).—SANDIWAY, 3 to 1.
ASTLEY STAKES (LEWES).—SUPERBA, 4 to 7.
YORKSHIRE OAKS.—BRITOMARTIS, 5 to 6.
HARTINGTON PLATE (DERBY).—LACEMAN, 5 to 2.
CHAMPAGNE STAKES (DONCASTER).—SUPERBA, 4 to 6.
PARK HILL STAKES (DONCASTER).—BRITOMARTIS, 4 to 1.
MANCHESTER AUTUMN HANDICAP.—WHIPPER-IN, 2 to 1.
ROUS MEMORIAL (NEWMARKET).—BUSYBODY, evens.
KEMPTON CAMBRIDGESHIRE TRIAL HANDICAP.—GEHEIMNISS,
   9 to 4.
CLEARWELL STAKES.—HARVESTER, 6 to 4.
MIDDLE PARK PLATE.—BUSYBODY, 15 to 8.
FRENCH DERBY.—FRONTIN, 5 to 4.

Headed the list of winning jockeys with 232 wins.

CHAPTER XVII

In the first season of his married life Archer started well by winning the Two Thousand Guineas with Galliard, after an exciting race, by a head from Goldfield, who was only a neck in front of The Prince. It was just before this race that Prince Batthyany dropped dead in the Jockey Club Stand. Galliard was a son of the Derby winner Galopin.

The Derby of that year gave rise to considerable controversy, for St. Blaise, Highland Chief, and Galliard finished so close together that only the judge could tell which had won, and he gave it to the first-named, whereas many thought that Highland Chief had proved successful.

There were many rumours that Archer had not tried, for it was known that his brother, Charlie, had £1,000 on Highland Chief, whom he had trained, and colour was lent to the suggestion when it was known that Lord Falmouth had decided to sell all his horses. But this had nothing to do with the riding of Galliard, as Lord Falmouth stated later. It was simply because he was getting an old man, and it is also said that Lord Falmouth had made up his mind to this sale some time before the Derby of 1883, although he did not do so until the following year.

Sir George Chetwynd attributed the success of St. Blaise to "the fearless way in which Wood sent him down the hill, hugging the rail and stealing several lengths. At the Bell, Highland Chief and Galliard were in hot pursuit, but neither could catch him, the former suffering defeat by a neck, and with Galliard half a length behind him. To this day some, who were very much less well placed than Judge Clarke, assert that the second won. Many people also thought that Archer rode a bad race, but I had more money on Galliard

than I ever had on a horse in the Derby before, and I am quite
satisfied that, owing to his heavy shoulders, Galliard would
not act down hill, and so lost too much ground ever to
make up."

The discussion as to whether or not Galliard ought to have
won at Epsom was renewed when at Ascot the colt cantered
away from Ossian in the Prince of Wales's Stakes, and the
next day, in the Ascot Derby, Ossian cantered away from
St. Blaise. Indeed, poor Archer seems to have caused as
much dissatisfaction by winning the St. Leger on Dutch
Oven as he did by losing the Derby on Galliard. The owner
of both his mounts was, at least at the last, equally satisfied
in both instances, and that, after all, was the chief thing.

Mr. Dawson, at least at first, seems to have had his doubts
about Archer's riding in the Derby, and in any case Galliard's
defeat was a bitter disappointment to him. "Lord Charles
Beresford told me," said a great authority on racing, "how
polite and respectful Mat Dawson always was. But he was at
Ascot the day Galliard won the St. James's Palace Stakes and
showed that he could win going downhill. Lord Charles felt a
tremendous slap on his back and his hat was shaken down
over his face. It was Mathew Dawson speaking his thoughts
aloud, and he said : "What the hell was my horse doing
at Epsom ?"

Lord Falmouth, whatever he may have thought in the heat
of the moment, certainly did not ultimately believe that
Archer had not tried on Galliard, and as proof of it the letter
he wrote to Mrs. Coleman, Archer's sister, after the jockey
had shot himself, may here be quoted :

Mereworth Castle   Nov: 9. 1886.

Dear M:: Coleman

The telegram which you
kindly sent me yesterday
morning was so reassuring,
that I can hardly describe
the shock the message which
followed it gave me in
the evening from M: Dawson
or the grief I feel at the
irreparable loss you have
sustained in the death of
your poor Brother —

Pray therefore accept
yourself & convey to your

Father & Mother, my most
heartfelt Sympathy at the
bereavement of so excellent
a Brother & Son —

For myself, I can only say,
that after the long & intimate
connection between us from
his boyhood — not an angry
word ever passed between us —

It is not everyone who
can make such an assertion
as this, & I mourn for him
as an attached friend —

His faithful services
to me were associated with
some of my happiest days,
& I shall always feel

that his zeal & best efforts
for my interests stood first
in his mind, whenever, &
wherever, they were put to
the test —

I regret extremely that
the malady from which I
have been for sometime ailing,
should be a bar to my being
present to pay a last sad
tribute of respect to his
memory, which I shall
ever cherish with the
most affectionate regard
Belive me dear Mr Coleman
& Mrs very faithfully
Falmouth

His best friends had implicit faith in Archer's honesty, and amongst those who wrote to him were Lord Grosvenor, who said :

"Saighton Grange, Chester,
"*December* 31, 1883.

"ARCHER,
"I see that there is a rumour going about that Lord Falmouth is going to give up racing, and that Mr. Dawson is going to train no longer. I am sure I hope there is no truth in this, for I think that no two men are more wanted on the Turf than they are just now. If it is true, I hope that you may succeed Dawson, and that at the same time you will not give up riding for training, as it seems to me there are very few jockey's now. Anyhow, I hope you will keep on riding for the Duke, and not forget me when you can ride Reprieve, who, I hear, cannot do better.

"I have been very unwell lately, or should have written earlier. Please send me an answer to this.
"GROSVENOR."
"I wish you many happy New Years."

In Mrs. Coleman's scrapbook there is a letter dated January 24 from the Duke of Westminster thanking Archer for his letter of sympathy on the death of Lord Grosvenor.

It was in 1883 that an important chapter was written in Turf history, because it saw the introduction to racing of St. Simon, whom Mathew Dawson bought for 1,600 guineas at the sale of Prince Batthyany's horses. Both Dawson and Archer, as has been said, thought St. Simon was the fastest and best horse they ever knew. "Whether the Saint was a real stayer I never knew," once remarked Dawson, "for nothing could go fast enough to make him tire himself."

Dawson thought that Ladas was the best-looking horse he ever saw, and he once said, "St. Simon could beat such as Harvester and Busybody as if they were common platers, and, though he and Minting never came together, I am satisfied from their trials that St. Simon would have beaten Ormonde. And Ladas is possibly as good as St. Mirin."

The following interesting description of Archer's home at

Newmarket appeared in the *Winning Post* of September 7, 1883, from the pen of Mr. W. Maycock (the late Sir Willoughby Maycock, K.C.M.G., who was kindly correcting the MS. of this book almost up to the time of his death) :

"FRED ARCHER AT FALMOUTH HOUSE

"HIS 'TIP' FOR THE GREAT ST. LEGER

"It is now some four and a half years ago since our esteemed contemporary, *The World*, in one of those series of graphic sketches entitled 'Celebrities at Home', which have gained for it such widespread and deserved popularity, portrayed Fred Archer at Newmarket ; a very able and excellent portrayal it was, too, for the class for whom it was prepared. But there are no doubt thousands who never saw it. Moreover, Freddy's domicile is no longer Heath House, and poor Harry Constable, who shared a valet with him, has gone over to the majority since 1879. We have long entertained a conviction that a peep at Archer 'out of silk' on a quiet day at home would prove interesting to our readers, among whom may be numbered some of his most ardent admirers ; so, availing ourselves of an 'off day', on Monday last we ran down to pay him a visit in his new home.

"Falmouth House, the building of which was only commenced some eighteen months ago, stands on the left-hand side of one of the Ely roads as they are termed—that which leads to Chippenham by Snailwell—about three-quarters of a mile from the centre of the town of Newmarket. Needless to say, it is named after the popular nobleman whose colours Archer has so often borne to victory, and for whom he entertains a regard which almost amounts to devotion. It is constructed of red brick, faced with white stone and gabled. At present it is entirely unsheltered, and a better place could scarcely have been selected to realize the force of the hurricane which raged on Monday last and swept over the bleak Heath and the Bedford Lodge estate, which lies on the opposite side of the road. The first thing that struck us on entering the gate was the admirable order in which the spacious garden, lawn, and gravel walks which surround the house were kept. A lawn-tennis net was having a rough time of it in the gale, and a well-defined court gave evidence that that popular pastime is not altogether despised at the headquarters of the Turf. In response to a ring of the bell, a dapper little maid ushered us into the breakfast-room, an elegantly furnished apartment, of which more anon, and two minutes later we were greeted with a warm welcome by the master of the house, and a grasp of the hand which has steered so many cracks to victory.

"Archer had just returned from a morning gallop on Highland Chief, a description of which, at the moment of our meeting, some scores of horse watchers were, no doubt, busily engaged up in the town in wiring to their respective employers throughout the kingdom. As all the world knows by this time, the quintette who took part therein consisted of the Leger favourite, with the 'elder brother' up, Lizzie, Ithuriel, Wallenstein, and Brayley, ridden respectively by White, Martin, Goater, and Luke. To use Archer's own words, 'the wind nearly turned us round', and few things affect some horses' form more. He seemed evidently pleased, however, with the result of the spin.

"In response to an invitation to 'have a look at the pictures', we repaired first to the dining-room, which is perhaps the most interesting feature in the house to a Turfite ; it is the first room on the left as you enter, and is capable of dining twelve or fourteen persons comfortably ; it is handsomely but quietly furnished, and, in common with the other rooms, everything is of the very best. The sideboard, surmounted by various magnificent pieces of plate and racing cups in gold and silver, might well inspire envy in the breast of a prince. The walls are papered with dark green, and in the centre opposite the mantelpiece is a large portrait in oils of the old grey Strathavon, admirably painted by Norton. As a work of art, perhaps, this carries off the palm of Archer's gallery. On the right of this is a portrait of Petronel, with Archer on foot in the Duke of Beaufort's colours, and Jewitt about to adjust the saddle. On each side of the bay window are paintings of Atlantic and Silvio, both by the late Harry Hall, and without their riders.

186

"On the right of the chimney-piece is a portrait of our hero's father, William Archer, on Thurgarton, a steeple-chaser of some renown thirty years ago, and which is conspicuous for the straight fetlocks and tucked-up withers that horse painters of that period delighted in. Valour, with Archer up, in Captain Machell's colours, by Hopkins, is a wonderful likeness of both man and horse, while Dutch Oven, by the same artist, Iroquois, by Harry Hall, and Bend Or, by Arnull, complete the dining-room collection, with the exception of the old favourite grey pony on which Archer learnt to ride, and which adorns the summit of the sideboard. Lying on each picture are cutting whips of various sorts and sizes, presented to the crack horseman on different occasions by his numerous patrons ; and another curio worthy of notice is a silver cartridge match-box, mounted on a portion of a shell which burst on the *Condor*, a present to Archer from Lord Charles Beresford.

"Returning to the entrance, the first thing that meets the eyes is a handsome German clock, about seven feet high, made of stained oak and brass, the gift of Count Festetics. On the right-hand side of the staircase are paintings of Parole and the well-known groups of the members of the Jockey Club. On the left of the entrance are paintings of Silvio, by Hall, and Beauminet, by Arnull, both with Archer up, while opposite to them on the right wall may be seen Spinaway, by Harry Hall, and Mathew Dawson on his favourite cob, by Arnull.

"Re-entering the morning- or breakfast-room, we have the honour and pleasure of making our bow to the mistress of the house, and, we should say, judging by the neatness and order which are everywhere conspicuous in her home, a very excellent mistress, too. The principal articles of furniture in this room are a piano and a handsome oak bookcase, the gift of Lord Rosslyn. The walls are adorned with large oil-paintings of Mr. and Mrs. Archer, senior, the illuminated testimonial presented to Archer at his wedding, the meet of the Royal Buckhounds, and a capital likeness of his old friend Constable in Lord Rosebery's primrose and rose hoops. On each side of the mantelpiece are photographs of Archer and Fordham, by Sherborn, of Newmarket, in the colours of Lord Falmouth and Mr. Leopold de Rothschild respectively, both admirable likenesses. Drawing aside a curtain, Archer shows us his Turkish bath, a real luxury to possess on the premises, and one that is very essential to a man the top of whose work it is to keep down to 8 stone 7 lb., when he would ride over a stone heavier when out of training. The bath is a neat arrangement, consisting of two rooms, one for sweating, the other for shampooing and a douche.

"But *the* room *par excellence* is the drawing-room, which is simple perfection on a small scale. No portraits of race-horses are allowed to profane the walls here. Over the door is a proof before letters engraving of the Prince of Wales, presented by His Royal Highness to Archer during the last July meeting, and rendered additionally interesting and valuable by his autograph attached to it. Besides this, there are two valuable prints of those departed Turf worthies, Admiral Rous and Mr. George Payne. The mantelpiece is a work of art in itself, being constructed of black marble, variegated with pink and yellow flowers inlaid. The grate is adorned with a Bend Or similar to the one Freddy wore on his sleeve in the Derby of 1880, painted in blue and black, and above the mantelpiece is a handsome glass, framed in gilt, with gilt supports on either side. At one end of the room is a gorgeous gilt-mounted mirror reaching from floor to ceiling, and at the other a cabinet which, like the King's daughter, is all glorious within, and contains among numerous nicknacks sundry fans, wedding presents from Count Kinsky and others. The drawing-room opens into a conservatory well stocked with choice plants, and a table and chair in the centre which suggest an after-dinner cigarette.

"Lighting a cigar, we face the elements again, visit a hot-house with an abundant supply of grapes, walk round a capital kitchen garden, and come to anchor in a well-kept four-stalled stable, in which are a couple of hunters, Mrs. Archer's pony, and a carriage horse, as well as a hunter in a loose box, which Mrs. Archer rides—a remarkably handsome, well-bred chestnut. A small saddle-room is kept in apple-pie order, and the carriage-house contains a pony trap, dog-cart, victoria, and a particularly smart brougham, built by Peters. The canine element is represented by a handsome

St. Bernard—Bernard by name; Sultan, a mastiff, a fox-terrier, and a little pet of Mrs. Archer's—custodians 'who would, collectively, make it pretty warm for a burglar should he venture to 'go a-burgling' at Falmouth House.

"Our attention was attracted by a quaint-looking object on the wall of the stable-yard, which, on closer inspection, proved to be a representation of Archer winning the St. Leger on Dutch Oven, done in wire on a wooden background. In answer to our interrogatory as to how he came by this curious relic, 'The Tinman' replied, 'Oh, some poor devil sent it me who won a few shillings on the race, I suppose.'

"The next move was to the paddocks, which, together with the groom's cottage and that occupied by the gardener, stand about one hundred yards from the house. Prince Maurice, an animal that was rather fancied by some for the last Derby, and another bay horse, are the only occupants of this portion of the establishment, and we stroll back to the house.

"About this period we fancy we hear our readers exclaiming: 'But how about this tip?' Well, well, boys, we're coming to it by degrees! All in good time! Keep your hair on and sit tight. We can't have it on the front page, you know or you'll be reading it on the bookstalls without buying the paper! We know your little game, and we don't mean to be done!

"We're back again in the dining-room, and sit down to a peach and a glass of sherry with our host. Who is the newcomer who has just dropped in? Why, none other than young John Dawson, the trainer of Leeds, Gareth, and some score others, Freddy's brother-in-law, a hearty, cheery young fellow as you would ever wish to meet. He has just dropped in to have a chat with F.A., as he calls him, on things in general and the gallop of the morning in particular. A very pleasant talk we had for an hour or so on past and future events. Needless to say, the back-end handicaps engage our attention to some extent, but it is not within the compass of this article to discuss them now, nor would it be fair to our host or owners to ventilate the opinions we formed on the respective chances of the various candidates. But Archer made no secret of the confidence with which he anticipates

189

the victory of Highland Chief next week. That he was asked to do something very big on Monday morning there can be but little doubt. That he so far succeeded in accomplishing that feat as to inspire every confidence in those immediately connected with him is equally certain. Archer is too old a hand, and withal too modest, to speak of the conventional 'certainties', especially when nearly a fortnight has to elapse before the decision of the event. But you may take it from us that he anticipates the victory of the second in the Derby on the Town Moor, on Wednesday next, with some degree of certainty, looking upon Ossian at the same time as the best place investment, coupled with Elzevir. If not claimed by Lord Falmouth for Grandmaster, Archer will have the mount on Royal Angus ; but as his experience of that animal is confined to the occasion on which his own mount, Beau Brummel, was defeated by him at Stockbridge last year, it was scarcely to be expected that he could form any reliable opinion as to his prowess, nor did we care to solicit it.

"Fred Archer has unquestionably achieved a position in life of which he may justly be proud, and which is mainly due to his untarnished integrity and indefatigable interest in his profession. He has now a home of which any nobleman might well be proud. The time may not be far distant when he will retire from the racket and fatigue incident to his present life, and devote himself, in conjunction with his old master and present partner, Mathew Dawson, to the less arduous duties of a training establishment. He may well be held up to his brethren as an example of what steadiness, thrift, and straightforwardness may attain even in a calling so surrounded by temptations as that of a jockey. Constant intercourse with the highest and bluest blood in the land has inculcated in him a modesty of demeanour and quiet manner which in themselves constitute an ineffable charm, and we can truly say that in the course of many and varied experiences we never recollect spending a more pleasant afternoon than that with 'Fred Archer at Falmouth House'."

The late Mr. Cecil Raleigh wrote of Archer and Lindsay Gordon, for the latter of whom, or at least for his poetry, he had a supreme scorn :

"No, I don't think there is any truth whatever in the Archer story. He was a very jealous horseman, and I do not think that the temptation existed that would have induced him to give up riding a Derby winner if it were possible. Even if he had offered to take a million before the race, I think he would have forgotten all about it when the finish came. If you want to solve a real mystery about him, try and discover why he was always called 'The Tinman', even in the sporting papers. Personally, I have not the faintest idea.

"Concerning Fred Jacobs, he may have known your Australian Mutton Laureate, but I should think he came along a little later (Jacobs, I mean), when the Homer of the Murrumbidgee had already left the Cotswolds for the classic country of Convicts and Kangaroos. . . ."

He wrote some lines himself, which he said reminded him of Gordon's verses. They ran something like this :

> The mare swept on to the finish,
> But the girl's eyes throbbed with tears.
> Another length meant victory,
> But the girl's heart burst with fears.

Prior to the opening of the season in 1884 there was an interesting interview with Fred Archer in the *Illustrated Sporting and Dramatic News*, and as it explains some of his methods of riding and views on starting, portions of it are quoted.

Archer in a way prided himself upon his weight, and the first thing he said was, "I could ride 8 stone 10 lb. to-morrow, and get a few more pounds off without very much trouble. I shall ride 8 stone 5 lb. in the course of the year, I have no doubt."

Discussing an unexpected win the previous year on La Trappe in the Molecomb Stakes, Archer said : "It was strange, I can't make out how I came to win now. I certainly did not think I had a chance. You may depend upon it that it was a false run race. We went no pace at first, and then the mare had just speed enough to get home with one run. It happens that way sometimes, you pull off when you haven't an outside chance."

When asked the secret of success Archer replied with a smile : "Well, I really don't quite know. I never throw away a chance in a race if I can help it, and am always looking out to see how I can steal a length or two by getting the rails, or anything of that sort, and then I generally manage to get well away. But what people say, and what I sometimes read in some of the papers about the starter favouring Archer, and his being off a couple of lengths to the good, is not true. In fact, it's rubbish.

"Of course, I don't mean to say that I don't do my best to get away when the flag falls, but it isn't the getting away first so much as how you get away—how you set your horse going. I mean, that makes all the difference. You can't set a horse going at once if you have a tight hold of his head. You often see a jockey at the post in a five-furlong race pulling at his horse, as nervous as he can be, watching the starter. The flag falls, and he lets go of the reins, ready to start off at his best pace. I've always got my horse ready to go, but not pulling at him, and then when we do start I'm off at full speed at once. If you watch you'll often see that some jockey was off a couple of lengths before me, but if his horse wasn't ready he doesn't keep his advantage."

There is a lot of good advice in this that might be assimilated by some of the present-day jockeys.

The interviewer suggested to Archer that he was not as severe on horses as he used to be. "You're quite right," he frankly replied. "It's a great mistake to knock a horse about, and I know that a few years back I was a severe rider. I've learnt better by experience. I rarely hit a horse more than twice in a finish now, and I rarely or never have rowels to my spurs. You can hurt a horse almost as much without, for the matter of that, if you want to, but it's bad policy to hurt them."

What a world of difference it might have made if Archer had adhered to the views he expressed that day, when he said : "I shan't put myself out and ride quite so much. I've headed the list for eleven years, but I've got so many things to look after that I can often do more useful work at home than in going about the country to ride. There's no fear of my not keeping fit with all the work I do, and I go most evenings into my Turkish bath."

This letter is out of Mrs. Coleman's old scrap-book :

> "Badminton,
> "*October* 16, 1883.

"ARCHER,

"Looking through the Criterion to be run on Monday, I see nothing you are likely to ride unless you have been specially engaged. My horse, Eastern Emperor, has been doing very well lately, and we hope and think he is much improved. I have some good tackle I can try with, and am going to give him a run.

"If I find he has improved, I shall run him, and should much like you to ride him for me. Royal Fern is an ugly customer, but we have a shade the best of the weights, and he has a nice turn of speed. I can try a bit, so, if he has improved as we think, he should run well and might beat the other. Will you write me a line to Manton House, Marlborough, and say if you can ride him? I have tried for thirty years and more to win the Criterion, and been second two or three times.

> "Yours faithfully,
> "BEAUFORT."

In Mrs. Coleman's book are the following :

> "Sutton, Loughborough,
> "*October* 29, 1883.

"DEAR SIR,

"According to promise, I send you a cheque for £50. I think I shall be at Worcester. I cannot get to Newmarket, so shall send two bad selling-platers to Worcester. You will not send yours, I suppose? I have bought Mr. Pennant's half of Ronald; it is no good having horses, particularly selling-platers, in halves. Wishing you good luck next week,

> "I am, yours faithfully,
> "G. PAGET."

"Mr. F. Archer."

There is a letter from Sir John Willoughby written from Hyde Park Barracks, S.W., on October 27, 1883, saying : "I send you £50 for Fast and Loose—and am much obliged to you" ; and another from Mr. Gerard enclosing a cheque for £50 for a win.

ARCHER'S PRINCIPAL WINS IN 1884

ESHER STAKES (SANDOWN).—THE LAMBKIN, 4 to 1.
NEWMARKET SPRING HANDICAP.—KEIR, 7 to 4.
WOODCOTE STAKES (EPSOM).—ROSY MORN, 2 to 5.
EPSOM GRAND PRIZE.—CHERRY, 6 to 4.
SALFORD BOROUGH HANDICAP.—ENERGY, 2 to 1.
HARTINGTON PLATE (MANCHESTER).—RENNY, 11 to 2.
NEW STAKES (ASCOT).—MELTON, 5 to 1.
WOKINGHAM STAKES (ASCOT).—ENERGY, 4 to 1.
ALEXANDRA PLATE (ASCOT).—CORRIE ROY, 4 to 7.
JULY HANDICAP (MANCHESTER).—FRIAR RUSH, 4 to 1.
STEWARDS' CUP (BRIGHTON).—BRAG, 5 to 2.
YORKSHIRE OAKS.—CLOCHETTE, 9 to 4.
KEMPTON PARK BREEDERS' STAKES.—LADY BEATRICE,
11 to 10.
CHAMPAGNE STAKES (DONCASTER).—LANGWELL, 10 to 1.
SEPTEMBER HANDICAP (MANCHESTER). — WHIPPER-IN,
11 to 10.
GREAT EASTERN RAILWAY HANDICAP.—ENERGY, 2 to 1.
MIDDLE PARK PLATE.—MELTON, 10 to 1.
CRITERION STAKES (NEWMARKET).—MELTON, 2 to 5.
DEWHURST PLATE.—PARADOX, 2 to 1.
LIVERPOOL AUTUMN CUP.—THEBAIS, 9 to 2.
RICHMOND STAKES.—ROSY MORN, 6 to 5.
CLEARWELL STAKES.—LANGWELL, evens.

Headed the list of jockeys with 241 wins.

CHAPTER XVIII

A SON was born in the January after Archer's marriage, but died almost immediately. Mrs. Archer was extremely ill for a while. The following letter was received at this time :

> "Taispitz, near Terain, Moravia,
> "*The 12th of January.*
>
> "DEAR ARCHER,
>   "I have just heard of the serious illness of Mrs. Archer, and I am sending to tell you I feel most sincerely for you, and would be very glad to hear better news very soon. I am *myself* very ill in consequence of a fall this spring.
>   "Believe me, yours truly,
>   "A. BALTAZZI."

The Viennese brothers Hector and Alexander Baltazzi, who are elsewhere mentioned in this book, were very popular socially and on the Turf. Mr. Hector Baltazzi could ride extremely well on the flat, and his brother owned Kisber, the Derby winner, who was named from his having been foaled at the Hungarian Government Stud at Kisber.

In this season Archer placed 241 wins to his credit out of 577 attempts, and for the eleventh successive year he distanced all competitors. But for the sad death of his wife early in November he would, no doubt, have established a record big enough to last for many years. Although he was not so fortunate as Wood this season in handicap events, Archer was well to the fore in two-year-old contests, among his successes being the Champagne, Autumn, Clearwell, New, and Richmond Stakes, and the Dewhurst and Middle Park Plates.

This was the year of the sale of Lord Falmouth's horses, and on this occasion Dawson and Archer presented to Lord Falmouth a beautiful silver salver, round the edge of which were graven his victories. Naturally, Lord Falmouth prized this beyond everything, and he stated it would always be preserved as an heirloom in his family. All the winners whose names were recorded on the salver were ridden by Archer, with the exception of Kingcraft in the Derby and Cecilia in the One Thousand Guineas, the mounts respectively of Tom French and John Morris.

But 1884 was a fatal year to Archer, and the day he rode Thebais to victory in the Liverpool Autumn Cup was probably the last happy day he spent. As has been said, his wife had had a little boy, who died immediately, and she was very ill ; now, on November 8, when he returned to scale from riding Thebais, a telegram was handed to him, informing him that he was the father of a daughter, and poor Fred rushed straight off to Newmarket.

The events of that day are described in a cutting in Sir Willoughby Maycock's scrap-book, headed "The American Tattersall on Archer", and written by Mr. William Easton. Part of it reads as follows :

"Some years ago scarcely a day passed that I did not spend some of it under the hospitable roof of Mr. John Dawson, the famous trainer at Newmarket. At that time Mr. Dawson's Nellie, afterwards Mrs. Fred Archer, was a child, and I of course knew her. Poor Archer, knowing this, seemed to find relief from his terrible grief after her death in talking to me about her. Hence the poor fellow's confidential conversation with me, which I will give in his own words.

"It happened when he was out here and we were returning from the Park, where he had been for a gallop. It was the only time that the great jockey ever mounted a horse in this country, and the beast he rode was a splendid-looking thoroughbred stallion called Pet Bud.

"As we walked our horses out of the Park, and into Fifth Avenue, hoping to direct his thoughts from his great trouble by talking about himself, I said to him : 'Fred, I should think you must sometimes feel tremendously proud and elated over your success and at the fact that you are a very great and important man in this world. It's a wonder that it has not utterly spoiled you, and made you a very disagreeable person, instead of the modest, unassuming man that you really are.'

"Turning in his saddle, face to face, he replied : 'No, you would be surprised how little I think of it all in that way. My life has not been a very long one, you know, and naturally I am gratified and thankful at my good fortune, or luck, it may be. Sometimes, when thinking it all over, I have thought to myself that it is only that I have been luckier than some of the other poor lads, who, very likely, would have been just as good as I am if they had had the same chances. That's about all the patting on the back I ever give myself.'

" 'To tell you the truth,' he continued, 'I am so thoroughly wrapped up in racing, my mind is so entirely upon it, that I really never think of anything else, not even of where I am, and of what is going on around me as I travel about from place to place.'

"He turned away, and nothing was said for several minutes, but his face assumed a most pitifully sad expression, and he went on : 'Ah, well, what does it all amount to after all ? It's all nothing to me now. Poor Nellie ! She was my glory, my pride, my life, my all, and she was taken from me at the very moment that my happiness did really seem to me to be so great and complete as to leave nothing else in this world that I could wish for.

" 'But the next moment ! What a change ! Then there was but one thing in the world that I wanted, and I would have gladly given up money, honours, and everything else, even my life, in exchange for only one word from her dear lips. I could not get it, and never can.'

"The poor fellow tried hard to conceal his emotion, but in spite of his efforts the tears rained down his face, and his terrible grief was pitiable to behold. Recovering himself in a minute or two, he said : 'How strange it all seems, and how odd that you should ask me that question about my feelings over my successes ! Do you know, I did feel something of what you must mean the other day. It was the day before my poor Nellie died.'

" 'I had just closed a brilliant season by winning the

199

Liverpool Cup on Thebais. I had received a telegram to say the baby was born, and that Nellie and the little thing were all right, and as the train whizzed me along towards home my whole career seemed to come up before me. I confess that I did feel a little proud at winding up my great season so brilliantly, and I was so happy about Nellie and baby, and everything generally, that I said to myself: "I wonder why I should be so blessed? There really does not seem to me to be anything in this world that I can or ought to want.'

" 'I arrived at home in due course, and everything seemed all right there. Nellie, you know, always liked to see me in my hunting-togs. So, as the hounds were going to meet somewhere near the next morning, I thought it would be a good excuse to dress myself in full hunting-rig, just to please her, and I meant to take lots of trouble to make myself as smart as possible on that account.

" 'I think I was the happiest man that evening that ever lived, and in that frame of mind as I thought of how I would go and show myself and say good morning to poor Nellie.

" 'Just then my sister came running towards me and cried out, "Oh, Fred! Fred! Nellie is dying!" I rushed into the room and found the poor little woman writhing in convulsions, which continued until she died. She did not know me and never spoke to me again.'

"He had to stop here again for a moment, but controlling himself by a big effort he went on to say, 'Do you know what my only real consolation is now?' Not waiting for an answer, he continued: 'I don't mind telling you that it is in prayer. I have, like other men, been careless about that sort of thing at times in my life, but since poor Nellie's death, when I am alone I spend most of my time upon my knees in earnest prayer. I get out of bed in the night when everything is still, and kneel and pray. It is such a comfort to do this—the only comfort I have now, in fact. I know it is what she would like me to do—she was so good, you know.

" 'And do you know, I think she is with me at those times.' "

When asked by his friends why he did not marry again, he would reply : "Oh, if I could only love a woman half so well as I loved her, I would, but I could not."

A friend of Archer's who lived on the Cotswolds said that Fred never had that very sad expression, so far as he remembers, before the death of his wife, and that it is particularly noticeable in the photograph Archer had taken in Dublin not long before he died. This friend said also that Mrs. Archer's death broke Fred up altogether ; he was never the same man afterwards.

Mrs. Archer was only twenty-three when she died, and the greatest sympathy was shown by high and low in England, and in fact practically all over the English-speaking world.

The following letters speak for themselves :

"1, Powis Square, Brighton,
"<i>November</i> 22, 1884.

"MY DEAR ARCHER,
"Ever since we first read in Saturday's evening paper a fortnight ago of the sad and grievous loss you have sustained you have been constantly in our thoughts, and most truly and sincerely have we sympathized with you. I much value the portraits of your wife and of yourself which she kindly sent me in the September of last year, and now I shall place with them the memorial card, for which I now wish to thank you, and which is a beautiful memorial of her short and bright life. Her portrait is so bright and so winning that I almost seem to have known her, and so to be better able to estimate your great loss.

"My inclination was to write to you on first hearing the sad news, but I am sure you must have been overwhelmed with letters, and I only now write to thank you for the card, and beg that you will not think of being at the trouble to send any reply. May God bless you and comfort you ; and believe me always very sincerely yours,
"J. BAGHOT DE LA BERE."

"MY DEAR YOUNG FRIEND,
"It grieves me very much to think of your sad loss. Pray bear up as well as you can. You have indeed my most sincere sympathy.

"Yours very truly,
"Marle Hill, Cheltenham." "W. LA TERRIÈRE."

"ARCHER,
        "I am so shocked and grieved at hearing the sad news I do to-day that I must write and tell you how sincerely I sympathize with you in your sorrow. News travels so slowly to us; it was only the other day I wrote to you, and now Lady Falmouth writes to me of your terrible loss.

"It seems hard to think that all is for the best—so easy to despair; but you, I am sure, even after such a blow as this, will think it and try to realize it.

"I know how deeply you will feel this, but there may be some little consolation in the thought that all your friends think of you in your trouble, and mourn with you in your loss.

"No one will do so more sincerely than I do.

        "Believe me, yours faithfully,
            "E. V. BOSCAWEN."

                                    "*November* 14, 1884.

"Only just one short line to assure you that Lady R. and I feel most deeply for you in your sad loss. Please don't trouble answering this. Try and bear it as well as you can.

                        "Ever truly yours,
                            "ROSSMORE."

                                "Rutland Cottage.
"ARCHER,
        "I am much obliged to you for your letter, but I am sorry you should have thought it necessary to write it. I can assure you we all sympathize very much with you in the great sorrow that has come upon you, and I can only hope that you may find consolation, although you can hardly hope just yet to obtain it. It must be a very trying time to you now, returning home, but you will find plenty of occupation, which is the best way of bearing life under your severe trouble.

                        "Yours truly,
"*March* 12, 1885."   "CADOGAN."

"ARCHER,

"I must write you a few lines to say how much I sympathize with you in the great loss which you have sustained, and I hope you will bear up as well as possible under what must be to you a most crushing sorrow.

"Believe me, yours truly,
"PORTLAND."

Lord Hastings wrote for himself and Lady Hastings "to express very deep sympathy with you in the great loss you have sustained. I am sure no amount of condolence from your friends can possibly lessen your extreme grief."

The Prince of Wales telegraphed his regrets, and other telegrams received were :

LORD LURGAN.—"Accept my sympathy in the great loss, which I was extremely sorry to hear about."

LORD FALMOUTH.—"I am profoundly grieved and shocked at your telegram. Pray be assured of my deepest sympathy, and Lady Falmouth's."

DUCHESS OF MONTROSE.—"Deeply feel for you. Have gone through it myself. Well know how you suffer."

DUKE OF ST. ALBANS.—"Accept the Duchess's and my most sincere sympathy in your grief. Have learnt your loss with much sorrow."

Although his sister, Mrs. Coleman, came to live with him, Fred became so depressed and sunk in melancholy that he determined to give up riding for a time. Archer had amazing powers of bodily endurance and capacity for self-denial and fasting, but he could not withstand mental suffering. Troubles and disappointments in racing or his domestic affairs completely upset and unnerved him.

Mr. Raleigh said that he had heard that they had a great piece of work at his wife's funeral to keep Archer from throwing himself into the open grave.

He possessed the artistic temperament in dress and deportment, and was one of the gentlest of human beings until he was astride a horse, and then his temper and language, coupled with his brilliant riding, often carried all before him. He had the curious and composite character we so often see asociated with genius.

Archer decided to travel for a time. He chose America for a trip, and one of the letters he received was from Lord Rosebery, who wrote on November 14, 1884:

"I was exceeding sorry to hear of your sad loss, and I think you are quite right to go for a change of scene to America. I only sent you one letter to Mr. Belmont, who is a great friend of mine and the president of the American Jockey Club. He will give you all the advice or assistance you want. If I were you I would first see the Falls of Niagara and then go to the Southern States, where you would find the most charming summer weather, and camelias flowering in the open air at Christmas.

"The hotel I go to is small and quiet. It is called the Breevoort House, and is kept by Mr. Waite. If you told him that you came from me I am sure he would make you comfortable. The Windsor Hotel is larger than the Grand Hotel here, but a great many English go to it, and I believe it is good.

"Take plenty of warm clothing, for all clothing there is very dear, and you will find New York very cold. I can't think of any more to tell you, but I hope you may have a pleasant voyage and a safe return."

"Belgrave House, London.
"*November* 15, 1884.

"MY DEAR MR. CUSHING,

"Mr. Fred Archer, the great jockey, is going to America to-day to try and recover from the grief of the loss of his wife. He is a personal friend of mine whom I hold in great esteem; he has asked me for letters of introduction to gentlemen whom I know in America. Your friends, who are in a great position there, could be of great service to him, and if you will I shall esteem it a great favour. I hope we shall see you and Mrs. Cushing soon back, and believe me,

"Yours sincerely,
"C. Stirling Crawfurd Montrose."

"Belgrave House, London.
"*November* 15.

"My Dear Mr. Reiver,
"If you can be of any service to Mr. Fred Archer, the great jockey, the bearer of this and a personal friend of my own, I shall take it as a great favour. He has just lost his wife and is trying to seek forgetfulness in your bright land.

"Remember me kindly to Mrs. Reiver, and believe me,
"Yours sincerely,
"C. Stirling Crawfurd Montrose."

Before going to America, Archer dashed off to Cheltenham to see Mr. Charles Jessop, his solicitor, and said, "I want to make my will, and to have it got ready by about two in the afternoon. I am off to America."

Mr. Jessop said he had only one letter to Fred in his possession, written by an aristocratic acquaintance, who said : "I am afraid I can't pay you the £100 I owe just yet." Mr. Jessop said that after Archer's death he had had a lot of letters like this from lords and others, and he kept them until he had made the writers pay back what they owed to the estate, and then he gave the letters back to those who had written them. But this one he happened to have kept, though he got back the £100. The writer went on to say : "Mind you don't flirt with the Duchess" (at some race-meeting Fred was going to).

Fred Archer's will read as follows :

"This is the last will and testament of me, Frederick James Archer, of Newmarket, in the county of Cambridge, gentleman. I appoint my friend, Robert Herbert Mills, and my brother-in-law, George Peddie Thomas Dawson, executors of this my will and trustees for the purposes hereinafter named. I direct that all my debts, funeral and testamentary expenses may be paid as soon after my decease as conveniently may be. I give and bequeath the following legacies, free of legal duty, viz:

"To my daughter, Nellie Rose Archer, £20,000, in addition to any other benefits she may take either under my marriage settlement or this will. To the said Robert Herbert Mills, £5,000; to the said G. P. T. Dawson, £500; to my brother, Charles Archer, £2,000; to my sister, Emily Collingwood Coleman, widow, £2,000; to my uncle, Albert Archer, £500; to my valet, William Bartholomew, generally known as 'Solomon', £1,000; to my sister-in-law, Annie Dawson, £2,000; and to my friend, Alexander Dawson Hogg, £500.

"I direct my said executors and trustees to invest upon some safe security a sum of money sufficient by its interest, income, and dividends to produce the yearly sum of £200 in such amounts and instalments, and at such times as they may think proper, for the maintenance and support of my father and mother and the survivor of them, and on the death of such survivor the said invested sum of money shall fall into and form part of my residuary estate.

"I direct my said executors and trustees in like manner to invest the sum of £2,000 and pay and apply the yearly interest, income and dividends to arise therefrom for and towards the maintenance, education, and bringing up of my nephew, Frederick Pratt, son of my sister, Alice Pratt, until he attains the age of 21 years, and on his attaining that age I direct my executors and trustees in like manner to pay him the said invested sum of £2,000 and all interests and dividends then due thereon.

"And I also direct my said executors and trustees in like manner to invest the sum of £5,000 and pay the yearly interest, income and dividends thereof to my sister, the said Alice Pratt, for her life, and at her decease I direct my said executors and trustees to pay the said invested sum of £5,000 and all interests and dividends then due thereon unto all and equally between all her children (except the said Frederick Pratt) in equal shares.

206

"All the rest residue and remainder of my estate, both real and personal and whatsoever not hereinbefore disposed of, I give, devise, and bequeath unto my daughter, Nellie Rose Archer, her heirs, executors, and assigns absolutely. And hereby revoking all former and other wills heretofore made by me, I declare this to be my last will and testament. In witness hereof I have hereunto set my hand this 14th day of November, 1884.

"Signed by the said F. J. Archer, and for his last will and testament, in the presence of us both present at the same time, who in his presence and in the presence of each other have hereunto subscribed our names as witnesses.

"F. J. ARCHER.

"Charles H. Jessop, of Cheltenham,
     "Solicitor.
"Wm. Jewell, his clerk."

Relating the incident afterwards, Mr. Jessop said : "So I drew it up very hurriedly. I did the best I could for little Nellie Archer, and for the family generally, and he left it very much to me to settle matters.

"I dare say some solicitors in my place would have suggested putting themselves down for £5,000 or so, but that was never my way. I suppose, though, I ought to have had a legacy ; at any rate, more than some of the people who did. Still, I made a very good thing out of the estate while it lasted. Naturally I should have drawn up the will better if I had had a little more time to think things over, and there were one or two little things I forgot.

"I think Fred would have done anything I liked, and left money to anyone I liked. I told him it was done in too great a hurry to be done properly, and Fred promised to come in again when he came back from America and have it all straightened up. But he never did. I told Fred he ought to appoint proper guardians for Nellie, and he did write (with infinite labour) a bit of paper saying that he wished the Dawsons to have charge of the child. On the strength of that I handed over Nellie to her Dawson grandparents. That bit of paper is the only writing of his, barring his signature, that I ever had. And even to write his name was a piece of work, I can tell you.

"When Fred died many people thought he had about half a million, but I, of course, knew better. He had had many very heavy expenses."

Fortified with numerous letters of introduction to friends across the water, Archer sailed for America in the *Bothnia* on November 15, 1884, and was accompanied by his friend Captain Bowling and his valet "Solomon", and as soon as he arrived he cabled inquiring after his little girl.

To an interviewer he said his trip was purely a sightseeing one. He was in search of distraction, wanted to get away from the long nights at Newmarket, and would not ride a horse for £5,000

Archer hardly went to a race-meeting while in the U.S.A. and Canada, but he travelled extensively. He went tobogganing in Montreal, visited the blue grass plains of Kentucky, inspected the pig-killing and canning factories of Chicago, saw the Great Exposition of New Orleans, and afterwards had five weeks' shooting.

At New York, he and Captain Bowling stayed at the Hotel Brunswick, Fifth Avenue, 26th and 27th Streets, and their bill for the week is in Mrs. Coleman's scrapbook.

She had this newspaper cutting, which probably amused her brother very much, to whom Mr. Justice Hawkins had sent a silver tankard as a wedding-present:

"'Who's Archer?' was the query of a learned judge when a witness ventured to mention the distinguished jockey of that name. Of course, his lordship desired the information in his judicial capacity only; for, as he happens to be a member of the tribunal which exercises jurisdiction over racecourses and their patrons, Mr. Justice Hawkins was well aware that Archer is a young man of slender build, who, by dint of a talent for taking a horse off Epsom Downs quicker than any other lad in the Newmarket stables, earns about twice the wages of an ambassador. This in itself is something, and proves the wisdom of the Universities which now affirm that a knowledge of Greek is an unnecessary equipment for the battle of life. However, if

208

anyone remains ignorant of the antecedents, merits, fame and opinions of Mr. Archer after the ample details with which the newspaper reporters have favoured us, it will be entirely his own fault. The 'Prince of the Pigskin', like other eminent men, has been starring it in the New World, and though, perhaps, not quite so lettered as Mr. Arnold, or scientific as Professor Huxley, or so worthy of applause as Mr. Irving, or Dr. Freeman, it is quite evident that he received much more attention than any one of these celebrities. The horse-jockey and his friend Captain Bowling appear to have been making quite a triumphal progress. They were feasted and fêted and lauded and saw everybody worth seeing, from the Newmarket point of view, and everything which a great Englishman, whose greatness hangs to the back of a horse, ought to see. In New York they were the guests of Governor Vanderbilt—who also, we believe, entertained Lord Coleridge. They were not dined by the President, probably regarding a person of so little account in the ring as unworthy of a visit. They were among the other eminent individuals received by Mrs. Lucilla Dudley, whose attempt to assassinate Mr. Jeremiah O'Donovan miscarried. Altogether the Captain and his friend seem to be having what no doubt they have by this time learnt to call 'a high old time of it'.

"All this is extremely entertaining, though possibly the Chief Justice, as he reads the story of Mr. Archer's doings, may feel that after all he was not made so much of as he had fondly imagined. It is only when the jockey begins to unburden himself to the interviewers that the world, whose sense of humour is not bounded by a paddock, begins to find the business so monstrously amusing. Mr. Archer, we learn, considers American theatres really A1, and the reporters gravely publish the fact. His opinion of the Americans, as a people, he showed his good sense by declining to formulate. All he could say was that to him— as to Lord Coleridge and Mr. Herbert Spencer—'they had been very kind and hospitable'—a dictum at which no one can cavil. Mrs. Dudley's cell was 'furnished like a drawing-room'. According to her account, she could have killed Jeremiah easily; and as soon as she is formally acquitted (a result of which she never entertains a doubt), it is her intention to take an office next door to this apostle of dynamite and 'frighten him to death'.

"It is also interesting to learn that, in the opinion of Mr. Archer, Mrs. Dudley is quite sane. From which it would seem that Epsom has supplied its principal ornament with the instinct and aptitude of a Lunacy Commissioner. Why not? Surely Archer is as competent to pronounce on the *mens sana* as on literary and political subjects. The absurdity of all this does not lie so much with the interviewed as with the interviewer. The 'lad', who is not without plenty of sound sense, by dint of flattery, and living in an atmosphere of horsiness, no doubt believes, like the Yorkshire 'tyke', that if a man 'knows the points of a mare he knows most anything'. When a Captain escorts him on his travels, and the reporters of newspapers hasten to record his dicta, it is but natural that Mr. Archer should imagine that every word which falls from his mouth is of interest to the world at large. The ludicrous side of the business is that the conductors of any newspaper can delude themselves into the belief that the views of a horse-jockey on the American Constitution are worthy of preservation, or that while the fact of the 'illustrious traveller' weighing 'nine stun ten pund' may be of concern to his employers, his comments as to the architecture of the American cities are of less value than the criticisms of the Chelsea Chicken on the Apollo Belvedere, or of the Southwark Slogger on the Cameroons question.

"And yet, though Mr. Archer's views on the American drama, his strictures on Transatlantic architecture, and his psychological study of Mrs. Lucilla Dudley of the Tombs Prison may be very ridiculous, it would be a mistake to imagine that the opinions of Mr. Archer and Captain Bowling are not of a great deal more value to some people than those of Mr. Bryce and Mr. Matthew Arnold.

"Fame is purely local. There is no such thing as universal celebrity. When the ostler begged the Bishop to shake hands with the bruiser in the stable-yard ('he'll let yer'), the worthy man simply gave expression to the relative opinions regarding prelates and prize-fighters held in his circle. When Victor Hugo witnessed a marriage at a Mairie, the registrar nearly brought on an apoplectic fit by mildly asking the 'Maitre' whether he spelt his name with or without a 't'.

.   .   .   .   .

"If the opinions of a jockey are laughed at by many of us, it is open to discussion whether on many a racecourse 'Fred's' ideas on democracy, art, insanity, and the New World at large may not be quoted with an appreciation which has never yet been accorded to those of De Tocqueville, or Winslow, or Anthony Trollope. It is even possible that the interest in Mr. Archer and the fêting he received may be the shadow of coming events. Has the craze for actors about attained its zenith? In Paris the circus-rider is displacing him, and in Madrid the greatest ambition of the Spanish 'Arry is to dress like a bull-fighter. In Germany the mediatized princes who used to make left-handed matches with opera-singers are now throwing their handkerchiefs at the sylphs of the flying trapeze. Is the jockey to be the next pet of English Society?"

The following telegram sent from St. James's, S.W., in 1885 is in Mrs. Coleman's scrap-book:

"FRED ARCHER, ESQ., Weighing-room, Racecourse.
    "Can you come to a theatre to-morrow (Friday)?
                                        "MONTROSE."

This letter is also in the scrap-book:

"ARCHER,
    "I will be over the Limekilns at 9 o'clock to-morrow. I never saw you this morning, although Sir Frederick tells me you were close to me. I was occupied with looking for Macheath.
                        "Yours faithfully,
            "C. STIRLING CRAWFURD MONTROSE."

"DEAR ARCHER.

"I shall be very glad to go to the meet of the 'Drag', and will with pleasure subscribe if you will tell me what to give.

"Yours sincerely,
"C. STIRLING CRAWFURD MONTROSE."

A sporting writer said in 1884 :

"At the time of the Craven Stakes, the Duchess of Montrose began to race as 'Mr. Manton'. It was about this time that I heard murmurs of a Jockey Ring—that is to say, of a supposed arrangement amongst a certain lot of jockeys, of whom Archer and Wood were supposed to be the head, that races were to be won by horses selected by the Ring. I went to both these jockeys and told them of the report, adding that as I did not believe a word of it I intended bringing the subject before the Jockey Club at their next meeting. Both expressed their willingness to be examined, and protested that there was not a word of truth in the report. The Jockey Club would not inquire into it, as no formulated accusation was made."

The following is in Mrs. Coleman's scrapbook :

SING A SONG OF ARCHER

DEDICATED TO THE CELEBRATED JOCKEY OF THAT NAME

A stands for Archer, the talk of the town ;
B for Bend Or, whom he rode to renown.
C for the Confidence in him that's placed ;
D is the Derby his riding has graced.
E is the Eminence firm that he's gained ;
F in the Front he for long has remained.
G breathes of Gladness when winners he lands ;
H is the Horse he so well understands.
I Iroquois he to mighty fame steered :
J is the then Yankee Joy that appeared.

K is the King that he is of the art ;
L the Low rung of the ladder his start.
M of his Might in the saddle will speak ;
N at Newmarket his home you may seek,
O is the Out and Out way he can ride ;
P the fair Principle ever his guide.
Q is his Quickness of arm, hand and eye ;
R his grand Rush when he wants to go by.
S is the sure Satisfaction he yields ;
T tells his Triumphs on numerous fields.
U is the Use of his knowledge of pace ;
V the great Valour he rode in the race.
W the Wonderment then to be seen ;
X stands for Xantho, on whose back he's been
Y is his Years yet to come of success ;
Z is the Zeal he has shown, you may guess.

—A. PARKER.

"Hammonds,
"October 21, 1884.   "High Street, Newmarket.
"ARCHER,

"I enclose you a cheque for £400, and at the same time let me add that I think it was very honourable of you to return me the £400.

"PORTLAND."

ARCHER'S PRINCIPAL WINS IN 1885

NOTTINGHAM SPRING HANDICAP.—ANTLER, 11 to 8.
CRAVEN STAKES (NEWMARKET).—EASTERLING, 4 to 6.
TWO THOUSAND GUINEAS.—PARADOX, 1 to 3.
GREAT CHESHIRE HANDICAP.—WHIPPER-IN, 8 to 11.
NEWMARKET SPRING HANDICAP.—NAUTILUS, 6 to 4.
PAYNE STAKES.—MELTON, 2 to 5.
WOODCOTE STAKES (EPSOM).—GAY HERMIT, 6 to 4.
DERBY STAKES.—MELTON, 75 to 40.
EPSOM GRAND PRIZE.—BIRD OF FREEDOM, 1 to 4.
THE OAKS.—LONELY, 85 to 40.
SALFORD BOROUGH HANDICAP.—MACMAHON, 5 to 4.
HARTINGTON PLATE (MANCHESTER).—THE BARD, 1 to 10.
JOHN O' GAUNT PLATE (MANCHESTER).—THE BARD, 1 to 5.
WHITSUNTIDE PLATE (MANCHESTER).—PHILOSOPHY, 40 to 75.
GRAND PRIZE OF PARIS.—PARADOX, 1 to 3.
GOLD VASE (ASCOT).—THEBAIS, 2 to 11.
INTERNATIONAL BREEDERS' STAKES (KEMPTON).—VOLTA,
    5 to 4.
GREAT EBOR HANDICAP.—MATE, 8 to 1.
CHAMPAGNE STAKES.—MINTING, 1 to 3.
ST. LEGER STAKES.—MELTON, 40 to 95.
MIDDLE PARK PLATE.—MINTING, 8 to 15.
CHAMPION STAKES (NEWMARKET).—PARADOX, 12 to 100.
CRITERION STAKES (NEWMARKET).—ORMONDE, 4 to 6.
DEWHURST PLATE (NEWMARKET).—ORMONDE, 4 to 11.

CHAPTER XIX

As showing something of what Archer's natural weight should have been, he was 9 stone 10 lb. when he returned to England, greatly improved in looks and buoyant in spirits, but as soon as he reached Newmarket he went into training and commenced the arduous task of getting weight off.

When he appeared on Mr. F. Robinson's Laceman in the Batthyany Stakes he was greeted by a storm of cheers, which were repeated again and again as he cantered down to the post. During 1885 he devoted himself, if anything, with even greater vigour to the duties of his profession, and may be said to have reached the zenith of his fame; for he beat all previous records and rode 246 winners in England, while he also won the Grand Prix on Paradox.

His series of important successes began when he had the mount on The Bard in the Molyneux Stakes at Liverpool. He rode Paradox in the Two Thousand Guineas, landing him a winner after a desperate and exciting race with Crafton, and on Melton accounted for Paradox in the Derby after another fine race.

Much of the history of the great jockey during this season is in a book of letters and cuttings, on the outside of which is written:

"The Derby, won by Melton, 1885. Private scraps collected by the Lady Hastings, and put in this book, 1902."

Of Archer, Lady Hastings says:

"I am very interested to hear that you are writing a book about Archer; I think he was the gallantest creature that

217

ever lived. He was simply afraid of nothing. Not that I think for a moment that he would ever be forgotten, but a book will help to make sure that he won't, and it is just an account of his life—not so much of his racing doings —that ought to interest people.

"Of course, I saw a great deal of him; he was always about the stables, and we were so anxious before the Derby that we almost slept in the stables.

"When Melton won the Derby we were all nearly off our heads with excitement. We were very young, both my husband and I, and while Lord Hastings lived racing seemed part of my very life. I had not been brought up to it and I never gambled, but after I was married I went into it with my husband, whose great interest it was.

"I could not go to see the Derby, because about a fortnight before it one of my sons was born. But afterwards they came up and told me that Archer was downstairs and would like to see me. I begged my husband to let him, and he came up. I was just up enough to be lying on the sofa, and he brought me the whip he had used in the race.

"Well, Archer told me all about it and then the baby was brought down to see him, tied up in our racing colours— —eau-de-nil and crimson. Of course, Archer was very pleased about it, for many people think it was one of his greatest, if not his greatest, race.

"Archer's was a very complex character. Generous to a fault in many ways, I did not admire him at all in the same way I did Mathew Dawson—not as a man, I mean. Of course, he was a genius—never was such riding seen—and many people thought him an angel as well. But I never did. He had always the same simple, unassuming manners— never wishing to put himself forward. He never would even come to lunch with my husband and me—he didn't think it was his place—though I think Lord Falmouth sometimes got him to go to him. That was partly why people liked him so much: he never put himself forward.

"Lord Hastings was very fond indeed of Archer. I think he knew that Archer, like everyone else, had his faults and I should not be too careful to ignore them. Archer was great enough to have the truth told about him. He had not always a nice expression ; indeed, at times I think it was almost diabolical. But I have always been a straight-spoken person.

"Nearly all Archer's acquaintances were, to put it vulgarly, titled people, and he practically spent his life among them. The way in which some women ran after Archer was amazing. They would not let him alone. People in society went simply mad about him and hunted after him. It was their fault more than his ; they would not let him alone. It's just the way with some people.

"He was a marvellous man, and a marvellous jockey. I should think there was never anybody a bit like him—one of the most extraordinary men that ever lived, and great enough to bear having the light thrown upon him. And through all the flattery—of course, one would like to describe the best as much as possible—and absurdity of all those ridiculous women, his manners remained quite unspoilt—just perfection.

"My husband used often to go about with Archer.

"Lord Falmouth—a shrewd, clever man—was always simply devoted to him. He would never hear a word against him, and though, as I say, I think Archer had his faults, my husband—if he saw them—ignored them and never spoke of them, and Lord Falmouth never would own he had any. And anything that is written about Archer is all to Lord Falmouth's honour and glory too."

Melton's first appearance of the year was in the Payne Stakes. The field only amounted to a quartette, and with Lonely, Kingwood, and Present Times saddled at the Ditch stables, the visitors to the Birdcage had to content themselves by obtaining a peep at Melton. This was merely a fleeting view, as he stayed in his box until the last minute, and was then led on to the course.

He looked so clean and healthy that the bookmakers dealt with their clients in a liberal vein, as it was more than 5 to 2 upon him according to the two-year-old running, although his penalty caused him to carry more weight than the others. With the pace little better than a crawl for two-thirds of the journey, Lonely was pulling so hard that Cannon could not prevent her from taking a good lead across the flat.

The issue was never in doubt, however, and the style in which Melton took himself to the front in the Abingdon Mile Bottom was simply perfect. Kingwood created a decided surprise by beating the other two, of whom Present Times was in an ungenerous vein, and gave Webb a very unpleasant ride.

The mere fact of Melton having beaten Kingwood by a length did not amount to much, but the artistic fashion in which he did his work made a deep impression, and scarcely had he passed the post than 3 to 1 was taken in "hundreds" for the Derby. At the same time Paradox was immovable at 7 to 2.

Dawson had a great opinion of the possibilities of Master Kildare as a sire when he was sent to the stud, but breeders disagreed with him, and although his fee was as low as 20 guineas they would have nothing to do with him. Consequently, in his first year he only produced three foals, all from mares belonging to Lord Hastings.

Two of these were colts, and one, out of Violet Melrose, was called Melton, and the other Pearl Diver, the former being named after Melton Constable, the home of Lord Hastings, in Norfolk.

It was obvious towards the back-end that Melton's chief opponent for classic honours in the following year would be Paradox, by Sterling out of Casuistry, who was bred at the Yardley Stud, near Birmingham, and was bought as a yearling by Captain Bowling and John Porter for 450 guineas.

Paradox soon showed that he was out of the ordinary, and so good was his first trial, and so impressed was the Duke of Westminster with it, that he bought the colt for £6,000. He was fancied for the Middle Park Plate, but was unruly and, whipping round at the post, lost so much ground that he could only dead-heat for third place with Royal Hampton, behind Melton and Xaintrailles.

A fortnight later Paradox reversed the form with Xaintrailles, and easily won the Dewhurst Plate, with the latter third and Cora second, but in the meantime the son of Sterling had been purchased privately from the Duke by Mr. Brodrick Cloete, who also had his horses at Kingsclere.

Paradox made his reappearance in the Two Thousand Guineas, but before this he had won a splendid trial in which he gave 21 lb. to Farewell. Odds of 3 to 1 were laid on Paradox, who only won by a head from Crafton, and the surprise of the Kingsclere stable can be imagined at the narrowness of the victory when Farewell won the One Thousand Guineas.

The blame fell on Archer, who rode Paradox. It was said he "waited" too long, but many of the public who saw the race drew their own conclusions. They recognized that Paradox was not an easy colt to ride and wanted a good deal of his own way, and this was reflected in the market, for when Epsom came along both Melton and Xaintrailles were backed in front of Paradox, who was now ridden by Fred Webb, while Archer was on the back of Melton.

Those who decried the riding of Archer at Newmarket had the chance to back their opinion at Epsom, but they were not at all anxious. The best description of the race has been written by Mr. Moorhouse, and according to him, when the field settled down, Royal Hampton (owned by Mr. Childwick), the *nom de course* of Mr. (afterwards Sir) Blundell Maple, made the running from Sheraton, Crafton, Xaintrailles, Red Ruin, Kingwood, and Paradox. Archer was content that Melton should lie nearly last.

After going half a mile Paradox became third. Descending the hill Royal Hampton was passed by Sheraton, Red Ruin, and Xaintrailles, and at this stage Melton began to draw nearer to the leaders. After reaching the straight, Xaintrailles took the lead from Red Ruin, Paradox, Luminary, Royal Hampton, and Melton, but the order quickly underwent a change, for Paradox assumed the command three furlongs from home, and drew out with a big advantage.

Presently Melton became second. Matters had worked out exactly as Archer hoped they would. He had ridden Paradox and knew his eccentricities. He was aware that the Kingsclere horse was better than his own mount, but he knew that the thing above all others which the son of Sterling hated was to be called upon to make his own running, and so in mapping out his plan of operations Archer had resolved to keep as far away from Paradox so long as possible. Here he was, then, carrying out this deep scheme.

As they neared the distance he noticed that Paradox was beginning to show signs of restiveness, the outcome of his sense of loneliness. The time for action had arrived. Melton had gradually been getting within striking distance.

The challenge was now made. Melton drew up to Paradox a hundred and fifty yards from home, and thenceforward to the winning-post the two horses were engaged in a terrific struggle for the mastery.

The Kingsclere colt had a shade the better of the argument when fifty yards from home; three strides from the post he still looked like winning by a head. Up went Archer's whip, once, twice! They were mighty swipes, and they achieved their object. Melton bounded forward, and in the very last moment got his head in front.

Never perhaps has a greater feat of jockeyship been witnessed than in Melton's victory in the Derby of 1885. The crowd instantly recognized the value of the achievement, and accorded Archer a tremendous ovation. Epsom Racecourse has been the scene of many enthusiastic demonstrations, but few that equalled this one. Webb has been blamed by some for not sending Paradox along more vigorously in the early part of the race, but the truth is that Archer took advantage of his rival's unavoidable helplessness.

It was a supreme instance of a race being won by brains. Webb knew well enough that Archer had in a sense tricked him, and he was naturally terribly annoyed when he found himself beaten. There was, perhaps, some excuse for a little exhibition of feeling, because this was the fifth year in succession that he had been on a horse finishing second or third.

Royal Hampton, who was ridden out for a place, finished a bad third, Xaintrailles was fourth, Crafton fifth, Sheraton sixth, and Red Ruin seventh. It so happened that the first four in the Derby were the first four in the Middle Park Plate, but they did not finish in the same order.

Melton's Derby was witnessed by the (then) Prince and Princess of Wales, Prince Edward and Prince George of Wales, and the three young Princesses. There was something specially appropriate in the presence of our present King, then Prince George of Wales, as this was his twentieth birthday, and he had never seen the Derby run before, though when the Derby was last run on his birthday, just eleven years before, it was won by a colt named after him, George Frederick, the grandson of Tom Oliver's Prestbury mare, The Bloomer.

Mr. Brodrick Cloete, the owner of Paradox, took his defeat like a man, and said to a friend, "Only fancy, being beaten by a nose—that much" (holding up his hands six inches apart). "I don't suppose I shall ever be so near to winning a Derby again."

Mr. Cloete had promised to give his reminiscences of Archer for this book, which was, however, laid on one side in 1914, and Mr. Cloete was drowned in the *Lusitania*.

The meeting of the two giants among trainers, Mat Dawson and John Porter, after the race is said to have been not one of the least pleasant features of the finish. "Well, Mat, I congratulate you, though you have beaten me," said Mr. Porter heartily. Lord Hastings might have won the Derby two years previously had not Beau Brummel broken down in training.

Lord and Lady Hastings received shoals of congratulations on Melton's Derby victory, and particularly Lady Hastings, because she was at home ill; but one of the most amusing sent to Lord Hastings was :

"I understand that Milton's 'Paradise Lost' is being revised, and will appear during Derby week and will be published under the title of 'Paradox Lost, by Melton'."

The first telegram sent away to Lady Hastings read :

"Joy! Joy! The most exciting race. We all thought here that Melton had won. Everybody congratulates, particularly Lord Rosslyn.—LILY CARRINGTON."

The same lady, writing the following day from Milburn, Esher, gave some idea of the excitement that prevailed among the members of the family and their friends on the Grand Stand at Epsom.   She wrote :

"Sweet Betty,—Thank you for your bow, which I wear with pride at the moment.   I hope you got my telegram, sent off, after a deal of fuss, by Lord Rosslyn.   He had to cross the course to do it, but I was determined you should have one from your representative in the Jockey Club Stand.

"Didn't George [Lord Hastings] tell you that C. was so overcome with emotion that he could not speak after the race ; he wept !   And Uncle Ned yelled at the top of his voice. They all tell me I turned quite white ; all I know is that I shook like an aspen leaf from head to foot.   How bad it would have been for you, my darling !   It was an excitement one expects to have only once in a lifetime.

"I could not sleep last night.   It all went round and round in my head, but, oh, if you could have seen it ! Melton looked simply beautiful in the preliminary canter, arched his neck, and went straight up the course with his bit as if he were a hack cantering up Rotten Row.

"Just at the top of the hill before Tatterham Corner he was last but three, and I could hardly breathe till I saw the beloved colours creeping up on our side of the course, and then the race began.   Paradox was half a length ahead when they passed the Jockey Club Stand, but he was gaining inch by inch.   One almost went mad, but here one is to tell the tale.

"What a glorious day, ever to be remembered, and what luck our seeing it, before we are off."

The second telegram to Lady Hastings was sent by her husband, who wired :

"Melton won a head, Paradox second, Royal Hampton third.   Had rather exciting moment.—HASTINGS, Grand Stand, Epsom."

One can imagine that Lord Hastings did have a "rather exciting moment", for, apart from the honour, a good deal of money was at stake.

There were dozens of other letters and telegrams from

friends, all of which Lady Hastings had pasted up in her "Melton Scrap-book".

The day following the race Lady Hastings sent the following letter to Archer:

"ARCHER,

"I must write and tell you how *perfectly delighted* I was when I heard our pet horse Melton had won the Derby with you on his back, and from all I hear his victory was greatly owing to the splendid way in which you guided him in the race. I only regret not having been there to see it, but pray accept my warmest thanks and congratulations. I do not ever remember seeing his lordship so pleased as he was on his return from Epsom yesterday, and I can assure you I was just as excited.

"Yours truly,
"ELIZ. HASTINGS."

Melton was always a difficult horse to train, and Dawson had many anxious periods with him; but all went well, and on St. Leger day it was written:

"Melton was one of the first of the St. Leger candidates in the paddock, and he threaded his way through the crowd as quietly as possible. He wore drab cloths on his hind and fore legs, which, however, it was plain to be seen were as perfectly clean as bars of silver.

"He has thickened immensely since he won the Derby, and the shine on his coat told its story as to his health and condition being as perfect as his most ardent admirers could possibly desire. Mathew Dawson had, in fact, very great reason to be proud of the appearance of his favourite when stripped, and of the result he has achieved through difficulties almost unparalleled in the intricacies of his calling as a trainer."

After the Derby, the St. Leger! There were ten runners, and odds of 95 to 40 were laid on Melton, while Isobar and Lonely were joint second favourites at 10 to 1. The race was started by Lord M. Beresford, and Melton was one of the first away, but Archer eased him until he was absolutely last. Melton, however, gradually improved his position, and when nearing the last bend except one Lonely and St. Helena went wide to avoid some new ground, Archer shot Melton in on the rails.

Coming into the straight Melton was two lengths to the front, but below the distance there came a determined challenge from Lord M. Beresford's Isobar. Archer just pricked Melton with his spur, and he bounded forward eventually to win in a canter by six lengths.

One of the treasured possessions of the Hastings family after the St. Leger was a telegram from the late King Edward, who was then Prince of Wales. He was then at Fredensborg, and he wired to Lord Hastings :

"Congratulate you on Melton's success.
　　　　　　　　　　　—ALBERT EDWARD."

Naturally the dual victory of Melton brought back memories of his great gambling predecessor, and "Vigilant and the Wizard" of his day wrote :

"Lord Hastings has now won the Derby and St. Leger, a fact which makes a man famous ; and yet the probability is that in the years to come, in looking back on the double victory of Melton, the popular mind will associate the horse with the memory of the last of the Plantagenets rather than that of the unassuming nobleman who is his proud possessor.

"The fourth Marquis of Hastings dying without issue the title became extinct. Looking back on the great chief of the plunging era, and remembering the space which he occupies in the popular mind, it seems almost incredible that he was only twenty-six years old when he was laid to his rest. From his short but marvellous career not one element of romance was lacking, and though he has now been in his grave nearly twenty years, but mention his name to one of the old companions and a look of sadness will come over his face, and in a far-off manner he will say, 'The very best of fellows.'

"The good fortune that was denied to the lord of Donington

has been amply vouchsafed to his namesake of Melton Constable. We wonder what the man who is dead would have done with the Ring, had he, say, in the year 1866, owned a horse of the calibre of Melton? In the language of the late Lord George Bentinck, he would not have left a cardseller with a shirt to his back.

"The owner of Melton is, as we have already said, a quiet, unassuming man, who does not bet, and he presents quite a pretty picture in the park driving with Lady Hastings, their little son, aged three, holding the reins. Like most quiet men, Lord Hastings is very firm of purpose, and last year, when his quasi-confederate the Duke of Portland severed his relations with Archer, Lord Hastings may well have thought, if he did not say, 'That may be all very well for you, but look at Melton, and the big races he is in next year. I shall enforce my claim.'

"Had Lord Hastings acted as the Duke of Portland did we should not now have to write of him as the owner of the Blue Riband, for if ever a race was won by the jockey rather than the horse it was the last Derby.

"Had Melton been sent to Newmarket as a yearling, without any reserve being placed upon him, he would not have fetched fifty guineas; and, more likely still, Mr. Tattersall, failing to obtain a bid, would have had to say, 'Take him away.'

"He had neither size nor breeding to recommend him, only exquisite quality. His excellence lies in his action, which is absolutely perfect, and as he moves over the ground he is a veritable thing of air. General Owen Williams, who is an old cavalry officer, is of opinion that the most perfect piece of machinery in action that was ever seen is the stride of The Bard; but, to our mind, we never saw a horse skim over the turf with the same ease and elegance as Melton."

"Warren House, Newmarket.

"*September* 29.

"Please accept the enclosed cheque as a small present for this year's Leger win.

"Yours truly,

"HASTINGS."

"DEAR ARCHER,
    "A few words only to thank you again for coming over last Sunday.
    "I am going to England next month, and hope to see you.
                    "Truly yours,
                        "MAURICE ESTERHAZY.
    "Paris, *April* 2, 1886."

ARCHER'S PRINCIPAL WINS IN 1886

THE DERBY.—ORMONDE, 4 to 9.
GOLD VASE (ASCOT).—BIRD OF FREEDOM, 3 to 1.
JULY STAKES (NEWMARKET).—ENTERPRISE, 85 to 40.
ZETLAND PLATE (LEICESTER).—SALISBURY, 5 to 4.
LEICESTERSHIRE CUP.—MELTON, 11 to 10.
GREAT YORKSHIRE STAKES.—GAY HERMIT, 9 to 2.
PEVERIL OF THE PEAK PLATE.—CRAFTON, 7 to 2.
ST. LEGER STAKES.—ORMONDE, 1 to 7.
SEPTEMBER PLATE (MANCHESTER).—FLORENTINE, 4 to 5.
SEPTEMBER HANDICAP (MANCHESTER).—CORUNNA, 4 to 1.
GREAT FOAL STAKES (NEWMARKET).—ORMONDE, 1 to 25.
CHAMPION STAKES (NEWMARKET).—ORMONDE, 1 to 100.
FREE HANDICAP (NEWMARKET).—ORMONDE, 1 to 7.
JOCKEY CLUB CUP (NEWMARKET).—ST. GATIEN, 8 to 11.

CHAPTER XX

In 1886—the last year of Archer's life—he won the Derby and the St. Leger on "the mighty Ormonde", whose history was highly romantic. Mr. Edward Moorhouse in his books gives some particulars of the breeding of one of the greatest horses of all time, and he states: "In the year 1844 old John Osborne, father of 'Honest John', the famous jockey, happened to attend Shrewsbury Races. During his stay in the old Border town he bought for 14 sovs. a brood mare named Annette, a daughter of Priam. She had at foot a filly foal.

"In due course the youngster received the name of Agnes and became the founder of the group of thoroughbreds known as the Agnes family, than which none more distinguished is to be found in the Stud Book. When the then Sir Tatton Sykes was forming his stud at Sledmere, on lines very different from those pursued by his venerable father, he bought from the Osbornes Miss Agnes (the second produce of Agnes), together with her daughter, Little Agnes.

"As the result of an alliance with The Cure, Miss Agnes produced Polly Agnes, who was so small and delicate a foal that Sir Tatton gave her to his stud groom, John Snarry, on condition that he took her away from Sledmore."

That was where the luck came in, for Sir Tatton never dreamed what he was parting with; but the romance of racing is full of such instances. Snarry sent the filly to his son at Malton, where she was brought up as a brood mare. She was eventually put to Macaroni, and produced Lily Agnes, the dam of Ormonde, and of Ornament, who later brought Sceptre into this world.

As a mare on the tracks, Lily Agnes was described as a "light-fleshed, ragged-hipped, lop-eared filly", but she could race, and won no less than twenty-one events, including such events as the Northumberland Plate, the Doncaster Cup, and the Great Ebor Handicap. She soon commenced to throw good stock, for her second foal, Farewell, was a winner of the One Thousand Guineas, and then came Ormonde, by Bend Or.

Ormonde was such a wonderful horse that he is worth an extended reference. Chapman, the Duke of Westminster's stud groom, said, "Ormonde was an extraordinary foal. When he came into the world his mane was already three inches long. His mother had carried him twelve months, although for two or three weeks she had shown the normal signs of approaching foaling.

"For several months Ormonde stood very much over at the knee. I have never before, and have never since, seen a foal with this characteristic so pronounced. It seemed impossible for him ever to grow straight. But he did, though the improvement was very gradual.

"He was one of the slow-maturing sort. In his early days he was a three-cornered beggar that might be anything or nothing. When he did begin to develop on the right lines he went ahead very quickly, and when he left Eaton to go to Kingsclere to be trained looked a high-class horse."

The late John Porter relates how when he received the colt he told the Duke of Westminster he was the best colt he had ever sent him, and he was quite right, although the Duke hardly thought so at the time. During the winter Ormonde had splints under both knees so badly that they prevented him flexing his knees properly. The trouble gradually disappeared, but the effects were such that in his first season Ormonde was not put into serious training until August, and after a few gallops was given a rough trial with Kendal.

Ormonde was nothing like fit, and giving a pound to Kendal he was beaten a length. But Kendal had good form at the back of him, and behind the pair of them were Whipper-In, a six-year-old giving 10 lb., and another two-year-old in Whitefriar.

John Porter knew from this trial that when he had got Ormonde fit he possessed something out of the ordinary. Lord Arthur Grosvenor says that Ormonde never won a trial the whole time he was in training. Porter goes on to say :

"By this time Ormonde measured sixteen hands. He had developed splendidly, and was a grand-looking horse. His quarters were exceptionally powerful, and though rather short his neck was the most muscular I ever saw a thoroughbred possess. He had good bone, beautifully laid shoulders, a very strong back, and rather straight hocks.

"Although in his slow paces he had not a very taking action, he was a free mover. There was immense propelling power behind the saddle. His ears were inclined to lop. The width of his head behind the ears was remarkable ; I never came across another horse that showed this characteristic to such an extent. Ormonde had a most amicable disposition and a wonderful constitution.

"He was a great 'doer', and never gave us any trouble. He would eat anything the man (Marlow) who 'did' him offered. Cakes, apples—everything seemed to be acceptable. When galloping he carried his head rather low, and covered an amazing lot of ground at each stride when extended.

"After Ormonde had shown himself to be a wonderful horse, the Duke of Westminster, when at Kingsclere one day, rode him a couple of canters. After he had pulled up I asked His Grace what he thought of his mount. He replied : 'I felt every moment that I was going to be shot over his head, his propelling power is so terrific.' Another day I myself got on Ormonde's back just to be able to say I had been there, but I never rode him on the Downs."

Lord Arthur Grosvenor wrote : "I happened to see the gallop of Ormonde with 'owner' up at Kingsclere. The distance was six furlongs, and when they started I thought I should never see 'owner' again that day, and supposed that the horse would go as far as Highclere, two or three miles further. Ormonde, however, knew where to pull up. I asked 'owner' how he enjoyed it, and he said he had little command over the horse. Ormonde had no shoulders, but a big bull-neck."

The day before Minting beat St. Mirin in the Middle

Park Plate, Ormonde made his first appearance in a Post Sweepstake over the Bretby Course, and, ridden by Archer, sailed through the mud and won easily. Little did the public think of this, and none realized that the following season Ormonde would be hailed as the "horse of the century", and that St. Mirin would be the cause of Archer's tragic death.

The Post Sweepstakes took place on October 14, and on October 26 Ormonde won the Criterion Stakes at Newmarket, and followed this two days later with the Dewhurst Plate, thus ending his two-year-old career.

During the winter the Derby provided plenty of discussion, but was this surprising when there were such horses as Minting, The Bard, an unbeaten winner of sixteen races, Saraband, and St. Mirin, to say nothing of Ormonde ?

For Ormonde's three-year-old career we are indebted to John Porter's book, in which he states the son of Bend Or wintered well, growing more muscular, especially about the quarters, which developed a tremendously powerful appearance. When the spring came round he did not think it necessary to subject him to a formal trial. They knew he was well, and that was all they wanted to know.

The Saturday before the Two Thousand Guineas saw Porter again at Newmarket. On the Sunday morning he took his horses on to the Bury Hill gallops by the side of the plantation, and there met Mat Dawson with his string. They were the only trainers on that portion of the Heath, and they discussed the relative merits of Ormonde and Minting, each trainer thinking his own the better horse.

Saraband and Ormonde were stabled in Aldcroft's yard, off the High Street. There were a few boxes between them. Saraband, owned by Mr. (afterwards Sir) Blundell Maple, was kept under the closest surveillance. A passage ran the whole length of the stable between the outside wall and the boxes, and in this, opposite Saraband's box, there was a bed on which an attendant slept. Outside there were two watchmen on guard.

Porter, too, looked well after Ormonde, and had a man sleeping in the passage. When he was at the stables on the Tuesday evening (the day before the race), Mr. Maple, who was then racing as "Mr. Childwick", went into the yard and inquired for his trainer, Robert Peck. Hearing him calling, Porter went out, and they began talking about the Two Thousand Guineas.

The owner of Saraband said his horse had a great chance of winning. John casually remarked that he ("Mr. Childwick") was certainly taking great care of the horse. Then, in a chaffing sort of way, added, "You take care of him to-night, and Ormonde will look after him to-morrow."

Mr. Maple had engaged Archer to ride Saraband both in the Guineas and the Derby, and paid the jockey a big sum down for the "claim". As it happened, Saraband did not run in the Derby, and Archer was able to ride Ormonde at Epsom, but at Newmarket George Barrett rode the son of Bend Or.

Having regard to what Porter had said to Mat Dawson and Mr. Maple, it follows that he must have looked upon Ormonde that day as a very sound 7 to 2 chance. The stable started Coracle with a view to his making the pace for Ormonde in the early stages of the race.

Viney, the rider of Coracle, was told to go along as fast as he could from the moment the flag fell. He conceived the idea of poaching several lengths' lead at the outset, and, in furtherance of his scheme, showed no inclination to line up with the other horses, but remained some way in advance.

The starter, the late Lord Marcus Beresford, ordered him to join them, and he exclaimed in an injured tone, "What is the use of me coming down there when I have to make the running for Ormonde?" He had, of course, to line up with the others, and, so far as Coracle was concerned, it only remains to be added that this pacemaking mission was a dire failure.

Ormonde, however, stood in no need of assistance. From first to last he was master of the situation. A long way from home the issue rested between Ormonde and Minting, and the latter was definitely and decisively beaten just where John had told Dawson he would be—coming out of the Dip a furlong from the winning-post.

The world at large now knew that Ormonde was a really great horse. Countless columns were written in praise of him. The people who knew him best were aware that it was impossible to exaggerate his merits. Between the Two Thousand and the Derby he progressed as well as his trainer could have wished, and there was no need to "try" him for the Epsom race.

Neither Minting nor Saraband opposed Ormonde in the Derby. Mat Dawson accepted the Two Thousand form as correct, and very wisely decided to keep Minting fresh for the Grand Prix du Paris, which he won in a canter. Mr. "Childwick" also realized the futility of running his horse, and so Archer was at liberty to ride the son of Bend Or.

Ormonde won the Derby easily enough by a length and a half from The Bard. The latter was a really good and game little horse, but Ormonde settled him in two strides. The Bard as a two-year-old was unbeaten, and won sixteen races that year. He had not been seen on a racecourse as a three-year-old before running in the Derby, so there was some excuse for the belief entertained in many quarters that he had a chance of beating Ormonde.

Coracle was again sent to the post to make the running for Ormonde, and was again of little or no use. The race was virtually a match between the first and second favourites all the way round. At the top of the hill, with seven furlongs to go, there were four or five horses in front of them. They drew nearer to the front approaching Tattenham Corner, coming round which Ormonde, close to the rails, gained a couple of lengths' lead on The Bard.

When heading for home the two horses began to draw away from the others. Running under pressure, The Bard ranged up alongside Ormonde, on whom Archer was riding a very confident race. It was not until he was inside the distance that Archer began to move; but the moment he called on his mount the contest was virtually over. Lengthening his stride, Ormonde shot ahead to win in a canter.

The judge, Mr. Clarke, afterwards declared that he had never seen a race won more easily than the Derby of 1886, in which Archer rode Ormonde to victory. Ormonde had a great reception when he returned to the weighing-room enclosure.

John Porter was now absolutely certain that in Ormonde he had the best horse that had ever been under his charge, though he realized this more strongly when he met and defeated Bendigo. Look at the horses Ormonde defeated! He was a giant among giants.

At Ascot, Ormonde won the St. James's Palace Stakes from Calais and Seaton, and in the Hardwicke beat Melton and three others. His next race was the St. Leger at Doncaster. The winning of the St. Leger was a very easy task for him.

After the race the Duke of Westminster offered Porter a present of £500 or Kendal. He decided to take the horse. Lord Wolverton was just then forming a stud at Iwerne Minster, near Blandford, in Dorsetshire, and wanted a stallion.

John leased Kendal to him for three years at £300 a year, giving him the option of buying the horse during that period for £1,200. Kendal's fee was twenty-five guineas. Lord Wolverton died before the lease had run its course, and Lady Wolverton asked John if he would mind taking the horse back. He agreed to do so, and sold him to Mr. John Gubbins for £3,000.

At the Newmarket First October Meeting Ormonde won the Great Foal Stakes, beating his stable companions Whitefriar and Mephisto. The same week he walked over for the Newmarket St. Leger. A fortnight later, with odds of 100 to 1 laid on him, he won the Champion Stakes from two opponents, and at the Houghton Meeting he won the Fall Handicap in a canter by eight lengths, carrying 9 stone 2 lb., and giving 2 stone each to Mephisto and Theodore. Having regard to what Mephisto had done, this was a wonderful performance.

The following day Ormonde walked over for the Private Sweepstakes of £1,000 each, half forfeit, Lord Hastings paying forfeit for Melton and Peck for The Bard. Melton (four years old) and Ormonde were to carry 8 stone 10 lb. each and The Bard 8 stone. The owners of Melton and The Bard were not anxious that Ormonde should have the opportunity of showing what he could do with their horses. He would have made a rare example of them. This was the last time Archer was on Ormonde's back.

It is of interest to interpolate here the opinion of one of the very greatest of all trainers on Archer, and Porter wrote :

"Archer was an extremely 'brainy' jockey, but not so finished a horseman as Fordham. He developed a style of his own. His body was short and his legs long, and he used the latter as if they were a pair of tongs gripping a horse's body. As a rule he rode with a slack rein, and sometimes at the finish of a race was half-way up the horse's neck. His success was largely due to his wonderful energy, his determination, and his pluck.

"His whole heart and soul were in the business he had in hand. He was almost invariably the first to weigh out, the first at the starting-post, the first away when the flag fell, and, as the records show, very often the first to pass the winning-post. I am afraid he was not too scrupulous. Very masterful, he generally had pretty much his own way, especially in minor races. If he did not want a horse to run he never hesitated to suggest to the owner that he should keep the horse in the stable that day. In short, Fred Archer was a powerful personality as well as a brilliantly successful jockey."

The satisfaction John Porter derived from Ormonde's performances that year was sadly discounted by a discovery he made on the Kingsclere Downs one misty morning shortly before he won the St. Leger. As Ormonde galloped past him he heard the horse make a whistling noise. John was dumbfounded.

The idea that the horse he almost worshipped was afflicted with wind infirmity distressed him very much. He hardly slept all the following night. His mind would dwell on the fact that Ormonde had become a victim of that scourge, roaring! He at once wrote to the Duke, who was naturally deeply grieved by the news. At that period the ailment was very slight, but it gradually grew worse.

As a four-year-old Ormonde did not run until Ascot, but before this he beat St. Mirin at even weights in a trial, and as the latter, receiving 10 lb., ran Minting to a length in the Jubilee Cup, Porter knew that, although Ormonde was a "roarer", he had not lost his form.

Ormonde continued to surprise owners of other horses. In the Rous Memorial Stakes he was set to give 25 lb. to Kilwarlin, then a three-year-old and later the winner of the

St. Leger, and before the race Captain Machell said to Porter, "The horse was never foaled that could give Kilwarlin 25 lb. and beat him."

The opinion of a judge like Captain Machell was entitled to the greatest respect, but he was wrong. Porter was so proud of Ormonde that he suggested to the Duke that Tom Cannon should come right through with the horse just to show the public what kind of a galloper he really was.

The Duke had no objection, and the public not only saw but marvelled. Ormonde not only beat Kilwarlin, but cantered home half a dozen lengths in front. The only comment Captain Machell could make to Porter was, "Ormonde is not a horse at all ; he's a damned steam-engine !"

Then came perhaps Ormonde's greatest feat, for on the following day Mat Dawson challenged with Minting in the Hardwicke Stakes, the pair meeting at even weights, while Bendigo conceded 2 lb. Mat Dawson was full of confidence, and he said to Porter, "You will be beaten to-day, John. No horse afflicted with Ormonde's infirmity can hope to beat Minting."

The public, however, stuck to their favourite and laid slight odds on Ormonde, but there was plenty of room for doubt, seeing that the race was a mile and a half with an up-hill finish. However, the faith of the public was justified.

Ormonde's performance was really a greater one than it looked on paper. George Barrett was jealous because Cannon was engaged to ride Ormonde, for he thought he should have had the mount. He rode Phil—the fourth runner—and coming round the bend into the straight bored his horse into Ormonde. Indeed, for a considerable distance Ormonde was practically carrying Phil.

After the race it was found that Ormonde's skin was grazed for three or four inches down the side of his near hind leg. That was where Phil had struck into him, and Cannon was unable to make as much of Ormonde as he could and would have done. When he returned to the paddock Cannon was very indignant, as it had taken Ormonde all his time to win by a neck.

There were scenes of tremendous excitement, the cheering being tremendous, while thousands of ladies waved their handkerchiefs as Ormonde was led in. The Duke was so proud that he led the horse twice round the paddock and half way down the course to the stables, for he did not seem to want to part with him.

Lord Arthur Grosvenor wrote :

"Ormonde as a foal stood over from his knees, which had the appearance of almost a deformity, but he soon grew out of it, and was a nice-looking yearling. When I went into his paddock he would come up to me at full gallop, stop just a yard in front of me, and stand there without moving. The wonderful action and the enormous stride he had were the cause of his winning all his races. He never showed any vice at all, was a most easy horse to train, and of course none of us knew how good he was till he ran his first race at Newmarket, late in the season, against a good mare called Modwena, whom he beat in a canter. Ormonde seldom ran in a home trial, but when he did he was always beaten, and he never won a trial during his racing career.

"There was much excitement over the Two Thousand of 1886. I remember well that Mathew Dawson was full of confidence over Minting ; and Saraband was always a big tip, but in the end Ormonde won in a canter by two lengths. Minting was a picture of power on that day, and full of muscle ; so was Saraband. We now knew that Ormonde was a real good horse, as whatever the going was, hard or deep, it made no difference to him, and his stride never altered.

"The next race against Minting was the Hardwicke Stakes at Ascot, in 1887, and we were very anxious about it, as Ormonde had then gone in his wind, and under these circumstances the one and a half miles and the hill were all against him. As the horses came out of the paddock the excitement was tremendous. Bendigo and Phil and the other runners looked well. They went off at a great pace, and I remember seeing the dust flying all round the bottom of the course, and really it was a desperate race between Minting and Ormonde. Ormonde won by a neck, and I have never seen such excitement on a course before or since.

"When Ormonde came into the paddock, I noticed that he had been cut just above his hocks, and found that Phil, with G. Barrett up, had done it, but it did not lame Ormonde, and

240

Phil was beaten off in the race. I think it was the most splendid finish I have ever seen on a racecourse. This race was the only one in which Ormonde was ever extended."

Fred Archer called Ormonde "a horse and a half".

Ormonde won the Imperial Gold Cup, and was then sent to the stud, but his career there is outside the scope of these memoirs.

As might be expected, Archer got many curious letters, and at any rate one incident can be vouched for.

An old widow in very poor circumstances, residing in a small country town, wrote to Archer a short time only before his death and asked him to put the sum of five shillings upon some horse for her in a race then coming off. In her letter the poor woman stated that she had a crown piece given to her by her mother, and that she, being very poor, wished to try to make some money out of it. She added that she could not afford to lose it, and wished Mr. Archer to place it upon a horse that would be sure to win.

Archer was kind enough to answer the epistle, and, what was better, gave the old dame excellent advice. He advised her to keep her crown piece, and by no means risk it, and not to dabble in horse-racing. Besides this, he enclosed in his letter a sovereign, as a solatium for the unpalatable advice he was forced to give. Poor Archer was always ready with his money when distress of all kinds tugged at his coat-skirts, and this was only a small one of the many generous acts on his part.

Towards the end of 1886 Archer sent photographs of himself and his little girl to some of his patrons, and amongst the replies he received were the following.

> "Abergeldie Castle,
> "Ballater, Aberdeenshire,
> "*October* 2, 1886.

"Colonel Teesdale is desired by the Prince of Wales to acknowledge the receipt of Mr. Archer's letter of the 29th September, and to thank him for the photograph of Mr. F. Archer in His Royal Highness's colours."

"Wateringbury, Mereworth Castle,
Maidstone.
"*October 9,* 1886.

"DEAR ARCHER,
    "Though I have charged Lord Falmouth to convey
to you my thanks for the photographs of yourself and your
dear little girl, which have been forwarded to me, I think it is
safer to write to you myself, lest he should forget to do so.
    "I was much pleased to get them, the more so as it showed
me that I am not forgotten.   I hope that the dear little girl
is nice and well, and able to enjoy the hot burst of summer
which we have been having—real fit weather for a child.
    "Wishing you all good luck, and especially when the
magpie jacket is—as I was so pleased to see last week—again
worn by you.
                            "Believe me, yours faithfully,
                                "M. F. E. FALMOUTH."

Lady Hastings wrote to Archer :

                            "Le Despeneer.

    "I feel I am indebted to you for sending me the photo-
graph of your poor wife and dear little child.   I am very
pleased to have them, and hope very much when I come to
Newmarket again you will allow me to see your little baby
girl.   I sincerely trust she may have a bright and happy future
in store for her, and that this year may be a prosperous one
for you.
    "Again thanking you very much for the photographs."

    In October Archer went to Ireland, and it was while there
he received what might almost in the light of after events be
described as the fatal telegram.   It was handed in at Newmarket on October 22, 1886, and read :

    "My horse runs in the Cambridgeshire.   I count on you
to ride it.—MONTROSE."

CHAPTER XXI

WHAT happened in Ireland is best described by Harry Custance, who in his book of recollections wrote :

"It was just three weeks before his tragic death that Archer and myself went over to Ireland together. We were accompanied by Captain De Vere Smith, 'Garry' Moore, James Henry Smith ('Jim the Penman') and George Haughton.

"Archer crossed the St. George's Channel to ride Cambusmore for Lord Londonderry, who was then Lord Lieutenant, and I went over to act as starter at the October Meeting at the Curragh. We arrived in Dublin on Tuesday morning, October 19, by the mail train, and after breakfasting and looking round the city we journeyed off to the Curragh. Archer had nothing to ride that day, but went down as a spectator.

"A busy time he had, too, as he couldn't stir without a crowd of the 'bhoys' almost mobbing him in admiration. As he had not been riding for a few days, and had been indulging a bit, he was rather anxious to know his weight, and asked me to go to the weighing-room with him, as he knew I had been over there before. We went together, and I put him in the scales, with his jacket and waistcoat off, and he weighed 9 stone 4 lb. He had only a thin pair of trousers and thin boots on, so I said, 'Why, you could only just about strip with your saddle.'

"He said, 'That is just what I could do ; but never mind, my old horse has only 9 stone 3lb. on, so I have only to get 1 lb. off. I looked at the list and said, 'You horse, Cambusmore, has only 9 stone on.' He answered, 'What nonsense !' So I bet him half a crown I was correct, and when he read

243

the conditions over two or three times he found out he was wrong.

"They had mixed them up in real Irish fashion, hence Fred's mistake. I believe these were the conditions of the race: 'The Lord Lieutenant's Plate, one and a half miles, for two-year-olds, 7 stone; three-year-olds, 8 stone 10 lb.; four-year-olds and upwards, 9 stone; 3 lb. allowed for mares and geldings.' In England it is the rule to put it: 'Mares and geldings allowed 3 lb.'; but unless anyone read it right through, and looked carefully into it, he might easily make the same mistake as Archer, and think the weight for a five-year-old would be 9 stone 3 lb.

"The next day being Wednesday he had nothing to ride, so he said he would not go down to the Curragh, but have a Turkish bath and get ready to ride Cambusmore. He was also asked to ride Mr. C. J. Blake's Isidore, who was thought to be a good thing at 8 stone 12 lb. in the race afterwards, a sweepstake for two-year-olds. He said he would try to do the weight, and he did it, without walking a mile.

"A rather amusing thing happened at this part of the visit. Mr. G. Haughton was staying at the Shelbourne, and wanted some medicine after his sea voyage. Archer said to him, 'Will you have some of this mixture? I am just going to take some.' He said, 'Yes. How much ought I to take?' Fred said directly, 'You don't want to take so much as I do,' and he gave him a tablespoonful, and took nearly a sherry-glass himself. The result was poor Haughton did 'walking exercise' all night and could not go to the races next day. I quote this to show the state poor Fred's stomach had got into with continual physicking.

"As mentioned in the earlier part of this story, he couldn't ride an ounce under 9 stone 4 lb. on the Tuesday afternoon, and on the Thursday afternoon he rode 8 stone 12 lb. This would not be considered anything to a man who walked with sweaters to get his weight off, but quite a different thing to a man who wasted on Turkish baths and physic.

"When Archer came to the post on Cambusmore—this was the first race he rode in Ireland—he thought he would like to win for the Lord Lieutenant, and on mounting he received such an ovation as is seldom heard on a racecourse.

It wanted five minutes to starting time, so we had a chat. I said, 'Well, Fred, I don't know if it is the excitement from the ovation they gave you, but I never saw you looking half so bad as you do now.'

"He turned round laughing, and said, 'Well, if I look bad now, what shall I look next Wednesday, when I ride St. Mirin in the Cambridgeshire?'

"Nothing more was said, as the time was up. I started them, and he won. Archer was also successful in the next race, riding 8 stone 12 lb., but was beaten into third place on Black Rose in the last race, the Welter Handicap, by Tom Beasley, on Spahi, and Mr. Cullen on Lord Chatham. I need hardly tell you Mr. Beasley had a most jovial reception on his return to the weighing-room.

"On board the mail steamer, on our way back, I said to Archer, 'You don't mean to say you are going to ride 8 stone 7 lb. next week?'

"He answered me: 'Cus, I am sure to ride St. Mirin, 8 stone 6 lb. or at most 8 stone 7 lb. I shall win the Cambridgeshire and then be able to come down into your country and enjoy myself this winter.' "

The two of them discussed plans for the winter, and Custance warned him he had seen many jockeys who wasted on physic, and especially at the back end of the season, go out like the snuff of a candle. Archer replied:

"Never mind if I go out or not. I shall do it."

It may be added to Custance's story that the horse which Archer rode at 8 stone 12 lb. was Mr. C. J. Blake's Isidore, whose proper weight was 8 stone 7 lb., so that Fred carried 5 lb. overweight. That was on the Thursday, but Archer, who never spared himself and drew big cheques on nature, crossed to England the same night, and on Friday rode at Sandown Park.

Then came days of wasting to ride St. Mirin—days of physic in the evening and mornings in the Turkish bath. Really he had made up his mind not to ride less than about 8 stone 10 lb. again, but he was tempted because the Cambridgeshire was the only big race he had never won.

"I never have won the Cambridgeshire," he said to a friend,

"and if I don't succeed this time I'll never try again." Prophetic words indeed !

Try as he would, Archer could not get down to scale 8 stone 6 lb., and although he had the lightest of saddles and nothing except a silk shirt, he was a pound overweight. Another few ounces for a woollen singlet, and he might not have caught that fatal chill.

It was a great race, but Archer was just beaten by a head by Mr. W. Gilbert's Sailor Prince, a six-year-old carrying 7 stone 7 lb., and ridden by A. White ; while Mr. Somer's Carlton, a three-year-old carrying 6 stone 13 lb., and ridden by Woodburn, was third. Carlton was favourite a 425-100, while St. Mirin figured at 100 to 9, and the winner at 22 to 1.

St. Mirin as a three-year-old was attempting an extremely difficult task to give the winner a stone and three years, but there were some who thought that Archer would have won if he could have put more power into his finish. That, however, was not the general impression, and the writers of the day in the *Sporting Chronicle* were of the opinion that Archer had never been seen to more advantage in the saddle.

On the Thursday he rode in six races, and won one, but on the last day of the meeting, including a walk-over, he was first past the post on five occasions, and finished up by riding the last winner, this being Lord Falmouth's Blanchland in the Houghton Stakes.

The people who cheered Archer for his fine performance in winning five races in one day little dreamed that Blanchland was the last winner he would ever ride.

On the morning of the last day of the Houghton Meeting Archer was visited by another well-known racing man, who, hiding his identity under the nom-de-plume "Philippus", later wrote a very interesting letter to the *Daily Telegraph*, in which he said :

"At nine o'clock on Friday morning, the last day of the Houghton Meeting, I cantered my hack up the road that leads to the handsome dwelling of Frederick Archer.

"Archer was just dressing after his Turkish bath. In a few minutes, with a smiling face, and a wonderfully bright expression, singularly clear eyes, and all signs of a marvellously healthy condition, he came into the dining-room, on the table of which, by the way, there was a plentiful repast, not any of which, however, was destined for the master of the house.

"He showed me pictures and photographs of his wife, whose death came upon him two years since with inextinguishable sorrow, of his child, and of other members of his family and friends. About each of them he had some agreeable reminiscence. There were pictures, too, of horses which he had ridden at various periods of his career, and he also showed me the whip of ivory, with the solid turquoise handle set with many hundreds of precious stones, that several of his French admirers had presented to him quite recently in Paris.

"I observed to him that so far as I could judge from his outward aspect he was in the best of health. At the same time I suggested to him that, notwithstanding his remarkable constitution, the time had arrived when it would be wise for him to make up his mind to give up much of the severely trying work which he was accepting.

"Let me just recall the fact that upon the day of my visit he rode, under the severe and self-denying conditions I have indicated, six winners, and some idea may be gathered of the physical tension to which his frame was habitually subjected, and which must have had no slight connection with the catastrophe which has made so deep an impression upon the minds of the entire community.

"I pointed out to him that with the money he had accumulated, with the profits he would derive from the produce of the brood mares in which he took such a keen interest, and with the companionship of his child, his future might now be one of happiness, activity, and enjoyment.

"Whilst I pressed these views upon him he listened very quietly. His replies were always characterized by great intelligence and modesty, but the sum total of them all was that he never felt so well as when he was in good hard training. Like most great artists whom I have ever known, I believe he was actually of a nervous and sensitive temperament, and that, like them, he was always inclined to estimate generously

247

the qualities of those behind him, but it was not so easy for him before the race to realize that the horse he had frequently steered to victory would be so easily disposed of.

"Before I left he took me through his little stables, pointing with affecting pride to the miniature victoria which he had bought for his child, and for which he had secured an infantile driver and the smallest pony in England. He conducted me over the paddocks, telling me as we went of some recent success he had achieved in the breeding department, and when we parted he went to the Heath to ride a trial or two before the day's acting commenced.

"At various times I have conversed on all sorts of topics with Frederick Archer, and I never met him in this way without being impressed by his retiring nature, his modesty, and, withal, his strong belief in his own powers. He was clearly an ambitious man, passionately attached to his calling, and intensely desirous to maintain his position as the un-disputed head of his profession. But he was always and at all times self-respecting and respectful in his bearing, and you could not talk to him long without being struck by his sin-gularly instinctive gentleness.

"Just before I left his home he told me with significant cheerfulness that he should be glad when the work of the year was over, as he contemplated making a tour of India. He looked forward with great gratification to this holiday—unhappily now forbidden to him—as likely to yield him much pleasure and permanent benefit to his health. There can be but one feeling in the public mind, that of profound regret that he was not spared to carry out his plan of restoring the vitality of his sharply tried frame."

"I remember hearing," said a great authority on racing, "that some time before his death Archer went to dinner with Webb and some other friends, and wandered out alone afterwards. He was found in a great state of mind afterwards because he thought someone was pursuing him in the dark. so much had all the wasting affected the nerves of a jockey who had not known what fear was. He was so tall, and for a man of his weight to ride 8 stone 7 lb. required a great effort."

"Burlington House,
"*October* 30, 1886.

"To FRED ARCHER, Falmouth Lodge.
        "Will you dine with me to-morrow (Sunday) at
eight ?   Come if possible ;   only a few people, and no
reporters.   Answer Paid.—LORD CAIRNS, 10, Bolton Street."

To return to Archer's racing, he missed Lincoln, but went
to Brighton on Wednesday and Thursday without riding a
winner, and on the first day at Lewes he finished by riding
Tommy Tittlemouse, who started at odds on in the Castle
Plate, but was unplaced.

That was his last mouth, for Archer was gradually feeling
worse.   He had caught a chill and he decided to return the
same night home, and did so.   As soon as the race was
over he communicated his decision to the trainer, Gurry, and
Archer must have been really ill, for he was afraid to travel
alone, and asked Gurry to go with him.

This Gurry consented to do, and on reaching Liverpool
Street Archer had a basin of arrowroot with a little brandy
in it.   In the train to Cambridge Archer went to sleep, and
on awakening said he felt quite a new man.

CHAPTER XXII

On the following day Archer became so ill that it was thought necessary to call in his local medical adviser, Dr. Wright, who was not at all satisfied with the condition of his patient, and he sent for Dr. Latham, of Cambridge. On Saturday they issued the following bulletin :

"Falmouth House, November 6, 1886, 6 p.m.—Mr. F. Archer has returned home suffering from the effects of a severe chill, followed by high fever.—(Signed) P. W. Latham and J. R. Wright."

On the Sunday Archer seemed rather better, but it was found that he was suffering from typhoid fever. On Monday morning the following bulletin was issued :

"Newmarket, November 8, 1886.—Mr. Fred Archer is suffering from an attack of typhoid fever. There is an improvement in his symptoms to-day.—(Signed) J. R. Wright."

The news of his illness soon spread, and one of the first men to write to him was Lord Alington, who, writing on the Sunday from Alington House, South Audley Street, said :

"I am very sorry to hear of your illness. Be careful and do not be foolish. No man can live on two oysters, one prawn, three doses of physic, and three Turkish baths daily !

"Health in this world is the first blessing—so take my advice and attend to yours. As I like you particularly I take an interest in you. All that I write is true."

Messages reached Newmarket from the greatest in the land. Lord Hastings wired : "Extremely sorry to hear of Archer's illness. Would like to know how he goes on."

Lord Rosslyn telegraphed to Archer's sister, Mrs. Coleman :

"Please let me know how your brother is to-day. If well enough, tell him how grieved I am to hear of his illness and earnestly wish a steady recovery."

Lord Falmouth telegraphed to Mrs. Coleman: "I regret to hear of Frederick's illness. Kindly let me hear how he goes on. Answer paid for."

> "Paris,
> "47, rue des Saslono,
> "Avenue du Trocadero.

"DEAR MRS. COLEMAN,

"I heard from Mr. Davis this morning that Fred was suffering from rheumatic fever. I sincerely trust he is going on all right, and should be very glad to have a line from you telling me of his getting better.

"Please give my kindest regards to him, and tell him to 'keep up his pecker'. I know it is out of the question of my being able to do anything for him, but if there should be anything you may want here, command me and it shall be attended to.

"With kind regards, trusting that he is going on all right,
> "Believe me to remain,
> "Yours sincerely,
> "W. WRIGHT.

"P.S.—I have had a lot of experience in rheumatic fever. If the doctor will allow you, give him plenty of Potash water."

The late Mr. E. H. Leach was talking to me about Fred Archer. He said, "He was *not* mean but *most* generous with his money.

"The morning of Fred's death I went round to inquire how he was, and Captain Bowling said he thought he was better.

"In the afternoon I was sitting talking to George Dawson at Heath House, and we saw Fred's grey hack galloping across The Severals. I said to George, 'Hallo, Fred must be worse.'

"He had shot himself."

The story of what happened on the fatal day is best told

by giving a report of the inquest, which was held at Archer's own house by the coroner, Mr. R. H. Wilson.

Captain Bowling said he was a retired captain, and frequently visited the deceased, and was very intimate with him. He identified the body as that of the late Fred Archer, the jockey, who was 29 years of age last birthday. Witness saw Archer on Saturday, when he was suffering from a severe illness. He conversed with witness, and spoke rationally enough, but at times his mind seemed to wander.

On Monday he appeared very much better, and there was every appearance that he would recover. Witness never heard him express any intention of committing suicide, nor did he think he was a man likely to do such an act. Witness left him about noon on Monday, and on his return, shortly after two o'clock, he found that Archer had shot himself. Witness did not notice anything unusual in his conversation during the morning.

Mrs. Coleman, his sister, after relating the circumstances attaching to the early part of his illness, said : "He wandered a little during his illness and seemed to forget things. He appeared better on Monday morning, but during a long conversation I had with him he occasionally forgot the subject and frequently expressed himself anxious about his recovery. At his bidding, a little after two, the nurse was sent out of the room, as he said he wished to speak to me alone.

"I noticed nothing unusual about this circumstance, as he had done so several times before. When the nurse went out I was looking out of the window, and he said, 'Are they coming ?' Almost immediately after I heard a noise, and, looking round, saw that my brother was out of bed, and had something in his hand.

"I ran to him, and when I saw it was a revolver tried to push it away. The revolver was in his left hand, and I hurt my hand in trying to push it away. He then threw his right arm round my neck and fired the revolver with his left hand. I saw him doing it, but could not stop him. He seemed awfully strong.

"He then fell flat on his back close to a chair. I was screaming, but he never spoke. The door was kept ajar, but in the struggle he forced me against it, closing it, and so my screams were not heard. I had no idea there was a revolver in the room ; it was in a pedestal by the side of the bed."

Charlotte Horinger, nurse belonging to the Cambridge Nurses' Institution, said she arrived on Monday morning and got to the sick-room at half past eleven. Captain Bowling and another nurse, Dennington, from the same institution, were there. She was in the room until Mrs. Coleman, at seventeen minutes past two, sent her to dinner. Mrs. Coleman, witness, and the patient only were in the room. He was alone for a few minutes several times in the four hours.

By the coroner : "When Mrs. Coleman came in the last time, did the patient speak to her ?"

Witness : "I asked the patient if he was comfortable. He said, 'Yes.' He said something to Mrs. Coleman which I did not catch. I left the room, and returned in one minute. I opened a bottle of eau-de-Cologne, and then went downstairs. The door was not quite closed. I had hardly been downstairs one minute when the bell rang, which the housemaid went to answer. I went upstairs. It kept on ringing violently. As I went upstairs, I heard cries of 'Help ! When I entered, the patient lay on the hearthrug quite dead. I smelt powder. I then turned him over to see his face. The manservant handed me the revolver which fell out of his master's hand. I produce the revolver."

"Had you any idea the revolver was in the room ?"— "No. I saw the box of cartridges in the pedestal. He was lying on his right side on the hearthrug. While I was nursing him he was very low-spirited. I had a conversation with him. He said he thought he was going to die. I told him to cheer up, as he would not die. He replied, 'I wish I was your way of thinking.' When I spoke to him he always answered rationally. He did not seem to wander in his mind. I saw he was bleeding in the mouth, but did not examine him further. I only looked at his eyes and felt his pulse."

Harry Sarjent, living at Exning, said :

"I was a groom and valet to Mr. Archer. I was in the house at 2.30 and heard my master's bell ring violently. I went up, and on entering the room I saw the deceased lying on the hearthrug. I saw the nurse turn him over and then saw the revolver produced fall from his hand. I gave it to the nurse. I could not tell from which hand it came.

"About a month ago deceased had a revolver repaired, because, as he told me, Mr. Hewitt's house had been broken into by burglars. He loaded it himself, and gave me directions to put it in the pedestal in his room when he was at home. When he was away I was to move it into my room, as I was directed to sleep in the house and have the revolver with me.

"There was no other man in the house. When my master returned last Thursday I put the revolver back in the pedestal. Before my master returned home on Thursday I heard that he had telegraphed that he was coming home that day. That led me to put the revolver where he had always ordered me. There is no lock to the pedestal."

Mr. J. R. Wright, of Newmarket, said :

"I have been Mr. Archer's medical man for 14 years. I have never attended him for any serious illness, with the exception of the injury to his arm. He had pretty good health, but was not a very strong man. I was called in to see him last Friday morning. I found him in a high state of fever. He was extremely restless. I prescribed for him and saw him again at 2 p.m. The feverish symptoms had increased.

"The temperature was so high that I suggested having a second opinion. He declined ; but I took it upon myself to send for Dr. Latham from Cambridge. He sent his carriage for me the next morning at half past seven. The temperature of the patient was the same. He was no better. He had a delusion that the dinner he had eaten three days before was still in his stomach. He said he did not want any other medicine but his wasting mixture.

"Dr. Latham came again on Saturday. We told Mr. Archer he had typhoid fever, and he then became quiet. On Sunday morning he was very depressed and continually told me he should die. His temperature fell on Sunday afternoon, and he was better on Monday morning. A little before eight his temperature was much lower, and he was better, though very low-spirited. He still had the idea that he must

die. I had a long talk with him, and left him about 9.30.
He spoke sensibly. I did not see him again alive.

"I went to the house again at 2.30. I met Mrs. Coleman
in the garden. She told me the facts, and I went upstairs
into the room. I saw deceased on his back on the floor.
He was covered with a sheet. He was quite dead. Finding
no external wounds, I looked into his mouth, and found that
there was a wound at the back of the mouth. On examining
the back of his head I found an opening between the two upper
cervical vertebræ. I was shown the revolver. It would be
possible for him to fire it with his left hand as described by
Mrs. Coleman. I have seen the bullet found on the dressing-
table, and have no doubt it is the bullet which passed through
the spinal column, dividing the spinal column and causing
instant death.

"He was not delirious in his fever, but disconnected in
his thoughts. It seemed from the commencement to take a
form of depression. I consider that in the weak state that he
was in, followed by the fever, his brain was so disordered that
he was not accountable for his actions. In other words, he
was temporarily insane at the time he committed the act."

After some remarks from the coroner, in which he stated
that in his opinion the evidence, more especially that of
Sarjent, went to prove that the rash act was quite unpremeditated, he left the verdict in the hands of the jury. Without leaving the room, they unanimously returned a verdict
"That the deceased committed suicide whilst in a state of
unsound mind."

The revolver, which was a six-chambered, formidable
weapon, bore the inscription, "Presented to Thomas Roughton on his winning the Liverpool Cup with Sterling." It
was Mr. Roughton who gave the revolver to Archer.

After the inquest the minds of Captain Bowling and Mr. W.
Manning, the well-known clerk of scales, were much exercised
as to what they should do with the revolver. They were afraid
it might be exhibited to a morbid-loving public, and so it is said
they buried it on Newmarket Heath ; but this seems doubtful.

At one time Archer is said to have been worth about a
quarter of a million, but the defeat of St. Mirin and other
heavy turf losses considerably reduced the value of the estate.

The news of Archer's sad end created the greatest consternation throughout the world.   In London special editions of the evening papers were issued, giving the bare announcement of Archer's death.   A large number of people crowded Fleet Street, and the omnibuses stopped to allow passengers to read the sad news posted up.   In the suburban trains, in the trams, and in the streets, it was almost the sole topic of conversation, and had Archer been a distinguished diplomatist, or even a member of the regnant crowned family, greater concern could hardly have been manifested.

Later on, special and extra-special editions of the evening papers were issued, and railways stations were thronged with boys offering them for sale.   So anxious were suburban travellers leaving town to obtain copies that silver coins in many instances were given for the sheets, as fast as the papers, without being folded, could be withdrawn from the bundles which each lad carried.

If the year of Archer's death is counted, he had headed the list for the last thirteen seasons, while in 1873 he was only two behind the late Harry Constable.   We append the full table :

Year.	Mounts.	Wins.	Year.	Mounts.	Wins
1870	15	2	1879	570	197
1871	40	3	1880	362	120
1872	180	27	1881	532	219
1873	422	107	1882	564	210
1874	530	147	1883	631	232
1875	605	172	1884	577	241
1876	662	207	1885	667	246
1877	602	218	1886	513	170
1878	610	229			

IN MEMORIAM

Fred Archer's dead !   The words ring out
    O'er verdant plain and valley wide,
And ears distended hear with doubt
    The news that he no more will ride.
His last race done, he sleeps in peace,
    And what may now his requiem be,
When all his efforts sadly cease ?
    He rode right well and gallantly !

His heart was stout, his hand was light,
    And riding swiftly through the day,
He rode into the shades of night
    By one dark, straight, and awful way.
So there is pity for him here,
    Since envy dare not touch him now,
And stooping o'er his open bier,
    We drop a laurel on his brow.
            The Sportsman, November 9, 1886.

F.A.

CHAPTER XXIII

THE funeral of Fred Archer was a most impressive affair, and the elements combined to make it even more so. Rain fell heavily during the morning, and though it was fine when the interment took place, dark, threatening clouds hung like a pall over the town.

Floral emblems arrived from all parts of the country, Ireland, and France, and three carriages were required to convey them. A simple but elegant wreath was sent by the Prince of Wales, through Lord Alington, but perhaps the most touching of all was a bunch of violets bearing the inscription, "With baby's fondest love to her father." The day before her father shot himself had been the anniversary of her mother's death, and the two-year-old girl had placed a similar bunch on the grave that day.

Amongst those who were present, apart from relatives, were Lord Alington, Lord A. Grosvenor (representing the Duke of Westminster), with John Porter, Mat Dawson, Hon. Captain H. Boscawen (representing Lord Falmouth), Mr. W. Evans (representing the Duchess of Montrose), Mr. John Hammond, Sir John Willoughby, and Lord Cardross.

As already stated, the death of Archer created a huge sensation, and from all parts of the world, from high and low, letters and telegrams of condolence and sympathy were sent to Mrs. Coleman, the sister of the jockey.

For the purposes of these memoirs only a few letters can be appended, and choice has been made of some of those from people with whom Archer was almost intimately connected on the racecourse and elsewhere.

"1, Powis Square, Brighton.
"*November* 9th, 1886.

"DEAR MRS. COLEMAN,
         "I must send one or two lines to say how deeply grieved I am at the sad news which the evening papers brought me last night.

"I was at Worcester, where I had gone to preach, and I am writing now at Oxford on my way home to Brighton. My sons saw your brother in Brighton last week, and three months ago his little daughter, so like himself in face, paid us a visit one morning. It will be in the future some comfort to you to read, as I have been reading to-day in the papers, the evidence which they write to supply of the universal affection, as well as admiration, with which he was regarded.

"I am unable to think of anything else, and most deeply do I sympathize with you as with all those nearest to him who are mourning one so deeply loved.

"Forgive my intrusion even with these few words at such a time, but I could not remain silent.
                    "Believe me, very sincerely yours,
                         "J. BAGHOT DE LA BERE."

"Burghley Paddocks,
         "The Lady Anne's House,
              "St. Martin's, Stamford.
                   "*November* 8, 1886.

"MY DEAR MADAM,
         "Since receiving your telegram I have heard the most melancholy news of your brother's death, and I beg you will accept Lady Rosslyn's and my sincere sympathy.

"I have known him from quite a boy, and I was personally sincerely attached to him, and, although so much younger than I am, I feel that I have lost a friend. He was a very remarkable man of singular energy, and would have made a distinguished mark—the very highest mark in any walk of life. He was the *very highest* in his own, and when on the pinnacle of his fame he has been snatched away suddenly from his friends and admirers, who are indeed innumerable, and to the great affliction of his family. It is inexpressibly sad, and

260

yet there is some consolation in his thus dying, as one may say, like a soldier in battle and at the moment of victory. Lady Rosslyn desires me once more to assure you of her sorrow and sympathy and the very tender feeling she had for his little orphan daughter, who will now be more precious to you than ever. With renewed assurances of our sincere sorrow.

"Believe me, very faithfully yours,
"ROSSLYN."

A facsimile copy of the following letter has been given earlier in the book.

"Mereworth Castle,
"*November* 9, 1886.

"DEAR MRS. COLEMAN,
"The telegram which you so kindly sent me yesterday morning was so reassuring that I can hardly describe the shock the message which followed it gave me in the evening from Mr. Dawson, or the grief I feel at the irreparable loss you have sustained in the death of your poor brother. Pray, therefore, accept yourself, and convey to your father and mother, my most heartfelt sympathy at the bereavement of so excellent a brother and son.

"For myself, I can truly say that, after the long and intimate connection between us from his boyhood, not an angry word ever passed between us.

"It is not everybody who can make such an assertion as this, and I mourn for him as an attached friend. His faithful services to me were associated with some of my happiest days, and I shall always feel that his zeal and best efforts for my interests stood first in his mind, whenever and wherever they were put to the test.

"I regret extremely that the malady from which I have been for some time ailing should be a bar to my being present to pay a last sad tribute of respect to his memory, which I shall ever cherish with affectionate regard.

"Believe me, dear Mrs. Coleman,
"Yours very faithfully,
"FALMOUTH."

"Liverpool.
    "*Tuesday*.

"My Dear Mrs. Coleman,
        "No words can tell you how much I have felt for you since I heard the dreadful intelligence yesterday at Rugby on my way here—and I cannot realize that we shall never see your dear brother again, and to you who lived with him and saw him daily and the last sad tragedy it must be indeed anguish.
        "I feel I cannot help dwelling on the horrible fact that wasting so much for St. Mirin must have done him harm, but for months I have not thought him looking well.   No doubt he laid down his life for his profession.
        "How we shall miss him!
        "Write and tell me everything and where you are going and how the child is.
        "I was ill also last week, and only saw in the paper on my return on Sunday night that he was ill, otherwise I should have written before.   Make Captain Bowling send me a few lines to London—I could not go to races to-day.
        "Ever believe me, your affectionate friend,
                        "C. S. C. Montrose."

                        "Melton Constable,
                            "East Dereham.
                                "*Thursday*.

"Dear Mrs. Coleman,
        "Although I do not really know you, I feel I must write you a few lines of sympathy.   I cannot tell you how deeply grieved we were when we heard the news of poor Mr. Archer's sad death, and how *truly* sorry we feel for you, his poor sister.   You must indeed need sympathy to help you to bear your great trouble.   I knew your poor brother very well, and it makes me terribly sad to think we shall no more see him when we come to Newmarket ; it seems almost impossible to believe that he is gone—and so young a man. One can only say, 'Thy will be done, O Lord.'
        "Both his lordship and myself would think it very kind if you would please place the small white cross we have sent on poor Archer's coffin as a last mark of our affection and esteem

262

for him. Trusting that you are bearing up pretty well under your sad trial, and again expressing my great sorrow for you.
"Believe me, yours very truly,
"Elizabeth Hastings."

"Cliveden,
"Maidenhead.
"Dear Mrs. Coleman,
"May I beg to offer you and poor Archer's family all sympathy on the loss of one whom we can so ill spare?

"I was *deeply* grieved to receive your telegrams this evening giving the disastrous news, and made all the sadder by the manner of the end, which must have been terribly shocking to you and to his friends.

"I had a very great regard for him throughout, as I hope he had for me, and it always gave me pleasure to see and talk to him through now many years.

"Racing will be a different thing for me now—so much *heart* cut out of it.

"He will be greatly and sadly missed, not only for his services, which were so remarkable in his profession, but for *himself*, and we can truly say we shall never see his like again!

"I should be much obliged if Captain Bowling or someone will kindly write or wire me to Grosvenor House and let me know the day, hour, and place of funeral, which, if possible, I should like to attend.
"I beg to remain, yours obediently,
"Westminster."

"Middleton Cottage,
"18-11-'86.
"Dear Mrs. Coleman,
"Alec wished me to write and say he called to see you this afternoon, to tell you the wreath was from Her Majesty the Queen of Naples. She also wished him to express her sincerest sympathy with you all.

"Trusting you are feeling better.
"I remain, yours very sincerely,
"Isabel Waugh."

263

"Sutton Valence.

"To Captain Bowling,
    "Please convey to Mrs. Coleman and all the house-
hold the sympathy I feel for you in your terrible loss.   I
grieve with you.
                                    "John Corlett."

Two of the most interesting letters are the following :

                            "Godolphin House,
                                "Newmarket.
                                    "*November* 18.

"Dear Mrs. Coleman,
    "The Prince of Wales is very anxious to have a
signature of your poor brother's in—if possible—any letter
of his that you could spare, as he wants to give it to some
friend of his who has a great wish to have your dear brother's
writing.   I went with H.R.H. to the cemetery this morning ; he was so interested in the grave and the flowers, and
remained by it just a quarter of an hour ; he made me tell
him every detail of the funeral, and showed real sympathy
and interest in speaking of the deplorable event.
    "I hope you are feeling better.
    "With continued sympathy.
                    "I remain, yours sincerely,
                        "Gertrude Clay Ker Seymer."

                            "Godolphin House,
                                "Newmarket.
                                    "*November* 19.

"Dear Mrs. Coleman,
    "I wish you could tell me that the change had done
you any good.   I do feel so sorry for you, and the loss is
so great to everyone that it is impossible to forget it for a
moment.   I hate bothering you about this autograph, but
when H.R.H. takes an interest in anything he never rests
till he gets it ; he has asked me a dozen times if I have not
been able to get it for him ; if, therefore, you can let me have

it in the course of an hour, I could then take it to him at Herringswell, where he is shooting, and where I join him for luncheon. Pray forgive me.

"Yours sincerely,
"GERTRUDE CLAY KER SEYMER."

"I have only just got your message about the baby; the Prince goes up from Kennett Station after shooting, so will not be back in Newmarket. If you did not think the drive too far, I am sure he would be pleased if her nurse could bring her to Herringswell Lodge at about two o'clock, but I shall say nothing about it."

Lord Arthur Grosvenor wrote on February 12, 1923:

"I saw a great deal of Archer, and he was a charming man to meet, and never got spoilt. He won two Derbies for my father, on Ormonde and Bend Or; on the latter he could only ride with one arm, as he was savaged by a horse called Muley Edris just before the Derby.

"I have got a photo of Archer on Ormonde on the Two Thousand race day—a photograph a little over two feet wide, but a good photo of Archer and his seat. I have also got a small etching of Ormonde by Emil Adam which is very good.

"Archer, I think, won three or four races at Chester in a day for my father, and in doing so, coming round one of the bends, caught an old lady with his leg, but it did not kill her. Archer and Bend Or always beat Robert the Devil on the Epsom course. I attended his funeral at Newmarket, and it just shows what he was, as all the old women all turned out at his funeral, and I believe he did a lot of good to the poor of Newmarket."

"35, Jermyn Street, S.W.,
"United Services Club, Pall Mall, S.W.
"*November* 11, 1886.
"MY DEAR MRS. COLEMAN,
"I have refrained from writing before, not from any want of affection towards my dear lost friend, but because I

did not want to trouble you at the first burst, in what I know must be your intense feelings of grief at the loss of your dearly beloved brother.

"For myself, I can honestly say that I admired and loved him with a pure and sincere affection, and I have often thought since that he was well aware of this himself. And then, when I come to think, if my feelings are so acute at the loss of the poor dear boy, what must yours and the rest of his family be? Of course, though, I feel myself too much prostrated to speak to anyone about him. The shock to me has been an awful one.

"And it might be some slight satisfaction for me to say that, even from those who did not know him as I had the pleasure of doing, I have overheard the warmest and most sympathetic remarks and feelings of the nicest description expressed about my dear Freddy; but how could it be otherwise regarding such a genial, gentle, kindly dispositioned boy like that? And, alas, how could anybody who knew him as I did, do anything but love him? I hope to-morrow to pay my last respect to my dear friend by attending his funeral. And expressing my deep sympathy with you and the rest of your family in your sore affliction,

"I remain, yours sincerely,
"H. Renny."

"Turf Club,
"Piccadilly.
"*November* 8, 1886.

"Dear Mrs. Coleman,
"I am so truly sorry to see in the papers, and also to hear privately, that your brother is so ill.

"I sincerely trust that he may very soon take a turn for the better and have a speedy recovery.

"As I am sure at this time you do not wish for additional trouble in the way of writing letters, please don't think of answering this, though of course I should be only too pleased to hear of any change for the better.

"Yours very truly,
"Carmarthen."

266

"Marle Hill, Cheltenham.
"*November* 9, 1886.
"MY DEAR MRS. COLEMAN,
"The sad news has just reached me. I am grieved indeed! You have my deepest sympathies, also Mrs. Archer and the other members of your family.
"Believe me to remain, yours sincerely,
"W. LA TERRIÈRE."

"51, Green Street,
"Grosvenor Square, W.
"*Tuesday, November* 9th, 1886.
"DEAR MRS. COLEMAN,
"I scarcely know how to write to you so as to be able in some way to express my intense feelings of sympathy with you and the rest of his family at the terribly sudden death of your poor brother; it seems so impossible to believe that one who only on Thursday last was with us should have been snatched away so suddenly. Truly, we may say, 'We shall never see his like again,' for not only did all his employers look on him as a most exemplary servant, but also regarded him in the light of a sincere friend. I should much like to know the date and time of the funeral, as I should like to send a wreath, and if my doctor will allow me (for I have been very unwell myself for the last fortnight), to come down and attend the last sad obsequies of one whom I shall never see or hear again. "Believe me, dear Mrs. Coleman,
"Yours very truly,
"H. H. HUNGERFORD."

"Kensington Palace, W.
"*January* 19.
"DEAR MRS. COLEMAN,
"I am *so* glad to hear from you, for I have so often thought of you, and felt so deeply for the great sorrow that has fallen on your life. You say truly how true a sympathizer, and I may say fellow-mourner, you have in me, for

267

your brother was to us a friend we shall regret to the last day of our lives. Neither Col. Chaine nor I have been to a race-meeting since his death, for it seemed too melancholy. If you come to London, do come and see me. Write me a line and tell me when you are coming. I am so glad dear little Nell is well. I shall look forward so to seeing her when I go to Newmarket ; it is fortunate the poor child is too young to realize her double loss, in, first the mother, and then the father.

"Time alone will do you good, dear Mrs. Coleman, and I think the thought that, constantly kept before us, reconciles us most to these partings is knowing we are the only sufferers, and that those we mourn are beyond any grief and any trouble. I hope your brother Charles keeps well and is regaining his health after his terrible blow. I have heard Captain Machell is very miserable, but I have neither heard from him nor seen him since the Duchess of Montrose has gone to the South of France. Col. Chaine begs his kindest remembrances to you, and believe me, dear Mrs. Coleman, always your sincere friend,

"Minnie Chaine."

"36, Oxford Street, London.
"November 9, 1886.

"Dear Mrs. Coleman,

"My feelings and the shock I have received to-day from the dreadful news will be nothing compared to yours. I have lost a good friend, you a brother.

"I pray God to give you courage in this dreadful hour of your life ; try and bear up for the sake of his child, for the sake of poor Fred.

"I cannot say much, for it pains me and it will pain you ; it was the will of God, and we are all bound to submit to destiny. My prayers are for him and his peace. My feeble consolation for you, 'May God be with you.'

"Believe me, your sorrowing friend,
"Con. K. Harropath."

"Known to you as C. Constantine."

"Newmarket.
"*July* 10, 1887.

"DEAR MRS. COLEMAN,

"It will give me great pleasure to put you ten pounds on. I fear Caster will beat Lizard at Liverpool, but we are certain to have something good soon. I never had such a good lot of horses, but do not care a bit about racing now without my old friend, and only buy horses for excitement, to try and get interested again in it, but I think I shall never care about racing again.

"Mrs. Dawson has promised to let little Nellie Archer come up to me at Crackenthorpe in Westmorland this autumn, and I fancy Mrs. Jewitt will come with her children for a week or so. I hope if you can spare the time you will come also; it is a funny old place. Little Nelly has just been up to see me; she seems well and has grown a good deal. I fancy that she will always be a nervous child.

"I remain, yours truly.
"J. O. MACHELL."

"Newmarket.
"*August* 1, '87.

"DEAR MRS COLEMAN,

"I am much obliged to you for returning the letter; it is the last I ever wrote to him. I shall not go to Brighton or Lewes this week, but am off to Yorkshire to-morrow, and shall rest until Doncaster. I did not put you on Sigurd; he had nasty cracked heels. If —— is as good as I think him, I will put you on him for the St. Leger. I will let you know if I can get my party right for Crackenthorpe. I think you will like the place, though there is not much to do; a change to a new place is always pleasant.

"I have taken Cheveley Paddocks for my brood mares and foals, and to-day moved all the animals from Moulton there.

"We won six races at Goodwood, but nothing big.
"I remain, yours truly,
"J. O MACHELL."

The late Mr. Wyndham B. Portman, the then proprietor

of *Horse and Hound*, whose writing under the *nom de plume* of "Audax" was widely known and read, wrote in that paper on Saturday, November 13, 1886 :

"The one absorbing topic of conversation in Turf circles this week has been the melancholy death of Fred Archer, and never have I noted more signs of genuine grief than when it transpired at Albert Gate on Monday afternoon that he had passed away by his own hand whilst under the influence of delirium. So much has been written on the subject that I will not fill our pages with a lengthened account of his career, but briefly express my own unfeigned sorrow for the death of the brightest ornament of his profession, and one who made many real friends by his undeviating truthfulness, his modesty under adulation which might have turned weaker heads, and his gentlemanly bearing in every relation of life.

"As a jockey I never saw his superior, and I have seen James Robinson, Sam Chifney, Frank Butler, Alfred Day, Custance, Tom French, Tom Aldcroft, and the immortal George Fordham show their brilliant skill on the pigskin. Many others may have shown as grand horsemanship in special instances, but as an all-round jockey Fred Archer has no equal, in my opinion. One main secret of his success was his undeviating attention to business, always seeing that his weight was right, his horse properly saddled, and that he reached the post in good time.

"The starters will miss him, as he set a bright example of submission to those in authority, never attempting to take advantage until the flag was dropped ; yet so skilful was he, so keenly did he watch the starter's movements, that he knew when to go, and won scores of races by his judgment at the starting-post. In the actual race, too, how different was his riding to that of the many headless horsemen that call themselves jockeys, and I pause to think how many races I have seen him snatch out of the fire, and drop a tear of unfeigned sorrow to think I shall never see his brilliant horsemanship again.

"Born at Cheltenham in 1857, when eleven years old he won a steeplechase at Bangor on a noted pony, Maid of Trent, and two years later, in 1870, he won a nursery at

Chesterfield on Athol Daisy. In 1872 he won the Cesarewitch on Salvanos for poor Joe Radclyffe, who has since joined the great majority, and from the moment that in 1874 he won the Two Thousand Guineas for Lord Falmouth on Atlantic, his name has been a household word, as he can claim that race four times, the One Thousand Guineas twice, and he can claim five Derbys, four Oaks, and the St. Leger six times, and I may mention that in all he has had in England 8,084 mounts, and ridden 2,748 winners, whilst he has won the City and Suburban five times, the Great Metropolitan once, Woodcote Stakes six times, Lincolnshire Handicap once, Northamptonshire Stakes once, Middle Park Plate thrice, Dewhirst Plate five times, Ascot Stakes once, Prince of Wales's Stakes (Ascot) three times, Royal Hunt Cup twice, Alexandra Plate twice, Great Ebor Handicap twice, Great Yorkshire Stakes once, Northumberland Plate once, Stewards' (Goodwood) twice, Great Yorkshire Handicap once, Champagne Stakes seven times, Portland Plate twice, Doncaster Cup once, Liverpool Autumn Cup thrice, and Manchester Cup once.

"Whilst dwelling on poor Fred's career, it is not too much to say that his success in life is in no small degree owing to the kindness of Lord Falmouth and his good friend and relative Mr. Mathew Dawson. Singularly enough, his first great success in the classic races was in the ever-popular magpie jacket of Lord Falmouth, and it was the last he wore to victory, when he won on Blanchland, the last race of the Houghton Friday. Would to heavens that, like the jockeys of old, he had wound up the year on that Houghton afternoon, as the cold, treacherous air of the Southdowns no doubt aggravated what would only too probably have proved a fatal illness. What hope there may have been was cut short, alas, by a fit of frenzy that has caused deep grief among racing men of every grade; for from the first gentleman in the land to the mildest punter at the street corner, his name was respected as the emblem of manliness and integrity.

"I fear that poor Fred Archer only adds one more to the list of those whose lives have been shortened by excessive wasting—at least, I can call to mind that poor Tom French, another of the best type of horsemen, wrecked his brilliant career by excessive wasting to ride in France. Men, how-ever wealthy, will run extraordinary risks to gratify their ambition in winning races, and Archer pinched himself cruelly to ride St. Mirin for the Cambridgeshire, as he fully thought he could win on him; whilst last week Mr. Abing-ton, one of the richest commoners in England, most fool-ishly faced the starter in a silk jacket, minus his shirt, to save half a pound when riding at a country meeting, in spite of the advice of his friends, who begged him to put on a thick flannel and declare the extra weight.

"I do not on this account desire a higher scale of weights, as there is no necessity for those who cannot get down to a certain standard to sport silk, and there are plenty of lads anxious to ride intermediate weights. Now that there is 'No Best' left in the riding world, owners need require no one to make special exertions on their account, and the almost superhuman excellence of one bright star will not confound the most careful calculations of handicappers; although I would not have it understood that I consider that many of the existing jockeys do not ride quite up to the average of past years."

"I remember", says Lord Rossmore on page 153 of his reminiscences, "telling Machell about an odd dream I had about poor Fred Archer, of whom he was very fond. After Archer's tragic death I dreamt that he appeared to me, and when I asked him what he wanted, he replied, 'I've come back for some more clothes, but chiefly to try to meet some-one I can trust. I know all the unkind things that have been said about me, and how I am supposed to have committed suicide rather than face an inquiry by the Stewards of the Jockey Club. I swear to you that I was right bang off my head when I shot myself.'

"I promised that I would repeat this to my pals, and Archer thanked me and said he wouldn't bother me again.

"I told Machell this strange dream, and to my great sur-prise he took it quite seriously: 'Do you know,' he said, 'that I couldn't get over that poor fellow's death for some time. I was unable to sleep, and one night when I was lying awake—and I swear I was awake—I saw Archer by my bed-side! I watched him for a few minutes, and I don't remember whether I spoke or not, but he put out his hand, patted me gently on the shoulder, and the action, strange to say, so soothed me that I went to sleep and have slept all right ever since."

Speaking of Archer Mat Dawson said that he was a marvellous boy, and had no equal except in George Fordham over the Newmarket Course, but there comparison ends; on other courses no one approached him.

A photogravure, after a painting by Archibald P. Tilt, was published in 1887 and is supposed to represent Archer's ghost on a white horse—presumably not his "Mascot" the grey Strathavon. Underneath the picture is written:

"Across the heath, along the course,
'Tis said that now on phantom horse,
The greatest jockey of our days,
Rides nightly in the moonlight's rays."

Towards the end of May, 1927, the *Morning Post* announced that Fred Archer's ghost was supposed to have been seen by one who knew him well, riding in a lane near Newmarket.

THE END

INDEX

Archer, William—*Continued.*
a pony, 39; takes Fred to
Newmarket, 43; and leaves
him there, 44; a well-known
jockey, 44; his signature, 46;
his pony, Chow, 62; comes to
see Fred at Newmarket, 64-8;
22-5, 34, 41-2, 71, 92, 101, 108-9,
111, 145, 153, 158, 171, 182,
187, 231
Archer, (Fred's brother), 27, 33,
40, 62; "the racing pony, Chow,
that old Billy Archer had won in
a raffle, and that young Billy
Archer generally rode, 66, 108-9
Arnold, M., 209-10
Arnull (painter), 187
Arnull, H. (jockey), 20
Argues, 94
Ascot, 45, 63, 89, 91, 95, 101, 113,
115, 128, 137, 139, 153, 177,
180, 195, 215, 229, 237-8, 271
Alexandra Plate, 177, 195
All-aged Stakes, 105
Coronation Stakes, 105
Derby, 91, 99
Gold Cup, 13, 229
Gold Vase, 95, 99, 101, 215
Hardwicke Stakes, 137, 237,
239-40
Jubilee Cup, 238
New Stakes, 58, 195, 197
Prince of Wales's Stakes, 113,
115, 131, 177, 271
Rous Memorial Stakes, 105, 161,
238
Royal Heath, the, 89-90
Royal Hunt Cup, 13, 75, 105,
137, 139-40, 153, 271
Stakes, 58, 195, 197
Three-Year-Old Triennial Stakes,
63, 90
Windsor Castle Stakes, 14
Wokingham Stakes, 105, 177,
195
Astley, Sir Jacob, 125
Astley, Sir John, 115, 139-41
Astley Stakes, Lewes, 99-177
Athol Daisy, 65, 271
Atlantic, 78-9, 85-6, 152

Atlantis, 64
"Audax", 270
Australia, 141, 148
Ayr Gold Cup, 76
Ayrshire, 53
Ayrshire Handicap, 76
Ayris, Harry, 41
Adventurière, 81-2

B

Baily's Magazine, 28, 41
Baird, Sir David, 55
Baird, George (Mr. "Abington"),
147
Bal Gal, 123, 125, 137, 160
Balliol, 164
Baltazzi, A., 83, 197
Baltazzi, H. ("Mr. Bruce"), 83,
197
Bangor, 64, 270
Baratzky, 22
Barcaldine, 117, 177
Barnton, 53, 55
Barrett, G., 235, 239-40
Bartholomew, W. (Solomon), 129,
206, 208
Bass Rock, 52
Bassoon, 92
Bates, F., 171
Batthyany, Prince, 56, 77, 82, 171
Batthyany Stakes, Lincoln, 217
Battlefield, 161-2
Bay Middleton wins the Derby, 49
Beasley, Tom, 245
Beau Brummel, 161, 190, 223
Beaufort, the then Duke of, 154-5,
186
Beauminet (par Flageolet et Beauty)
123, 125, 187
Becher's Brook, 29
Beckford, 38, 41
Belinda, 177
Belisarius II., 155
Bell, Mr., 55
Bell's Life, 37-8, 72
Bella, 89
Belle Lurette, 137
Belleisle, 55

D

Festetics, Count, 169, 187
Fife, Duchess of, 222
Fife Hills, 52
Figaro, 101
Filho da Puta, 57
Findon Stakes, 177
Fire King, 113
Fishfag, 21
Fitzhardinge, Earl, 41. (*See under* Berkeley, Colonel W. F.)
Fitzhardinge (Berkeley) Hounds,41
Flatman, 155
Fleet Street, 256
Fletcher, Squire, 118
Fleur-de-lis, 57
Florentine, 229
Fobert, 58
Foley Arms, Malvern, 17
Fordham, George, 66, 69, 85, 91, 101, 107-8, 130, 145, 150, 153-5, 157, 187, 238, 270, 273
Fortissimo, 161
Fox, Charles James, 18
Foxhall, 140, 146, 151
France, 93
Fredensborg, 226
Freeman, Dr., 209
French Derby (Chantilly), 123, 125, 177
French, Tom, 70, 76, 78, 85, 155, 189, 198, 270-2
Friar Rush, 161, 195
Frontin, 177
Fullerton, 14

G

GALLIARD, 13, 56, 130, 147-8, 157, 161, 177, 179-80
Galopin, 56, 89, 179
Gambier, Mr., 23
Gareth, 189
Garterly Bell, 84
Gay Hermit, 215, 229
Gee, Mr., 101
Geheimniss, 13, 147, 163-5, 175, 177
Gelding by Wamba out of Truth, 81-2

Geologist, 147
George IV., 19, 57
George V., 71, 222-3
George Frederick, 49, 83, 223
Gerard, Mr., 193
Gilbert, W., 246
Gertrude, 64
Glasgow, Earl of, 57
Glen Arthur, 11
Gloucester, the Duke of, 19
Glover, Tommy, 81, 93
Goater, 130, 186
Godding, —, 56
Golby's at Northleach, 42
Golden Cross Hotel (Charing Cross), 127
Goldfield, 179
Goodrych, Anne, 28
Goodwood, 113, 119, 123, 125, 137, 163, 177
    Chichester Stakes, 95, 99
    Cup, 57, 59
    Halnaker Stakes, 119, 148
    Ham Produce Stakes, 69, 89
    Molecomb Stakes, 177, 191
    Nassau Stakes, 123
    Prince of Wales's Stakes, 89, 95, 99
    Rous Memorial Stakes, 123, 137
    Richmond Stakes, 105, 113, 115, 119, 123, 125, 137, 195, 197
    Sussex Stakes, 137, 163
Gordon, Adam Lindsay, 18, 23-4, 28, 31-4, 42, 50, 61, 190-1
Gordon of Gicht, Sir Alexander, 50
Gordon of Gicht, Catherine (Countess of Dunbar), 50
Gordon of Gicht, Miss (Lady Byron), 50
Gordon, the last Duke of, 19
Gorgate Hall, 64
Gould, Nat, 130, 141, 145
Granby, John, Marquess of, 51
Granby, Frances, Marchioness of, 51
Grand Prix de Paris, 94, 140, 151, 161, 215, 217, 236
Grandison, 155
Grandmaster, 177, 190

Hurricane, 64
Hutton, Mr., 132-3
Hyde Park Barracks, 193

I

I'Anson, W., senior, 27, 52-3
I'Ansons, the, 27, 52-3
Illustrated Sporting and Dramatic News, 34, 53-4, 115, 154-5, 173, 191
Ilsley, 55
India, 248
Inheritor, 52
Ireland, 242
Iroquois, 137, 139, 146-7, 151-2, 187, 212
Irvine, 53
Irving, Mr., 209
Isidore, 244-5
Isobar, 225-6
Ithuriel, 186
Iwerne Minster, 237

J

Jacobs, F., 24, 191
James I., 50
Jannette, 99, 105-6, 111, 113, 116
Jarvis, J., 109
Jenner, Dr., 18
Jennings, Tom, 107-8, 160, 171
Jermyn Street, 175-6, 265
Jessop, C. H., 205, 207
Jewell, William, 207
Jewitt, Mr., 173, 186
Jewitt, Mrs., 269
Joel, S., 121
Jones, Herbert, 29
Jones, John, 28-9
Joneses, the, 37
Julius, 58-9, 118
Julius Cæsar, 99, 101, 105

K

Keene, J. R., 151
Keir, 195
Kelbourne, Lord. 54-5 (*See under* Glasgow, Earl of)

Kempton Park, 113, 116, 140, 156, 161, 177, 195, 215
Cambridgeshire Trial Handicap, 177
Cup, 113
International Breeders' Stakes, 195, 215
International Two-Year-Old Plate, 161
Kendal, 232, 237
Kennett Station, 265
Kensington Palace, 267
Kentucky, 208
Ker Seymer, Mrs. G., 168, 264-5
Ker Seymer, Colonel E. Clay, 168
Kerr, Andrew, 42
Kidderminster, 29
Kilwarlin, 238
King, Mr., 171
King, Mrs., 171
King Cole, 20, 173
King Lud, 84
King Tom, 64, 97
Kingcraft, 64, 86, 198
"Kings of the Turf", 131
King's Heath (Birmingham), 34
Kingsclere, 127, 220-2, 232-3, 237-8
Kingsclere Downs, 237-8
Kingwood, 219-21
Kinsky, Count, 169, 188
Kisber (Hungary), 197
Kisber (horse), 78, 83, 197
Kismet, 120
Kitchener and Fenn, Messrs., 46
Kitchin, Jim, 53

L

Laceman, 217
Ladas, 184
Lady Adelia, 21
Lady Beatrice, 195
Lady Betty, 64
Lady Coventry, 97
Lady Golightly, 91, 95, 97, 99, 102, 105
Lady Lurewell, 58
Lady Masham, 139
Lady Patricia, 95
Ladylove, 79, 83-4, 89, 90, 92
La Terrière, "Dick", 18, 42-3

McGeorge, James, 141
McGeorge, Tom, 127, 141
McGeorge's Hotel, Newark, 141
Machell, Captain J. O., 13, 15, 48, 84, 125, 140-1, 187, 239, 268-9, 272
Macmahon, 215
Mackenzie, Mr., 11
McOrville, 24
Mac Rae, Mr., Police Superintendent, 27, 29-30
Madrid, 211
Magpie Colours, the, 63-4, 85
Maher, Danny, 12, 91
Maid of Trent, 64, 270
Maiden Plate (Goodwood), 119, 148
Maidenhead, 263
Maidment, 65, 69, 77, 83
Maidstone, 242
Mairie, a, 211
Malcolm, Sir J., 24
Malton, 51, 54, 65, 231
Malton of Scotland, the, 51
Malvern, 17, 41
Manchester, 13, 71, 90, 103, 128, 130, 132, 137, 139, 140-3, 166, 177, 195, 215, 229, 271
    Autumn Cup, 13, 90, 130, 132, 137, 139, 140-3, 166, 229, 271
    Autumn Handicap, 177
    Great Foal Stakes, 103, 161, 229
    Hartington Plate, 177, 195, 215
    John o'Gaunt Plate, 215
    July Handicap, 195
    Queen's Hotel, 71, 128
    September Handicap, 195, 229
    September Plate, 229
    Whitsuntide Plate, 177, 215
Manifold, 63
Manœuvre, 102
Manning, W., 171, 255
Manton House, Marlborough, 193
Maple, Sir B., 221, 234-5
Marden, 164
Margaret of Anjou, 50

Marlborough, 193
Marlow, 233
Marsh, Richard, 43, 130, 136, 158
Marshall, Frederick, 32, 46
Martha Lynn, 53
Martin, —, 186
Mason, Finch, 28
Master Kildare, 113, 121, 123, 125-6, 145, 220
Mate, 215
Maycock, Lady, 121
Maycock, Sir Willoughby, K.C.M.G., 15, 20, 25, 31, 50, 120-1, 198
Meiklam, Mr., 57
Melbourne Argus, the, 103
Melton, 39, 130, 145, 195, 215, 217, 220-3, 225-7, 229

Melton Constable, 220, 262
Melton Scrapbook, 217, 225
Melton's Derby, 11-12, 217, 225
Melton's St. Leger, 225, 227
Mephisto, 237
Mereworth Castle, 63, 181-3, 242, 261
Merry, James, 55-6, 58
Merry-go-Round, 91
Merthyr, 176
Middle Park Plate, Newmarket, 63, 176-7, 195, 197, 215, 220, 233-4, 271
Middleton Cottage, 263
Middleham, 55
Miller, the late Lieutenant-Colonel, E. D., C.B.E., D.S.O., 153
Mills, R. Herbert, 39, 158-9, 205-6
Mills, Mrs. R. Herbert, 159
Mills, Wyndham, 158-9
Milton, John, 223
Minting, 184, 215, 233-6, 238-40
Miss Agnes, 231
Mrs. Barnet, 57
"Mr. Childwick", 221, 234, 236
"Mr. Manton", 212
Modena, 79
Modwena, 240
Monachus, 95
Montgomerie, Lord, 53, 55

Montrose, then Dowager Duchess
   of, 12, 15, 67, 203, 205, 211-12,
   259, 262, 268
Moore, Garratt, 243
Moorhouse, E., 221-3
Morbey, C., 133
Moravia, 197
Morgan, H., 49, 90-1
Morgan la Faye, 58
Morris, J., 102, 198
Mostyn Mile, the, 52
Moulton, 263
Mousquetaire, 95, 99
Mowerina, 139, 161
Muley Edris, 11, 75, 85, 123, 130-1,
   145-6, 265
Muriel, 123
Murray, G., 53
Murrumbidgee, the, 191
Mytton, J, 33-4

N

NAPLES, Queen of, 263
Napoleon, 33
Naunton Inn, 42
Nautilus, 215
Navarino, the battle of, 49
Naylor, Mr., 64
Nelson, G., 57
Neptune, 109
New Orleans, 208
New York, 152, 198, 208-9
   Brevoort House, 204
   Fifth Avenue, 198, 208
   Park, the, 198
   Twenty-Sixth and Twenty-
      Seventh Streets, 208
   Windsor Hotel, 204
Newark, 141, 147
Newcastle, 232
Newcastle, Duke of, 58, 63
Newcastle Journal, 82
Newman, H. J., 171
Newmarket, 11, 38, 43-51, 55-6,
   59-60, 62-3, 69-70, 75, 77,
   83-6, 89, 92, 95, 97-8,
   105, 107, 109-11, 113, 118-19,
   123, 130, 134, 137, 145,

Newmarket—*Continued.*
   149-50, 152, 155-6, 158, 161,
   170-1, 185, 187, 195, 198,
   205, 209-11, 215, 217, 221,
   227, 229, 234, 237, 240,
   242, 246, 264-5, 268, 273
Abingdon Mile Bottom, 220
Aldcroft's Yard, 234
Newmarket All Saints, 51
Bedford Lodge, 55, 115, 140, 185
Bretby Stakes Course, 119, 234
Bretby Plate, 108
Newmarket ; Buckenham Stakes,
   69, 89
Bury Hill, 58, 134, 234
Bushes Handicap, 119, 107-8
Bushes Hill, 73, 84, 107-8, 119
Cambridgeshire, The, 12-13,
   51, 56, 71-2, 76, 90, 151,
   242, 245-6, 272
Cesarewitch Stakes, 64, 75-6,
   81-2, 84, 89, 95, 97, 146-7,
   151, 271
Challenge Cup, 48
Champion Stakes, 105, 137,
   139, 229, 237, 161
Changes in, 56
Chesterfield Stakes, 63, 87, 89,
   105, 161
Chesterfield Cheveley Paddocks,
   269
Chesterfield Chieveley Hundred,
   51
Clearwell Stakes, 69, 79, 83,
   87, 89, 95, 99, 101, 123, 137,
   177, 195, 197
Coffee Rooms, 49
Course, the, 150, 273
Craven Meeting, 69, 92, 97, 107
Craven Stakes, 177, 215
Criterion Stakes, 84, 99, 110,
   193, 195, 215, 234
Crown Hotel, 48
Derby, 95
Devil's Dyke, 50
Dewhurst Plate, 105, 123, 125,
   195, 197, 215, 220, 234, 271
Ditch Mile Handicap, 84, 108
Ditch Stables, 219
Drag Hounds, 71, 212

Reiver, Mr., 205
Remedy, 57
Renny (horse), 195
Renny, H., 79, 266
Repentance Colt, 83
Reprieve, 177, 184
Reputation, 154
Retreat, 161
Reviewer, 54
Rhidorroch, 11
Richards, Gordon, 16
Rieff, —, 70
Rieff, J., 70
Ripon, 63
Ripon Great Northern Handicap, 63
Rob Roy, 11
Robert the Devil, 11, 130, 134-5 136, 139, 146, 150-1, 265
Robinson, James, 155, 270
Rogers, Sam, 155
Ronald, 193
Rookery, 161
Rose, Mary (Mrs. Mathew Dawson), 57-8
Rosebery, Lord, 77, 187, 204
Rosebery, 95, 97
Rossiter, A., 11, 120, 146, 150
Rosslyn, Lord (in 1819), 19
Rosslyn, Lord, 187, 223-4, 250-1, 260-1
Rosslyn, Lady, 260-1
Rossmore, Lord, 202, 272
Rossmore, Lady, 202
Rosy Cross, 125, 143
Rosy Morn, 195
Rotten Row, 224
Rouge Rose, 135
Roughton, Thomas, 255
Rous, Admiral, 15, 49, 81-2, 105, 113, 120, 123, 137, 161, 188, 238
Rowlands, C. (*See under* Cecil Raleigh)
Rowlands, Dr. F., 28, 38
Rowlands, Mrs. F., 38
Royal Angus, 190
Royal Buckhounds, 187
Royal Fern, 193
Royal Hampton, 11, 220-2, 224

Rufford, Mr., 77
Rugby, 64, 262
Russian Government, 21
Russley Park, 115, 135
Rutland, Dukes of, 51
Rutland, Francis, Sixth Earl of, 51
Rye House Plot, 50
Rylstone, 121

S

SACHEM, 164
Sailor Prince, 246
St. Albans, 31-3
St. Blaise, 147, 175
St. Clair, Hugh, 42
St. Gatien, 229
St. George's Cottage, 17 19, 24, 26-7
St. George's Place, 17-19, 24, 26-7
St. George's Channel, 243
St. Helena, 226
St. James's Palace, 169, 211
St. James's Palace Stakes (Ascot), 161, 177, 180
St. James's Park, 51
St. Leger. (*See under* Doncaster)
St. Mirin, 12, 184, 233, 242, 245-6, 255, 262, 272
St. Pancras, 62
St. Simon, 115-19, 148, 184
Salford Borough Handicap, Manchester, 195, 215
Salisbury, 229
Salvanie, 109
Salvanos, 75-6, 271
Sandiway, 177
Sandown, 127, 161, 177, 195
  Esher Stakes, 113, 195
  National Breeders' Stakes, 177
  Great Sapling Stakes, 113
  Royal Stakes, 161
Sanford, M., 151
Sanguinetti, Mr., 33
Saraband, 234-6, 240
Sargent, H., 253, 255
Sayers, Tom, 31, 34, 37, 71
Sceptre, 231
Scotland, 57
Scott, Bill, 155

Thirsk (Russia), 22
"Thomas", Mr., 28, 31, 34
Thormanby, 82
"Thormanby," 131
Thunder, 95, 97-8
Thurgarton, 187
Tilt, A. P., 273
"Tom Cribb", 52
Tomahawk, 79, 82-3, 86
Tombs Prison, 210
Tommy Tittlemouse, 157, 249
Torquay, 173
Touchet, 143
Touchstone, 21
Town Guard, 151
Tramp, 23
Trelawny, 23
Trent, 86
Tsarkoe Selo Palace, 21-2
Tudor, F., 157
Turner (jockey), 23

U

Unicorn Inn (Winchcomb), 41

V

Valour, 13, 130, 132, 137, 139-43, 166, 187, 213
Vanderbilt, Governor, 209
Vanguard, 23
Vanity Fair cartoon, 103-4
Vegetarian, 127
Vevette Colt by Wamba, 77
Vliemann, Mr., 38
Victoria, Princess, 222
"Vigilant," 69
Villar, W., 29, 31, 39, 61, 103
Viney, —, 235
Violet Melrose, 220
Vivid, 63
Volta, 215
Voltigeur, 53
Vyner, C., 89, 97

W

Wagon and Horse Hotel, Newmarket, 172
Waite, Mr., 204
Walker, Johnny, 52
Wallenstein, 186
Walters, Mr., 20
Wamba, 77
Warren House, 56, 165, 172
Warwick races, 78
Wasp Nest, 129
Waterloo, battle of, 21, 32
Waterloo Bridge, 156
Watts, J., 14
Wauchope, Sir John Don-, 58, 117
Waugh, Alec, 263
Waugh, Isabel, 263
Weatherby, Messrs., 134
Webb, Fred, 78, 90-1, 132-3
Weever's at Bourton-on-the-Hill, 42
Wee Willie, 52
Wellington, Duke of, 32
Wells, Mr., 171
Wendell Holmes, Dr. Oliver, 41
Westminster, Duke of, 119, 133-36, 146, 176, 184, 220, 232-41, 259, 263
Wheatear, 89
Wheel of Fortune, 105-7, 113, 115-18, 232
Whipper In, 155, 161, 177, 195, 215, 232
Whirlwind, 113
White, A., 246
White (jockey), 186
Whitehall, 51
Whitefriar, 232, 237
Whitewall, 54
Wilcox, Mr., 40
Wild Tommy, 97-8
William le Gros, 57
William IV., 57
Williams, Mrs. (Miss Hughes), 35-6
Williams, General Owen, 227
Willins, Mrs., 64
Willoughby, Sir John, 193, 259

294

Lightning Source UK Ltd.
Milton Keynes UK
UKOW051813121111

181959UK00001B/135/A